About the Author

MADELINE LEVINE, PH.D., has been a practicing clinical psychologist in Marin County for the past twenty-five years. She is
the author of *Viewing Violence* and *See No Evil: A Guide to
Protecting Our Children from Media Violence*. She is a frequent
lecturer on child and adolescent issues, and lives in California
with her husband and three sons.

The Price of Privilege

How Parental Pressure and Material Advantage
Are Creating a Generation
of Disconnected and Unhappy Kids

Madeline Levine, Ph.D.

HARPER

NEW YORK · LONDON · TORONTO · SYDNEY

This book is dedicated to the four amazing men in my life.
To my husband, Lee, for his good-humored love,
support, and encouragement. And to our three sons,
Loren, Michael, and Jeremy who inspire me daily and
whom I love beyond words and reason.

HARPER

The names and identifying characteristics of individuals discussed in this book have been changed to protect their privacy, as have the locations of certain events.

A hardcover edition of this book was published in 2006 by HarperCollins Publishers.

HarperCollins books may be purchased for educational, business, or sales promotional use. For information, please e-mail the Special Markets Department at SPsales@harpercollins.com.

FIRST HARPER PAPERBACK PUBLISHED 2008.

Designed by Nancy B. Field

The Library of Congress has catalogued the hardcover edition as follows:
Levine, Madeline.
    The price of privilege: how parental pressure and material advantage are creating a generation of disconnected and unhappy kids / Madeline Levine.—1st ed.
      p. cm.
    Includes index.
    ISBN-10: 0-06-059584-1
    ISBN-13: 978-0-06-059584-5
    1. Child rearing. 2. Parenting. 3. Wealth—Psychological aspects. 4. Teenagers—Conduct of life. 5. Adolescent psychology. I. Title.
HQ769.L394 2006
649'.156—dc22   2005057725

ISBN 978-0-06-059585-2 (pbk.)

23 24 25 26 27 LBC 67 66 65 64 63

CONTENTS

PART TWO
HOW THE CULTURE OF AFFLUENCE WORKS AGAINST THE DEVELOPMENT OF THE SELF

PART THREE
PARENTING FOR AUTONOMY

PART FOUR

WHY YOU HAVE TO STAND ON YOUR OWN TWO FEET BEFORE YOUR CHILDREN CAN STAND ON THEIRS

PART ONE

AMERICA'S NEW "AT-RISK" CHILD

· CHAPTER 1 ·

The Paradox of Privilege

It was 6:15 P.M. Friday when I closed the door behind my last unhappy teenage patient of the week. I slumped into my well-worn chair feeling depleted and surprisingly close to tears. The fifteen-year-old girl who had just left my office was bright, personable, highly pressured by her adoring, but frequently preoccupied, affluent parents, and very angry. She had used a razor to incise the word EMPTY on her left forearm, showing it to me when I commented on her typical cutter disguise—a long-sleeve T-shirt pulled halfway over her hand, with an opening torn in the cuff for her thumb. Such T-shirts are almost always worn to camouflage an array of self-mutilating behaviors: cutting with sharp instruments, piercing with safety pins, or burning with matches. I tried to imagine how intensely unhappy my young patient must have felt to cut her distress into her flesh.

As a psychologist who has been treating unhappy teens for over twenty-five years, I wondered why this particular child left me feeling so ragged. I live and work in an upper-middle-class suburban community with concerned, educated, and involved parents who have exceedingly high expectations for their children. In spite of parental concern and economic advantage, many of my adolescent patients suffer from readily apparent emotional disorders: addictions, anxiety disorders, depression, eating disorders, and assorted self-destructive behaviors. Others are perplexingly and persistently unhappy in ways that are more difficult to quantify easily. The fact that many of these teens are highly proficient in some areas of their lives helps mask significant impairments in others—the straight-A student who feels too socially awkward to attend a single school dance, the captain of the basketball team who is abusive toward his mother, the svelte homecoming queen who consistently sees a "fat ugly duckling" in the mirror. While I love my work, it is also quite demanding and I usually greet the end of the day on Friday with a mixture of relief and anticipation, not sadness. Sinking further into my chair, I flipped through my appointment book, searching for clues to my emotional weariness.

I was not surprised by the seriousness of many of my cases. After two decades of treating unhappy kids, and the publication of a couple of books on how the media influence child development, I had become a "senior" psychologist and am often referred difficult cases. I enjoy working with troubled adolescents and seem to have a knack for developing an easy rapport with them. The eating-disordered girls who are enraged by their mother's submissiveness and yet mimic it in their own self-defeating behavior. The junior high school girls with pitiable self-esteem who regularly give oral sex to boys behind the school gymnasium, while insisting that they are not sexually active—an astonishing redefinition of sexual activity shared by most of their generation. The substance-abusing boys who attempt to ward off depression with drug use but ultimately end up in out-of-the-way places for a year or two of rehab. Many of these teenagers suffer from obvious emotional illnesses: depression, anxiety disorders, eating disorders, and substance abuse. Often there is a family history of depression or bipolar illness or alcoholism. These teens "look" troubled. Their grades are usually poor, their relationships volatile, and their behavior floridly risky. Their parents are terrified when they haul them in for treatment.

But I was puzzled by the fact that an increasingly large number of my hours were filled with cases that initially seem to be rather garden-variety adolescent problems. When parents make calls to my office for these kids, there is often little sense of urgency. Some parents may have a vague sense that all is not well and ask me to "take a look" at their child. A few have discovered drug paraphernalia or perhaps an unsettling diary entry and call, hoping I will allay their fears since these same teens are doing well in school and are compliant at home. They may note that their child appears "less sunny," or seems somewhat withdrawn, but these parents don't see their children as troubled—unhappy maybe, but not troubled. More than a few parents call not out of their own concern, but at the insistence of their teenager.

In fact, many of these teens have a notable ability to put up a good front. Absent the usual list of suspects—bad divorces, substance abuse, immobilizing depression, school failure, or delinquent behavior—their parents are frequently surprised by their request to see a therapist. It would be a stretch to diagnose these kids as emotionally ill. They don't have the frazzled, disheveled look of kids who know they are in serious trouble.

Nevertheless, they complain bitterly of being too pressured, misunderstood, anxious, angry, sad, and empty. While at first they may not appear to meet strict criteria for a clinical diagnosis, they are certainly unhappy. Most of these adolescents have great difficulty articulating the cause of their distress. There is a vagueness, both to their complaints and to the way they present themselves. They describe "being at loose ends" or "missing something inside" or "feeling unhappy for no reason." While they are aware that they lead lives of privilege, they take little pleasure from their fortunate circumstances. They lack the enthusiasm typically seen in young people.

After a few sessions, sometimes more, the extent of distress among these teenagers becomes apparent. Scratch the surface, and many of them are, in fact, depressed, anxious, and angry. Quite a few have been able to hide self-injurious behaviors like cutting, illegal drug use, or bulimia from both their parents and their peers. While many of these teens are verbal and psychologically aware, they don't seem to know themselves very well. They lack practical skills for navigating out in the world; they can be easily frustrated or impulsive; and they have trouble anticipating the consequences of their actions. They are overly dependent on the opinions of parents, teachers, coaches, and peers and frequently rely on others, not only to pave the way on difficult tasks but to grease the wheels of everyday life as well. While often personable and academically successful, they aren't particularly creative or interesting. They complain about being bored; they are often boring.

Treating these teenagers can be more difficult and less rewarding than treating my "sicker" patients. Parents are more likely to deny the fact that their child has run into psychological trouble because the historical markers of adolescent disturbance—failing grades, withdrawal, and acting out—are not readily apparent. Yet, as my appointment book confirmed, my practice was increasingly filled with kids from comfortable homes who, in spite of superficial appearances to the contrary, are extremely unhappy, disconnected, and passive. The kind of independence historically coveted in adolescence is strikingly absent from their agendas.

Sensing their children's vulnerabilities, parents find themselves protecting their offspring from either challenge or disappointment. Fearful that their kids will not be sturdy enough to withstand even the most mundane requirements of completing homework, meeting curfew, straightening their rooms, or even showing up for dinner, discipline becomes lax, often nonexistent. While demands for outstanding academic or extracurricular performance are very high, expectations about family responsibilities are amazingly low. This kind of imbalance in expectations results in kids who regularly expect others to "take up the slack," rather than learning themselves how to prioritize tasks or how to manage time. Tutors, coaches, counselors, and psychotherapists are all enlisted by parents to shore up performance and help ensure the kind of academic and athletic success so prized in my community. While my patients may seem passive and disconnected, their parents are typically in a frenzy of worry and overinvolvement. They tend to shower their children with material goods, hoping to buy compliance with parents' goals as well as divert attention away from their children's unhappiness.

A superficial reading of this type of teenager might suggest that they are simply spoiled or overindulged. It is tempting to trivialize the problems of kids who have been the recipients of exhaustive parental intervention and have been liberally handed both material and educational opportunities. Yet the depletion I felt that Friday afternoon came not from treating spoiled or indulged kids, but from treating troubled ones.

Regardless of how successful these kids look on the surface, regardless of the clothes they wear, the cars they drive, the grades they get, or the teams they star on, they are not navigating adolescence successfully at all. Modest setbacks frequently send them into a tailspin. A talented thirteen-year-old seriously considers hacking his way into the school computer system to raise his math grade. An academically outstanding sixteen-year-old thinks about suicide when her SAT scores come back marginally lower than she had expected. A fourteen-year-old boy cut from his high school junior varsity basketball team is afraid to go home, anticipating his father's disappointment and criticism. He calls his mother, and tells her that he is going to a friends' house. In fact, he is curled up on my couch, red-eyed and hopeless. He believes he has nothing to live for. While it is tempting to attribute scenarios like these to the histrionics of adolescence, it would be a mistake. Adolescent suicide has quadrupled since 1950.[1]

My mood continued to sink as I scanned my appointment book and realized that the week that had just passed was not significantly different from the week before, or the month before—or the year before, for that matter. For several years now my practice has been increasingly filled by teenagers whose problems seem out of proportion to their life circumstances. Kids who, by luck and fortunate genetics, are smart and talented, who have well-intentioned, highly involved parents, and who enjoy the opportunities that their financially secure parents can provide. Kids who should be striding, but find themselves stumbling through life. Like all of us who scramble to provide advantages for our children, I had assumed that involvement, opportunity, and money would help safeguard the emotional health of children. **Yet my appointment book forced me to consider quite the opposite: some aspects of affluence and parental involvement might be contributing to the unhappiness and fragility of my privileged patients.**

WHY KIDS WHO HAVE SO MUCH
CAN FEEL EMPTY

In what therapists are fond of referring to as an "aha moment," I realized that I had been so profoundly affected by my cutter, with her oozing, desperate message, because with the single, raw word EMPTY she had captured the dilemma of many of my teenage patients. "Empty" in what way? Many of my patients have teachers, coaches, and, most of all, parents who have actively poured enormous amounts of attention and resources into these children. Paradoxically, the more they pour, the less full many of my patients seem to be. Indulged, coddled, pressured, and micromanaged on the outside, my young patients appeared to be inadvertently deprived of the opportunity to develop an inside.

Parents who persistently fall on the side of intervening for their child, as opposed to supporting their child's attempts to problem-solve, interfere with the most important task of childhood and adolescence: the development of a sense of self. *Autonomy*, what we commonly call independence, along with *competence* and *interpersonal relationships*, are considered to be inborn human needs. Their development is central to psychological health.[2] In a supportive and respectful family, children go about the business of forging a "sense of self" by being exposed to, and learning to manage, increasingly complex personal and interpersonal challenges.

"Mommy is so proud that I can tie my shoelaces all by myself," is the pleased statement of a youngster who has been allowed the opportunity to master a difficult task on her own, knowing that her mother is also pleased by her growing competence and independence. Similarly, the adolescent who says, "I decided that it was more important to work things out with my best friend than study for my geometry quiz. My mom might not agree, but I think she'll understand," is also honing a sense of self by taking up the challenge of making a decision in the face of competing personal, academic, and parental expectations. The fact that her connection with her mother is secure enough to withstand a difference of opinion allows her to make a decision that feels authentically her own because she is not diverted by her mother's needs or anxiety.

It is easy to see how always tying shoelaces for a toddler would be impairing her autonomy. No parent wants to still be tying shoelaces for a twelve-year-old. The rationale behind "staying out of it" is less clear with the teenager (often the stakes seem higher—academics, peer choices, drugs, sex), and parents are far more likely to chime in: "You can talk to your friend after the test. It's important to keep up your grades." The fact that the stakes *are* higher is all the more reason to provide teenagers with as many opportunities as possible to make their own decisions and learn from the consequences. Just as it was critical for the toddler to fumble with her shoelaces before mastering the art of shoelace tying, so is it critical for the adolescent to fumble with difficult tasks and choices in order to master the art of making independent, healthy, moral decisions that can be called upon in the absence of parents' directives. We all want our children to put their best foot forward. But in childhood and adolescence, sometimes the best foot is the one that is stumbled on, providing an opportunity for the child to learn how to regain balance, and right himself.

When we coerce, intrude on, or take over for our children unnecessarily we may be "spoiling" them, but the far more significant consequence is that we are interfering with their ability to construct a sense of self. My patient was empty because she had not been able to develop the internal resources that would make it possible for her to feel that she "owned" her life or could manage her feelings. She felt little control over what happened to her and had no confidence in her ability to handle the curveballs of adolescence. Cutting was one of the few things over which she felt control. Cutting allowed her angry feelings to seep out in a measured way rather than explode.

The reason that so many of my patients feel empty is because they lack the secure, reliable, welcoming internal structure that we call "the self." The boredom, the vagueness, the unhappiness, the reliance on others, all point to kids who have run into difficulty with the very foundation of psychological development. While the houses my young patients live in are often lavish, their internal homes are impoverished. Well-meaning parents contribute to problems in self-development by pressuring their children, emphasizing external measures of success, being overly critical, and being alternately emotionally unavailable or intrusive. Becoming independent, and forging an identity becomes particularly difficult for children under these circumstances.

The popular press has devoted rivers of ink to chronicling the "epidemic" of narcissistic, overinvolved parents producing spoiled, entitled children with poor values. But my experience leads me to a very different conclusion. Most of my patients are deeply troubled, not spoiled; most of their parents are not narcissistic but are struggling, often quite alone, with their own problems. The suffering felt by parents and children alike is genuine, and not trivial. The kids I see have been given all kinds of material advantages, yet feel that they have nothing genuine to anchor their lives to. They lack spontaneity, creativity, enthusiasm, and, most disturbingly, the capacity for pleasure. As their problems become more evident, their parents become confused and worried sick. As they either withdraw or ratchet up their involvement, their children seem less and less able to accomplish the tasks of childhood and adolescence—developing friendships, interests, self-control, and independence.

The traditional trajectory of adolescence—withdrawal, irritability, defiance, rejection of parental values, the trying on and discarding of different identities, and, finally, the development of a stable identity—seems to have given way to a far less successful trajectory. Fewer and fewer affluent teens are able to resist the constant pressure to excel. Between accelerated academic courses, multiple extracurricular activities, premature preparation for high school or college, special coaches and tutors engaged to wring the last bit of performance out of them, many kids find themselves scheduled to within an inch of their lives. Criticism and even rejection become commonplace as competitive parents continue to push their children toward higher levels of accomplishment. As a result, kids can't find the time, both literal and psychological, to linger in internal exploration; a necessary precursor to a well-developed sense of self. Fantasies, daydreaming, thinking about oneself and one's future, even just "chilling" are critical processes in self-development and cannot be hurried. Every child has a different time table, and most are ahead of the pack in some areas and behind in others. We would do well to remember "late bloomers" like Albert Einstein, John Steinbeck, Benjamin Franklin, and J.R.R. Tolkein. Sometimes a nudge is helpful, but a shove rarely is.

What looks like healthy assimilation into the family and community—getting high grades, conforming to parents' and community standards, and being receptive to the interests and activities valued by others—can be deceptive. Kids can present as models of competence and still lack a fundamental sense of who they are. Psychologists call this the "false self," and it is highly correlated with a number of emotional problems, most notably depression.[3]

Psychological development goes awry when children are pressured into valuing the views of others over their own. A young girl works madly to maintain her high GPA because "my mom would have a breakdown if my grades dropped." This girl might be an enthusiastic student under other circumstances, but her need to keep her mother's anxiety at bay is bound to interfere with her capacity to work independently and with pleasure. Ultimately, motivation for any venture needs to feel like it comes from inside. When it does, it feels "true"; when it comes from outside, it feels "phony." Working *primarily* to please others and to gain their approval takes time and energy away from children's real job of figuring out their authentic talents, skills, and interests. The "false self" becomes particularly problematic in adolescence as teens are required to confront the normal proliferation of "selves" ("I'm so cheerful with my friends, but I feel like a different, unhappy person with my parents") and figure out who is the "real me." Authenticity is not aided when kids have to battle against parents who are implanting other, often unrealistic "selves"—stellar student, outstanding athlete, perfect kid—into their teenager's already crowded psychological landscape.

Adolescents need tremendous support as they go about the task of figuring out their identities, their future selves. Too often what they get is intrusion. Intrusion and support are two fundamentally different processes: support is about the needs of the child, intrusion is about the needs of the parent. This difference will be highlighted throughout this book because, without a full appreciation of the desirability of support, warmth, and involvement on the one hand, and the damage of intrusion, rejection, and criticism on the other, parents will continue to undermine their children's psychological progress in spite of good intentions. As long as kids are not afforded the opportunity to craft a sense of self that feels authentic, a sense of self that truly comes from within, psychologists like myself will continue to see more and more youngsters at risk for profound feelings of depression, anxiety, substance abuse, and emptiness.

WHY WE CAN'T AFFORD TO TRIVIALIZE THE PROBLEMS OF PRIVILEGED KIDS

Psychologists are taught to be careful about the conclusions they reach. Just because my practice is filled with a perplexing assortment of teenagers who are desperately unhappy in spite of the seeming advantages of both money and parental concern doesn't necessarily mean that I've uncovered a new trend. The history of psychology is littered with accurate observations leading to inaccurate conclusions. When I was in graduate school we were taught that one of the markers for schizophrenia was a high blood concentration of sodium; that was until further research showed that institutions tend to heavily salt the bland food they serve their patients.

Unhappy teenagers are hardly remarkable, and I needed to be certain that what I was observing in my own practice was not simply a puzzling local phenomenon. While it certainly seemed odd that parental concern and financial resources were not having the expected protective effect on the mental health of the kids in my community, I had no evidence that this paradox extended any further than my county line. After all, I live in Marin County, California, the target of endless stereotypes, some inaccurate, some deserved. My community is relatively homogenous (white, upper-middle-class, well educated), with parents who tend to be highly involved, competitive, and extremely anxious about their children's performance. But what, I wondered, was going on in the rest of the country? Were other mental health professionals also seeing the empty, unhappy, hovered-over child of privilege that made up the majority of my practice? Was there any data to substantiate my observation that privileged children with well-educated and financially secure parents were experiencing higher rates of psychological impairment than before? Was it accurate that many of these problems stemmed from a poorly developed sense of self?

I began calling colleagues around the country, talking to mental health workers in urban, suburban, and rural areas. I spoke to clinicians who exclusively treat the children of the affluent as well as those whose practices are made up squarely of middle-class families. Privilege is a relative term in this country. While the term "wealthy" might be reserved for the top 1 or 2 percent of families earning high incomes, many more people in this country are relatively affluent. Researchers studying "affluence" use annual family incomes of approximately $120,000–$160,000. Marketing magazines target an income of $75,000 and above, slightly over one in four households in this country, as placing people in a category called "mass affluence."[4] A substantial group of children enjoy high levels of privilege—televisions, computers, video games, and cell phones—though their parents have rather modest incomes. The fact is, the United States is one of the most affluent countries in the world, and large numbers of our children lead lives of privilege unimagined in many places.

The results of months of phone calls were surprisingly consistent. In spite of regional variations in language—in metropolitan Chicago they were "vacant"; in a suburb of New York, "evacuated"; in a rural community in Vermont, "bland"—it was clear that my smart, privileged, dependent but disconnected and empty patient was showing up in every part of the country. Not one here and there, but in droves. Like myself, the majority of child and adolescent psychologists and psychiatrists I called have outgoing messages on their answering machines saying, "At the present time I am no longer able to see new patients in either treatment or consultation." Worked to the gills, our practices overflowing, we may be helping individual children, but we are ignoring the larger issues.

- Why are the most advantaged kids in this country running into unprecedented levels of mental illness and emotional distress?

- Is there something about such factors as privilege, high levels of parental income, education, involvement, and expectations that can combine to have a toxic rather than the expected protective effect on children?

- Why are children of privilege, in record numbers, having an extraordinarily difficult time completing the most fundamentally important task of adolescence—the development of autonomy and a healthy sense of self?

We need to examine our parenting paradigm. Raising children has come to look more and more like a business endeavor and less and less like an endeavor of the heart. We are overly concerned with "the bottom line," with how our children "do" rather than with who our children "are." We pour time, attention, and money into insuring their performance, consistently making it to their soccer game while inconsistently making it to the dinner table. The fact that our persistent and often critical involvement is well-intended, that we believe that our efforts ultimately will help our children to be happy and to successfully compete in a demanding world, does not lessen the damage.

We need to become familiar with the research showing that privileged children from affluent families are experiencing disproportionately high levels of emotional problems, and we need to learn more about why this is the case. We have to examine the disturbing social structure, the "culture of affluence," that surrounds both ourselves and our children. While this book focuses on those children who are most clearly damaged by this culture, it is likely that all kids are vulnerable to one degree or another when pressure is excessive, parents are preoccupied, and values are poor. We have to be acutely attuned to our own psychological issues and our own happiness, or lack of it. We have to be willing to take an unflinching look at our parenting skills. And finally, we have to begin to develop the kinds of relationships, homes, schools, and communities that can act as a safety net not only for kids with "problems" but for all kids. We have to stop pouring our resources into the problem and begin pouring them into the solution.

This book is the outcome of evaluating over a hundred studies on child development, speaking with dozens of knowledgeable clinicians and researchers, and sifting through my own twenty-five years of experience both as a psychologist and as a parent. It is for those parents who are courageous enough to take a hard look at the way they are parenting, the culture they have bought into, and the difficult but necessary modifications they must make to help their children grow into autonomous, moral, capable, and connected adults. Mental health crises refuse to be ignored. They come back, often in stunningly ugly ways, to haunt us, our children, and our communities. Like my cutter's arm, this book is meant to be an exclamation mark highlighting a problem that refuses to be misrepresented, trivialized, or swept under the rug. Quite simply, we can no longer afford to ignore the epidemic of serious emotional problems in our well-manicured backyards.

· CHAPTER 2 ·

The Not-So-Hidden Mental Health Epidemic Among Privileged Youth

Speaking to child and adolescent psychotherapists throughout the country was both informative and confirming: I wasn't the only one puzzled by the increasingly large number of unhappy, deeply troubled, privileged kids in my practice, and by the lack of serious attention to this problem. The psychologists, psychiatrists, and mental health workers I spoke with were all eager to share stories about their young patients and theorize about what factors were contributing to the surprisingly high rates of emotional distress among a group long considered to be at low risk for emotional problems. Phone calls often lasted for hours as difficult cases were discussed and "big picture" issues were explored. While the stories I heard from clinicians around the country were intriguing and disturbing, they were still only what researchers somewhat disparagingly call "anecdotal evidence." Scientists depend on research with large groups of subjects, not individual cases, no matter how compelling, in order to draw conclusions. Where was the research on these kids? And why, in spite of hearing so much about how "spoiled" America's kids are, weren't we hearing about how troubled they are?

Several months of investigation at the University of California/ San Francisco medical library helped clarify why discussion about the emotional problems of affluent youngsters is sparse at best. The fact is that children from well-educated, financially secure homes are among the last group of children to be studied by researchers. The field of psychology has long been focused on the problems of middle-class families. In the last few decades, the focus of research has shifted to the problems of those children conventionally considered to be at risk—children of poverty. There is a vast body of literature documenting the fact that poverty imposes such severe financial, emotional, and social challenges that parenting skills are often compromised and as a result children in poverty have high levels of emotional and behavioral problems.[1] The corollary has long been assumed to be true: if a lack of income can imply poor parenting, then ample income should imply good parenting. It is only recently that social scientists have considered that this corollary, while logical, might not be correct and have turned their attention, finally, to children and teens from well-educated, financially comfortable families. Their findings are new, consistent, and extremely disturbing.

Researchers, led by Dr. Suniya Luthar of Columbia University's Teachers College, have found that America has a new group of "at-risk" kids, or, more accurately, a previously unrecognized and unstudied group of at-risk kids. They defy the stereotypes commonly associated with the term "at-risk." They are not inner-city kids growing up in harsh and unforgiving circumstances. They do not have empty refrigerators in their kitchens, roaches in their homes, metal detectors in their schools, or killings in their neighborhoods. **America's newly identified at-risk group is preteens and teens from affluent, well-educated families. In spite of their economic and social advantages, they experience among the highest rates of depression, substance abuse, anxiety disorders, somatic complaints, and unhappiness of any group of children in this country.**[2] When researchers look at kids across the socioeconomic spectrum, they find that the most troubled adolescents often come from affluent homes.[3] We know little about whether or not younger children from affluent families are equally at risk because no one has yet systematically studied their incidence of emotional problems. But it is becoming increasingly clear as research accumulates, that past age eleven or twelve, increases in material wealth do not translate into advantages in emotional health; on the contrary, they can translate into significant disadvantages.

These new findings should in no way minimize concern about those children traditionally considered to be at risk. Rather it should open our eyes to the fact that money, education, power, prestige, and material goods offer no protection against unhappiness or emotional illness. We need to seriously examine the culture of affluence—what it values, what it neglects, and what it disparages—to find clues to the disrepair of so many of its children. We need to investigate the possibility that some aspects of this culture: materialism, individualism, perfectionism, and competition may actually contribute to psychological problems. And we need to understand more about parenting in affluent communities. Why are children in the highest income brackets no more likely to view their parents as available, affectionate, or capable than children whose parents are at the bottom of the economic and social scale?[4] Why are the high levels of parental involvement and expectations, factors long considered to be positive for healthy child development, not having the expected protective effect on kids from affluent homes?

THE MAGNITUDE OF THE PROBLEM

Studies of public school students have shown that as many as 22 percent of adolescent girls from financially comfortable families suffer from clinical depression. This is three times the national rate of depression for adolescent girls. By the end of high school, as many as one-third of girls from these families can exhibit clinically significant symptoms of anxiety.[5] Boys from affluent families also have elevated rates of anxiety and depression early in high school, although less pronounced than their female counterparts. However, once these boys enter eleventh and twelfth grade, their most significant problem appears to be the regularity with which they use drugs and alcohol to self-medicate their depression.[6] This is a particularly disturbing finding, because teens who use drugs to self-medicate, rather than for experimentation or to fit in with peers, are at significantly higher risk for becoming long-term substance abusers.

Also worrisome is the fact that many of the most popular adolescent boys are heavy users of illegal drugs, and that their peers support this risky behavior. When groups of young adolescents are asked who they like most in their classes, they often choose classmates who openly display delinquent behaviors and substance use. This peer admiration of rule-breaking behaviors is *equally* prevalent among urban kids in poverty and affluent suburban kids, challenging the stereotype that it is "tough" inner-city boys who are most likely to endorse delinquent behavior.[7] In addition to depression, anxiety, substance use, rule breaking, and psychosomatic disorders are all elevated among affluent teens.[8] Affluent teens may also be prone to eating disorders and cutting.[9] When do these problems begin and who are the children most likely to be affected?

In a particularly noteworthy study, sixth- and seventh-grade junior high school students in a moderately affluent suburban community outside New York City were studied (average family income $120,000).[10] These students all attended the local public school. While the sixth-grade students looked particularly good—that is, their levels of psychopathology were *below* the national average for children this age—seventh-grade boys and girls showed *unexpectedly high* levels of anxiety, depression, and substance use. Perhaps most notable were the findings on rates of depression among girls. Depression among the seventh-grade affluent girls was twice as high as the national norm for girls this age.[11] While not yet as high as the 22 percent rate of depression found in affluent high school girls, it is striking that with an age difference of just one year, junior high school girls went from low levels to markedly high levels of depression.[12] As many researchers have pointed out, early adolescence seems to represent a period of accelerated vulnerability for girls.[13] It appears that affluent girls are at particularly high risk for depression and anxiety beginning at about age twelve.

Private school kids do not fare any better, despite the fact that parental income and level of education can be even higher. While younger private high school boys and girls are only modestly more depressed and anxious than the general population, their levels of distress shoot up over the last two years of high school. Anxiety, depression, somatic complaints, thought problems, attention problems, and rule breaking can be two to five times more prevalent among private high school juniors and seniors than among the general population of high school juniors and seniors.[14] Anxiety, depression, and somatic complaints lead the way for both boys and girls; girls are more prone to suffer internally, boys to act out with drugs and conduct problems. It may be that private high school freshmen and sophomores are initially more protected from stress, but that achievement pressure on juniors and seniors is particularly intense. In addition, among wealthy private school students there may be greater access to money for drugs at the same time that busy and preoccupied parents are unavailable to monitor their teenagers' social life.

Seventeen-year-old Catherine is a senior at a competitive private high school in my area. She has worked extremely hard for the past three years and is focused on her goal of eventually working in the field of international banking. She is set on Wharton, Sloan, or Haas, the three top-ranked undergraduate business schools in the country. I point out that these schools are extremely difficult to get into, and that Catherine has never mentioned whether the schools themselves or the towns they're located in are appealing to her. Catherine dismisses my concern. "I want to get a good job when I graduate. One of those schools will be my ticket," she insists.

While Catherine spends every available minute during the week studying, she spends the better part of many weekends high on cocaine, both because the drug is popular among her peer group, but also because it allows her to stay up after partying and still study. To avoid the inevitable "crash" that follows cocaine use, she takes sleeping pills to get to sleep on Sunday night. Catherine's parents, who view her as "almost out the door," are unaware of their daughter's drug habit, partly out of denial and partly because they are not around enough to monitor her comings and goings. They see her single-minded academic focus as positive and an indication of emotional maturity. Successful professionals themselves, they are well aware of Catherine's high GPA, yet quite unaware of the fact that without intervention she is likely to develop a full-blown substance-abuse problem, one that will ultimately prevent her from achieving either personal or academic success, regardless of the school she is admitted to.

The Centers for Disease Control, in Atlanta, define an epidemic as "The occurrence in a community or regions of cases of an illness, specific health related behavior, or health related events clearly in *excess of normal expectancy.*"[15] Depression, anxiety disorders, and substance abuse are all hitting kids from comfortable homes at a rate clearly "in excess of normal expectancy." Our most current data suggest that as many as 30 to 40 percent of twelve- to eighteen-year-olds from affluent homes are experiencing troubling psychological symptoms.[16] This epidemic, in addition to causing great suffering for children and their families, also carries a significant risk for premature mortality. Ten to 15 percent of those who suffer from depression eventually commit suicide.[17] This same 10- to 15-percent mortality rate is associated with anorexia.[18] Drug and alcohol use are factors in an extremely high percentage of accidental adolescent deaths, typically motor-vehicle accidents (the leading cause of adolescent death) and overdoses.

Researchers studying this group of financially comfortable kids regularly note that their findings are "surprising" or "startling." No one expected that children of privilege would be exhibiting rates of emotional problems significantly higher than the average child, and certainly not rates comparable to, or greater than, children living in dire poverty. **It is now clear, however, that children of privilege are exhibiting unexpectedly high rates of emotional problems beginning in junior high school and accelerating throughout adolescence.** These findings are in line with what I and many other mental health professionals are seeing in our offices on a daily basis. So *why* are children from financially secure homes exhibiting epidemic levels of emotional distress? The only "privilege" that many privileged children appear to have is financially comfortable parents. We cannot afford to draw any optimistic conclusions about a child's emotional health based on either their parents' education or financial standing.

The media, the primary source of public health information for most Americans, has put us on notice that there is a mental health crisis by providing a constant stream of disturbing stories about upper-class kids. While the shock value of many of these stories helps to sell newspapers and magazine, and hypes interest in some television "specials," the stories are rarely presented in a context that could help us understand what is driving such high levels of bad behavior and psychological distress. Because the media prefer sound bites to sound analysis, we are given little or no thoughtful information about the underpinnings of what is often appalling behavior.

For example:

- In Westchester County, an affluent suburb of New York City, Harrison High School lets out early because of a power failure. An impromptu beer party ensues, during which a seventeen-year-old boy is punched in the face and hits his head on a concrete patio. As he lies unconscious, other teens try to hide evidence of the party rather than call for help. The boy dies.[19]

- In Northbrook, Illinois, an affluent suburb of Chicago, a high school "powder-puff" football game between intoxicated seniors and junior girls turns ugly. The older girls pummel the younger ones with feces, fish guts, and paint cans, sending five girls to the hospital with broken bones and serious lacerations.[20]

- A *Frontline* special on PBS investigates an outbreak of syphilis in a prosperous town outside of Atlanta, Georgia. Over 200 youngsters are affected, some as young as twelve. In interviews, the town youngsters describe binge drinking, sexual promiscuity, peer pressure, a desire to fit in, and an absence of adult supervision as the contributing factors to the epidemic. "We heard a lot about emptiness," comments one of the researchers on the program.[21]

What is striking about all of these stories is not simply the absence of adult monitoring, but that all three instances of "bad," even lethal, behavior take place with the consent of a large peer group. While most parents work to instill good values and help their children make honest and safe choices, the peer group, a potent and ubiquitous socializing force in adolescence, is increasingly endorsing deviant behaviors. Researchers have found that young adolescents in the "popular crowd" at school—those who often set the standards of desired and acceptable behavior—demonstrate notably high levels of social aggression, which is both admired and approved of by their peers.[22] This applies not only to the "studs," who tend toward substance use and rule breaking, but also to the "queen bees," who are deliberately unkind to girls of "lower" status. And the more these students increase these negative behaviors across the middle school years, the more likely they are to end up with high social status as they head into high school.

The fact that affluent teens are increasingly immersed in a peer culture that values substance use, rule breaking, and delinquency is particularly concerning since researchers have found that adolescent friendships can involve "deviancy training," which in turn predicts increases in delinquency, substance use, violence, and psychopathology in adulthood.[23] In other words, who your teenager hangs out with really does make a difference. **Teens are particularly likely to be drawn to other teens with poor values when they are experiencing high levels of stress, either within or outside the family.**[24] The young adolescent who finds himself caught between two parents in a hostile divorce and the high-achieving high school student who is expected to come home with nothing less than straight A's are both vulnerable to making poor peer choices.

While it is tempting to dismiss disturbing stories about affluent teenagers as unfortunate anomalies, or as the antics of spoiled, unsupervised kids, such stories have become too commonplace to be ignored. The factors that are promoting high levels of psychological impairment in some children are also likely to be contributing to stress and unhappiness in many more children. What we are learning from research, what we see in our families and communities, and what we read about in the papers makes it clear that without understanding the contributors to the high levels of problems among privileged youth, we will remain powerless to help them.

Fortunately, there is a recent surge of interest in the topic by thoughtful people from many related fields—psychology, psychiatry, pediatrics, neurobiology, sociology, and education—that allows us to begin to piece together the contributors to this mental health crisis. As we are increasingly able to identify these factors, we can also identify the personal, parenting, and social solutions that hold the key to helping our kids get back on a track that leads to an emotionally healthy adulthood.

DON'T KIDS "GROW OUT OF" ADOLESCENT ANGST?

It may be tempting to dismiss depression as normal adolescent turmoil or a "case of the blues," and substance use/abuse as typical, even healthy, experimentation, but the long-term consequences of parental denial about adolescent adjustment problems are ominous. When depression occurs in adolescence, there is a strong likelihood that it will recur later in life as well. More than half of all depressed teens have a recurrence of depression within five years.[25] Depressed adolescents followed into adulthood show an elevated risk for additional episodes of depression, as well as for poor social skills and marriage choices, impaired academic and job performance, and increased risk of substance abuse, suicide attempts, and both psychiatric and medical hospitalization.[26] Kids often do not grow out of depression, and when in doubt, a parent should always consult with a professional.

Similarly, substance use/abuse that is unaddressed can have serious long-term consequences. Many teens experiment with drugs and alcohol at younger ages than their parents did. Parents need to keep in mind that early experimentation can easily develop into addiction and dependence given the particular features of the adolescent brain. Current research on brain development shows that the brain continues to develop far longer than we previously thought, well into our twenties. Teens in particular have brains that are prone to sensation seeking, have trouble with impulse control, and are vulnerable to toxins in the environment, whether that's alcohol or a bad relationship with a parent. When teenagers chronically use drugs to alleviate feelings of depression and anxiety, they can experience short-term relief. Unfortunately, however, they will also experience brain changes, which in the long run will worsen the very psychiatric symptoms that were initially alleviated by drug and alcohol use.

Drug use in adolescence can become a vicious cycle, and parents need to be alert to this potential. This past year I treated six young teenagers who had become methamphetamine addicts; this is more than the total of all the methamphetamine-addicted teens I previously had treated in twenty-five years of practice. Drugs like cocaine, ecstasy, methamphetamine, even heroin have become popular among affluent youth. These drugs are strongly linked with anxiety disorders, with potentially serious negative impact on brain development, and even with death.[27] The adolescent brain is exquisitely sensitive to drug and alcohol abuse. Even marijuana, regularly used, impairs adolescent functioning on tests of attention, memory, and processing of complex information. These cognitive deficits can last for months or even years after marijuana use has stopped. And alcohol, the drug of choice for most adolescents, also shows continuity of abuse over time. Almost 40 percent of alcoholics are already drinking excessively between the ages of fifteen and nineteen.[28] In affluent communities, where substance use is high, both among parents and their children, there is simply not enough public recognition of scientific advances documenting the debilitating impact of drug and alcohol use on adolescent brain development.

Psychological problems, particularly when they are untreated, tend to endure over time. It is dangerous to assume that the emotional problems of affluent preteens and teens will resolve more readily than those of any other group of children. On the contrary, affluent children are at risk of having their problems glossed over or trivialized, increasing the likelihood that when their problems are finally acknowledged, they will be more severe and more difficult to resolve.

DON'T KIDS FROM AFFLUENT FAMILIES GET ALL THE HELP THEY NEED?

While affluent kids may experience a particularly turbulent time during adolescence, isn't it likely that their parents' financial resources and concern, along with school and community mental health services, will ultimately protect them from serious disturbance in adulthood? The answer appears to be no. Researchers tell us that parents generally know when their children are troubled, but that they are reluctant to seek professional help unless the problems are flagrant and disruptive.[29] The kid who plays truant, gets in fights, or has run-ins with the law is much more likely to get help than the child who is quietly despondent, drinking regularly, and cutting herself in private.

Affluent parents hesitate to seek professional help more than other groups of parents. They have strong feelings about protecting privacy and fears about sullying their children's academic records. School psychologists and counselors say that when they recommend outside help for children's mental health or substance-use problems, wealthy parents react much more defensively and negatively than do middle- and low-income parents. The fear of litigation is also higher when dealing with high-income parents. As a result, the children of the most affluent families are often the *least* likely to be referred for therapy.[30]

Unfortunately, affluent parents often have difficulty publicly accepting the fact that there are problems in their households, and they tend to blame the messenger. It is not unusual for the school to have identified emotional problems in one of my patients three, four, or five years before parents are willing to entertain the idea that the problem lies not with the teaching staff or the administration, but with their child. This delay in obtaining help does not serve children well, as valuable time is lost and developmental issues become more complicated and harder to treat.

Sean, a fourteen-year-old patient of mine, had tried unsuccessfully over the course of two or three years to draw his parents' attention to his increasing unhappiness. He began asking for help soon after entering junior high school and was told repeatedly by his parents that he was "going through a stage." When his depression, withdrawal, and teariness did not activate his parents, he turned to substance use and hanging out with the "bad" boys at school. Still his parents denied that anything was seriously wrong; his father had also hung around with a "tough crowd" and saw this more as an achievement than a call for help. Finally Sean came home with a gun, and his parents called me that night. As he astutely observed in therapy, "I guess they needed a gun to their head to 'get' what was going on with me." By the time Sean landed in therapy, he was no longer just a mildly depressed youngster; he now came with a drug problem and some pretty angry, antisocial attitudes. Early on, his therapy would most likely have been brief and successful; three years later, Sean is a tough case.

While Sean's parents simply couldn't acknowledge his obvious distress, other parents are seduced into denial by their child's outward successes. The straight-A student, the cheerleading captain, the popular, well-liked kid—how could *these* children be desperately unhappy? A colleague of mine in Chicago tells of a capable student in one of Chicago's most affluent suburbs who was selling pot at the local high school. She went to school high every day and conducted business in the parking lot at lunchtime. When she was not abusing marijuana she was dabbling in cocaine or drinking. Calls to her parents from concerned friends and neighbors were met with resistance. Her parents pointed out her popularity and high grades as evidence of her emotional stability. Not until she copied the keys of a neighbor's Ferrari, stole the car, and led the police on a high-speed chase, ultimately driving herself into a stone wall and a month in the intensive care unit in the local hospital, were her parents able to acknowledge how terribly troubled she was.

THE TOXIC BREW OF PRESSURE
AND ISOLATION

Having documented the high rates of emotional problems among children of well-educated, affluent parents, researchers have turned their attention to the possible causes of their surprising findings. Regardless of whether research has focused on younger kids, older kids, or has followed youngsters throughout their adolescence, two factors repeatedly emerge as contributing to their high levels of emotional problems. The first is *achievement pressure* and the second is *isolation from parents*.[31] While achievement pressure and isolation from adults appear to be mutually exclusive (*somebody* has to be putting the pressure on), they are not. In fact, achievement pressure often comes from parents who are overinvolved in how well their children perform and inadequately involved in monitoring these same children in other areas. **We can be overinvolved in the wrong things, and underinvolved in the right things, both at the same time.**

Achievement Pressure

In my community, children's grades are available 24/7 on the Internet, on a program called PowerSchool. In spite of the school's injunction not to use this program injudiciously, children complain that their parents know how they did in school that day even before the child reaches their front door. "Powersnoop," as one of my wry young patients calls it, can be summoned at any time of the day to give a bird's-eye view of how your child did on her last pop quiz or her daily homework assignment. Certainly children benefit from having their academic progress monitored, but not on an hour-by-hour, or even a daily basis. The creativity and flexibility required to become a true learner is inhibited by excessive focus on every inch of progress, or lack thereof. It may keep a kid's nose to the grindstone because she is anxious about her performance, but it certainly does not encourage real love of learning.

Research and common sense tell us that anxious parents make anxious children. Children take their cues from their parents. Whether their parents experience the world as benevolent, threatening, or unpredictable impacts a child's developing sense of how likely he or she is to be successful out in the world. Kids whose parents typically say, "Go for it," are being encouraged to have a very different attitude about challenge than kids whose parents list all possible catastrophic outcomes. Anxiety is particularly disturbing to children since it disrupts their basic sense of security.

Of all the things parents are likely to be anxious about, academic performance is invariably near the top of the list. Parents' anxiety about school performance leads to children who are pressured and anxious, but perhaps most dangerously it also leads to children who are perfectionists. Research shows that parents' emphasis on achievement is linked to their children's *maladaptive perfectionist* strivings. Maladaptive perfectionism (that is, perfectionism that impairs functioning—the child who can't sleep, who throws up, or who feigns illness because he is anxious about a test) is highly correlated with depression and suicide.[32] When parents place an excessively high value on outstanding performance, children come to see anything less than perfection as failure. While most kids hang in and try to meet these high expectations, more and more kids are opting out. Cindy Goodwin, the director for Youth and Family Services on Mercer Island, an affluent suburb outside of Seattle, notes that there has been a significant increase in school phobias and school refusal. "So many kids are pressured to be perfect—we're a small community and everyone knows how everyone else is doing—so first kids try to be perfect, and then they become anxious, and finally phobic."

Notably, there is a particularly strong relationship between perfectionism and suicide among those adolescents who are gifted.[33] Adolescent suicide is often precipitated by a perceived failure—at school, with parents, or in a relationship. Adolescents are idealistic and highly self-critical; additional parental pressures to meet harsh performance demands, while perhaps temporarily successful in driving academic achievement, are ultimately destructive. This does not mean that high expectations for children are potentially lethal. On the contrary, high expectations are found to promote achievement and competency in children. **It is when a parent's love is experienced as *conditional* on achievement that children are at risk for serious emotional problems.**[34] These are children who are driven to be "perfect" in the hope of garnering parental love and acceptance. Their inevitable missteps activate intense feelings of shame and hopelessness.

This unrealistic pressure to achieve gives birth to the tearful, hunched-over child I see in my office who in spite of hard work and good, solid B grades, says, "I've let my parents down." Dr. Neil Jacobson, a psychiatrist with a large practice of children and adolescents drawn largely from the suburbs of Dallas, observes, "Affluent parents seem to have forgotten Mendelian genetics. There is always regression to the mean." It is critical that parents who may be particularly bright, successful, or driven themselves remember that the odds are *against* their turning out children who are as gifted. Unremitting academic pressure leads to depression, anxiety, even suicide in some children, and a debilitating sense of not being able to keep up in many more.

Isolation from Parents

Another consistent finding on the unhappiness of affluent youth is the fact that they feel both physical and psychological isolation from adults—from their parents in particular.[35] The finding that, as a group, affluent teens are less likely to feel close to their parents than children in poverty—less likely than any other group of teens, for that matter—surprised me. After all, I have an entire shelf full of "overparenting" books saying that we are too involved in our children's lives. So why would affluent teens feel isolated when there are adults swarming around them?

Kyle, a fifteen-year-old patient of mine succinctly clarified my confusion: "It's so odd that I feel my mom is everywhere and nowhere at the same time." Being "everywhere" is about intrusion; being "nowhere" is about lack of connection. While affluent kids often feel that adults are crawling all over their world, intruding into territory that rightfully belongs to the child and directing their development with something approximating military precision, this does not mean that kids feel connected. Parents can be overinvolved and children can still feel isolated. Controlling and overinvolved parents typically leave kids feeling angry or alienated, neither of which is conducive to emotional closeness. **And it is emotional closeness, maternal warmth in particular, that is as close as we get to a silver bullet against psychological impairment.**

The dilemma of the working mom deserves some attention here. As has been well documented in numerous books and studies, working mothers shoulder the lion's share of childcare and household responsibilities, in addition to the hours demanded by their jobs or careers.[36] Yet the sight of overwhelmed mothers dropping their children off at various activities, their ears glued to their cell phones, tends to evoke ridicule rather than empathy. The fact is that these are mothers who are doing their best to meet the competing needs of family and work—typically with remarkably little social or community support. But a distracted, exhausted mother is not likely to be experienced as genuinely involved by her child.

Disconnection is not the sole province of working moms, but of all parents who are overwhelmed, either literally or emotionally. This kind of frantic, disconnected shuffling of children from one activity to the next is a good example of what my perceptive young patient meant by "everywhere and nowhere at the same time." Running around like chickens with our heads cut off stresses both us and our kids, and, most important, schools them in a parenting style that will not stand them, or our future grandchildren, in good stead. Our children benefit more from our ability to be "present" than they do from being rushed off to one more activity. Try to slow down. It is almost always in quiet, unpressured moments that kids reach inside and expose the most delicate parts of their developing selves.

Study after study shows that teens want more, not less, time with their parents, yet parents regularly overestimate the amount of time they spend with their teenagers.[37] Dr. Joseph Jankowski, Chief of Child and Adolescent Psychiatry at Tufts Medical Center in Boston, sees extremely troubled children from some of the most affluent communities in this country—Newton Center, Beacon Hill, and Brookline—and is struck by how lonely, even neglected, many of these kids are. He makes a distinction between parents who are not capable (those with significant impairments of their own) and parents who simply are not available. Dr. Jankowski notes, "These parents certainly want the best for their children. But they want it in a mechanistic way. They want buttons pushed, and pushed quickly, so that their kids get better with little effort. But helping troubled kids takes a long time and what these kids really need are their parents *themselves.*"

In affluent families, where social and professional demands can be highly time consuming, there is often a lack of "family time." In what some researchers call the "silver spoon syndrome," affluent kids are often painfully aware that they rate low on their parent's "to-do" list.[38] As a result, there is an *inverse* relationship between income and closeness to parents.[39] Lower-socioeconomic kids are far more likely to report feeling close to their parents than kids from high socioeconomic homes.

In one study, only 13 percent of preadolescents from affluent homes felt close to their parents, rating their relationship as "optimal," while an additional 27 percent said their parents were "adequate."[40] This leaves 60 percent of eleven- and twelve-year-olds who were studied feeling distant from their parents. This is not simply a harmless example of preadolescent whining. Follow-up studies on the 60 percent of youngsters who reported low levels of closeness to their parents showed particularly high rates of depression, anxiety, delinquency, and substance use.[41] Because affluent, well-educated parents often consider themselves enlightened about parenting issues, they are often shocked to find that their daughter had an abortion without consulting them, or their first hint that their son was substance abusing came when the police picked him up for dealing. Kids who don't feel close to their parents are unlikely to confide in them, and affluent parents have to be alert to the fact that, as a group, we underestimate the impact of our absences and overestimate the degree of closeness our children feel toward us.

Children simply cannot be parented in absentia. Material advantages do not lessen the sting of unavailability. Kids get in trouble when no one is paying attention. In the words of Dr. Suniya Luthar, who has extensively researched both ends of the economic spectrum, "Parents' emotional and physical absence is related to compromised well-being of children in inner city ghettos and in exclusive gated communities alike."

Friends, nannies, housekeepers, au pairs, or older siblings cannot fill the role that a concerned and involved parent occupies. There are certain aspects of family life that pack a lot of "bang for the buck" for busy families. For example, parents need to remember that kids love rituals and depend on them for a sense of continuity and connection. Perhaps the single most important ritual a family can observe is having dinner together. Families who eat together five or more times a week have kids who are significantly less likely to use tobacco, alcohol, or marijuana, have higher grade-point averages, less depressive symptoms, and fewer suicide attempts than families who eat together two or fewer times a week.[42] Eating together reinforces the idea that family members are interested, available, and concerned about each other. It provides a reliable time and place for kids to share accomplishments, challenges, and worries, to check in with parents and siblings, or simply to feel part of the family.

WHY PARENTS' GOOD INTENTIONS ARE NOT ENOUGH

What's so wrong with putting pressure on kids to achieve? After all, failed educational experiments like Summerhill, the flagship of "do your own thing" education in the 1960s, suggest that, left to their own devices, kids are not necessarily disciplined or even creative learners. Isn't it part of a parent's responsibility to make sure that they set the bar high for their children, teaching them the benefits of hard work and the pleasures of mastering difficult tasks? When does encouragement become unhealthy pressure?

As for isolation from adults, haven't children, especially teenagers, always formed their own "societies," with private codes for dress, attitude, and language so that adults would be forced into isolation by their lack of familiarity with the young group's culture? When does the normal waxing and waning of parent-child closeness threaten to become isolation? It is very difficult to pick a single point on the continuum of parenting and say, "This is when you're heading for trouble." Certainly parents need to be alert to persistent patterns of sadness, anxiety, lack of motivation, irritability, or self-destructive behavior in their children. These can signal serious problems, and consultation with a child or adolescent therapist is in order. Adolescent depression can look like adult depression: teary, hopeless, self-destructive, disengaged; but it can also look quite different, with adolescents often being far more angry than sad.

Every family is different, and what one child experiences as acceptable pressure or involvement, another experiences as egregious. Being free enough from your own preoccupations to be attuned to the *needs of your particular child* is one of the greatest contribution to their healthy psychological development you can make. Certainly parents are expected to be involved, to provide standards, guidance, and goals for their children. Alternatively, children are expected to separate themselves from their parents, align with their peers, and even discard some of their parents' standards, guidance, and goals as they develop their own. **This book is not about low standards or disengagement. Quite the opposite, it is about how to help children develop the very skills that will lead them to set their *own* bar high.** Sometimes parents understand how this process works, and sometimes, in spite of the best intentions, we don't. We worry that without our constant intervention and vigilance our kids will not achieve, and unwittingly we set the stage for their failure.

Most of the adolescents I treat, as well as many of their parents are well aware that something is terribly amiss. While parents may resist incorporating less stressful standards in their homes for fear their child might "fall behind," there is a growing awareness that, in spite of tremendous external accomplishment, many kids are both dreadfully unhappy and impaired in their ability to function autonomously. Well-developed autonomy allows kids to reliably and confidently see the world through their own eyes without fear of disappointing their parents. For many "star" children in comfortable communities this is a difficult, if not impossible, task. Not only are many of these kids expected to perform at the highest levels, they are also expected to make it look easy. Heavily dependent on their "public" success for a sense of self, many of these youngsters have little in the way of authentic purpose in their lives, leaving a void where conscience, generosity, and connection should be. Parents know this in their hearts, from their communities and from the local newspapers.

In my own community, a methamphetamine lab is discovered in the neighboring town, an alternative prom is held for the hotshot athletes barred from graduation for plastering digitally altered pornographic pictures of their teachers on car windshields in the school parking lot, and three high school boys are arrested for abducting and raping a female classmate. Instead of being outraged at this ugly and deplorable behavior, panicked parents scurry to find lawyers to defend their children. No parent in his or her right mind can really believe that this kind of parenting will turn out healthy, responsible, loving adults.

No matter how worried we are about our child's future we must always emphasize integrity over prerogative. Children of privilege frequently grow into positions of authority and philanthropy. They are likely to be our doctors, lawyers, CEOs, government officials, and policy-makers, not to mention our caretakers. A sturdy, moral, internally motivated sense of self is in their best interest, but it is also in ours. Dr. Susan Day, Chair of the Department of Ophthalmology at California Pacific Medical Center in San Francisco, observes that applicants for their highly competitive residency program increasingly have "a terrific paper pedigree, but on interview, often reveal a misguided tendency to choose 'pre-programmed' advancement over genuine curiosity and good values." The directors of counseling centers at many of the most prestigious schools, colleges, and universities in this country are reporting an "unprecedented" increase in the number of students who are seeking out services for emotional problems.

It makes no sense to say that children of privilege are running into epidemic levels of emotional problems simply because their parents are financially comfortable. While "money doesn't buy happiness" rings true, it seems like a stretch to say that it buys unhappiness. Painting serious social issues with a broad brush is not helpful, particularly when the issues involve the emotional health and even lives of our children. Researchers call it "fine-grained analysis," the effort to look at a problem in detail, to better understand its complexity so that the best possible solutions can be offered. Laying aside whatever preconceptions we may have about money, let's turn to a "fine-grained analysis" of whether it's actually our affluence, or something related to affluence, that is causing privileged children to have skyrocketing rates of emotional problems.

CHAPTER 3

Why Money Doesn't Buy Mental Health

While research may show that our current parenting style exacts a psychological price from both parents and kids, we seem to feel that whatever price is being exacted in the short run is outweighed by benefits in the long run. We are hopeful that our intense, pressured, and often controlling involvement will ultimately reap a personal, intellectual, and financial bonanza for our children. Is it possible, in spite of the well-documented negative psychological effects of intrusion, control, and pressure, that "overparented" kids will ultimately become particularly successful either professionally or financially? And if they do, will they become happy adults? In spite of the aphorism that "money can't buy happiness," more and more Americans are pouring time, effort, and personal resources into making more money, assuming that there will be some positive payback for all their hard work.

The fact is, this particular aphorism is correct. Money cannot buy happiness. Or, more precisely, once you have enough money to meet basic needs, money does not make you happier. Money certainly can buy all kinds of "stuff." It can make it easy to purchase services, and it can buy unique and interesting experiences, but research is very clear on this: money buys *neither* happiness nor unhappiness.[1] So if money itself is essentially neutral in terms of mental health, then why are the children of affluent families so disproportionately unhappy?

Casting a dispassionate eye on the subject of money is challenging. Bombarded by a lifetime of exposure to advertising, whose sole job it is to create anxiety and then assuage it by selling us cars or toothpaste or deodorant, most of us have had our thoughts about money influenced in multiple ways by those who profit most from consumerism. "Whoever said money can't buy happiness, doesn't know how to spend it," reads a Lexus ad brought to you by Madison Avenue, not the American Psychological Association. As a result, most of us have reached conclusions about money by having our perceptions manipulated, not by being exposed to what researchers know.

In addition, our thinking about money is influenced not only by our current socioeconomic standing, but by our socioeconomic history as well. I'm just as likely to look at the world through the blue-collar eyes of my childhood as through the upper-middle-class eyes of my middle age. As we try to untangle the factors that are leading to elevated levels of emotional distress in affluent families, we would do well to inventory our own often ambivalent views about the role of money in our lives. Bearing in mind that we come to this topic with biases and conflicts, we are fortunate to have a large body of research, spanning over thirty years, to help us understand the relationships between money, psychological adjustment, and happiness.

MONEY DOESN'T MAKE US HAPPIER

Two researchers, Drs. Ed Diener and David Myers, have looked at the issue of money and happiness, by pooling data on this subject on over a million people in forty-five countries. Most people in most countries report themselves as being "pretty happy." In addition to income, factors such as literacy, political freedom, and civil rights all influence a person's happiness, what researchers often call "well-being."[2] Not surprisingly, people who live in nations with high levels of poverty and low levels of civil rights report lower levels of happiness. However, the majority of people worldwide, regardless of age, race, or socioeconomic status appear to be relatively happy as long as their basic needs are met. It's noteworthy that happiness does not necessarily rise in direct proportion to the wealth of any particular country. For example, in the 1990s, the Irish reported higher levels of life satisfaction than both the Japanese and the West Germans, in spite of the fact that the Japanese and the West Germans had twice the average income of the Irish. Summarizing years of work on the relationship between money and happiness, one prominent researcher writes: "People who go to work in their overalls and on the bus are just as happy, on the average, as those in suits who drive to work in their own Mercedes."[3]

In spite of these findings, most people in this country believe that having more money would indeed make them happier. Interestingly, as our incomes rise, we believe we need more and more money to maintain a minimal standard of living. In this country, poorer people and wealthier people give very different answers to the question "How much money would you need to be happy?" In a study designed to answer this question people who earned less than $30,000 a year said that $50,000 a year would fulfill their dreams, while those making over $100,000 said they would need $250,000 to be satisfied.[4] While it can be tempting to conclude that those with more money are simply greedier than those with less, there is an important alternate explanation. Most parents try to provide "the best" for their children, and many upper-middle-class parents are driven to work hard, not primarily for material goods, but to be able to provide their children with superior educational opportunities. The umbrella of "education" can become quite broad for affluent families and often includes a host of travel and cultural opportunities unimagined by less financially well-off families.

As for some of the very richest people in this country, those among the Forbes 100 wealthiest Americans, their level of happiness is only slightly happier than the average American's.[5] For most people, the correlation between income and personal happiness is "virtually negligible."[6] In spite of short-lived changes in mood, the accumulation of more money or goods has essentially no impact on how we feel. Studies on lottery winners show that within approximately *eight weeks*, most of these individuals return to pretty much the same state of mind they were in before their windfall.[7] Certainly we may get a shot of euphoria from a raise or a new purchase, but such satisfactions are temporary and surprisingly fleeting. We each seem to have a "set point" of happiness, and return to it quickly even after substantial positive changes in our financial status.

In the words of David Myers, whose research informs much of this discussion, "Thanks to our capacity to adapt to ever greater fame and fortune, yesterday's luxuries can soon become today's necessities and tomorrow's relics."[8] I grew up in a working-class family, in a small house with one bathroom and a backyard the size of a postage stamp. My husband and I, both reasonably successful professionals, live in a large home with a sprawling backyard. Am I happier? Not at all. This is not a comment on my marriage or my life circumstances. Rather, it is simply an acknowledgment that my own level of happiness has not been impacted in any substantial way by my rising economic standing.

Take a moment and think about your own life and whether or not changing economics has had a *lasting* effect on your happiness. A significant part of your level of happiness was determined before you were born, by your genes and your parents. Studies show that approximately 50 percent of happiness is inherited, leaving 50 percent to be determined by parenting, life experiences, and luck.[9] While researchers in the field of optimism/pessimism find that it is possible to cultivate a more optimistic outlook, this is a personal and therapeutic endeavor, not a financial one.[10]

In 1958, when John Kenneth Galbraith wrote his landmark book about prosperity in the United States, *The Affluent Society*, the average American's per capita income expressed in today's dollars was $9,000. Today, the average American income is more than double that, at $20,000 per person. Since most Americans believe it is "very important" to be financially well off we would expect a real ratcheting up of happiness in a country that has more of everything: leisure, money, cars, home ownership, air conditioners, televisions, computers, etc. [11] We are twice as rich as when Galbraith was writing; are we twice as happy? Well, no, not at all actually, and many of us are twice as *unhappy*. Teen suicide has quadrupled in this period of time and rates of divorce have doubled. In addition, we are seeing a far higher incidence of many serious emotional illnesses, such as depression, anxiety disorders, behavioral disorders, self-mutilation, and substance abuse.[12] Apparently economic growth has not improved our psychological condition one bit. And, paradoxically, it appears that the group that is at highest risk of psychological impairment is comprised of the very children we would expect to be benefiting from this upswing in the standard of living.

It's hard to understand how the kinds of special opportunities enjoyed by affluent families can possibly be the source of a host of negative psychological outcomes for children. Surely tutors, private schools, top universities, and experiences abroad can only broaden our children's experiences and expose them to greater opportunities. Sure, it may not turn an unhappy child into a happy child, but is it really possible that something about our affluent lifestyle is actually *lessening* the likelihood that our children will lead happy, secure, interesting lives? These thoughts may be particularly difficult for financially comfortable parents to entertain. After all, many of us have worked overtime our whole adult lives in order to ensure our children a prosperous future. If research shows that it is not money per se that impacts mental health, then what about our affluent lifestyle is so emotionally toxic to our children? The following story illustrates how part of the answer to this question resides in the values of the culture of affluence.

ALLISON:
HOW AFFLUENCE CAN GET IN THE WAY
OF EMOTIONAL DEVELOPMENT

Sixteen-year-old Allison is typical of a new breed of teenager finding their way into my office. She is a delightful young lady, articulate, charming, and bright. Unlike most of my patients, Allison was brought to therapy by her parents, not for any particular psychological problems, but because her parents noticed how many of her friends were running into trouble and they wanted to make sure that Allison would have someone to talk to, "just in case." Both parents had high-pressure jobs and were frequently unavailable to Allison. While years ago I might have considered this a trivial request, I no longer do. When parents request that I fill the role of sympathetic advisor, it typically means that the parents are either too busy, too insecure, or simply not up to the job. Some parents rightfully surmise that their own depression, anxiety, or alienation is getting in the way of their parenting skills. I then become an ear for the child as well as a resource for the parent.

Allison's parents couldn't "put their finger" on any particular concerns about their daughter, but they worried that she was "too dependent" on them and that they had cultivated this dependency by happily managing or outsourcing most of the details of Allison's life. After all, she was such a trouble-free kid, well liked, good grades, why shouldn't they make her life as easy as possible? Besides, they were often guilty about their frequent absences due either to work or social demands.

While they showered Allison with material goods, she had few responsibilities. Lately they admitted that Allison seemed somewhat "low-key" but was easily perked up by shopping sprees when her mom could find a few hours to spend with her. Many of her acquisitions hung in her closet unworn. Her parents were only mildly concerned about this, feeling that Allison's unused purchases were a small price to pay for the temporary lift she seemed to get from buying things.

Allison was happy to come to my office and run through the typical tribulations of adolescence. We easily fell into a comfortable relationship. Free from the kinds of truly worrisome problems I so often see in my office, I looked forward to my sessions with Allison. I thought she was an indulged and materialistic child, but I assumed that, like most of my adolescent patients, Allison's concerns with the superficial would lessen as she became more comfortable and trusting with me.

Allison's life revolved around pleasing, taking her cues from and evaluating herself through the eyes of others. Our comfortable relationship was partly due to the fact that Allison was amazingly compliant and dependent on me. Unlike many teenagers, she never missed an appointment, proudly showed me her outstanding academic work, and was anxious to know my opinions on everything from how many advanced-placement courses she should take to how she looked in her latest Juicy Couture sweat set.

On one level Allison was a dream child (and patient), never angry or challenging; but there was also something strikingly absent about her. While Allison talked a lot in session, she rarely talked about anything interesting or important. Pleasant and cheerful, she nonetheless seemed devoid of substance, chattering about clothes and cars and vacations, but rarely about her own conflicts or aspirations. Adolescent therapists are accustomed to hearing the endless details of adolescent life, and our genuine interest in these details typically leads our young patients to begin revealing deeper feelings. Therapy always begins with what *matters* to your patient, and for teenagers what matters is how they look or who they hang out with or whether they will "hook up" or not. As therapy moves forward, these concerns typically give way to issues of dependence and independence, sense of self, or relationship problems. Allison never moved forward into deeper territory.

Allison's identity was conferred entirely by the things she owned and the people around her. She never struggled with the core issue of adolescence: autonomy. She was a child whose sense of self was crafted by the outside world, by those she worked so hard to please and charm. As I found myself becoming increasingly distracted during our sessions, I realized that nothing much was happening in therapy, and that I had struck a bad deal with Allison. She would be a pleaser as long as she could rely on my approval for her self-definition and as long as I allowed her to avoid confronting her inner life. Admiration for her clothes, hugs for her grades, and pats on the back for her "easy" nature had all been a mistake. I was humbled, as a seasoned psychologist, to see how easily I had aided and abetted Allison's truncated development.

No one slides through adolescence that easily. While the myth that adolescence is a time of "sturm und drang" has been laid to rest, it certainly is a time of defining, redefining, and fine-tuning a sense of self. What is important about Allison's story, unlike so many of the stories in this book where suffering and impairment are obvious, is how easily she was able to "pass." Casual observation would never reveal that anything was wrong with Allison; but her parent's unease was well founded—behind all her well-honed social skills, Allison's sense of self was thin as air.

As I backed off being so eager to tell Allison what I thought, as I began limiting my admiration of her possessions and performances, Allison became at first confused and then angry and finally depressed. She wanted to stop coming to see me. She said she no longer knew what I "wanted from her." She was irritated at my notion that I had made some mistakes in her therapy and that we should turn our attention not to what I wanted but to finding out more about what she wanted. Trying to downplay Allison's superficial, facile exterior and find "the real" Allison was difficult, not because Allison was "hiding" her real self, but because there was very little self-development behind the façade. Allison's whole life had been defined by well-meaning parents, relatives, and teachers, robbing Allison of the opportunity to think about what she wanted for herself. Like the material goods that substituted for real connection in Allison's life, her reliance on others substituted for the real psychological work of self-development.

I had waited too long to correct my mistakes with Allison. She stormed out of therapy one day, declaring the whole endeavor "boring." What was really boring to Allison was Allison herself. She had evaded growing into a complex, robust, conflicted, normal adolescent. Allison had neither the internal resources nor, more important, the motivation to begin working on her outsized dependence on others to affirm her fragile sense of self. I tell this case in spite of its poor outcome because it taught me a lot about how eager we can be to have our children (or our patients) look good and how pleasurable it can be to remain the center of their lives. Unfortunately, the price they pay for our gratification is impairment in their capacity to be independent.

It struck me that something about Allison's reliance on others was a common state of affairs among many of my affluent adolescent patients. Was there actually something about living in an affluent family that made these kids more dependent on others? Were their parents more easily fooled into believing that things were doing well when they weren't? Allison's case, seemingly easy, ultimately unsuccessful, was one of the reasons I became interested in the issues of affluence and emotional problems. How come our seemingly warm and useful relationship unraveled so easily when I put the slightest pressure on Allison to stand on her own two feet?

It was not money per se that impaired Allison's development; rather it was a parenting style that emphasized the importance of external motivation while promoting materialism as a substitute for the hard personal and interpersonal work that adolescence demands. While this parenting style is by no means restricted to affluent families, it is often found there because affluent parents have the resources to default to materialism when their own problems or pressures make meaningful connection with their children difficult. This is a bad bargain all around; it transmits poor values and leaves our kids in the lurch emotionally because it encourages them to forgo the development of internal motivation, keeping them dependent on others and on material goods for a sense of self. And for affluent parents, who often value external markers of success themselves, it can be tempting to let a bit of unease slide when our kids seem to be performing well.

MATERIALISM: THE DARK SIDE OF AFFLUENCE

Materialism is not the same as having money. As we've seen, once basic needs are met, there is no relationship between money and happiness. *Materialism, on the other hand, does predict a lack of happiness and satisfaction.*[13] Materialism is a value system that emphasizes wealth, status, image, and material consumption. It is a measure of how much we value material things over other things in our lives, like friends, family, and work. It keeps us wedded to external measures of accomplishment for a sense of self—prestige, power, money for adults; grades, clothes, electronics for kids.

The tendency to accumulate objects and to seek prestige may have served our ancestors well. Groups of people with more "stuff," particularly livestock, tools, and weapons, were certainly more likely to survive than those who did not value or seek to accumulate those things. Having a prestigious leader with "the most stuff" helped the group in two ways: it provided organized leadership and presented a formidable opponent to enemies or those looking to steal the group's "stuff." But in this country most of us are long past needing to accumulate things for the sake of survival. That is, unless we broaden our notion of survival to include "I'll just die without those Manolos."

As a young and inexperienced therapist I was part of a team counseling a very wealthy couple going through a divorce. The wife would spend hours in my office lamenting the loss of her lifestyle. She wept most about her sheets. She had spent years sleeping on the finest Egyptian cotton, carefully ironed and scented by the laundress. As a twenty-eight-year-old financially struggling intern, I was at a total loss to understand her sorrow about her sheets. Now I understand that those sheets were a stand-in for the many things she was losing: her marriage, home, family, friends, and status. Decades later, I understand her upset about losing her costly cotton sheets. "Yesterday's luxuries become today's necessities." We all have things, luxuries really, that we've become attached to and would feel deprived without. Liking stuff isn't the problem; liking stuff more than people is. My patient was losing a lifetime of connection, and yet her grief centered on the things, not the people, she was losing. While often associated with affluence, materialism is found among people in all socioeconomic groups.

Affluent people get to indulge their penchant for accumulating "stuff" more than most, making their materialism more obvious. A father in a neighboring town has a young daughter with a drug problem. In response to a question about her well-being he responds, "We had to put her in rehab for a month, and it cost us a

BMW."[14] When money is no object, blatant expressions of materialism can make us wince.

Materialism may be unappealing and suggest superficial values, but how does that lead to unhappiness or psychological problems? Materialists may not be saints, but what about materialism makes people unhappy?

One of the largest and most disturbing studies done on the trend toward an increasingly materialistic orientation among young people comes from the annual survey conducted by the University of California at Los Angeles and the American Council on Education. Researchers at UCLA have studied nearly a quarter of a million students entering college over the past forty years.[15] When asked about reasons for going to college during the 1960s and early seventies, most students placed the highest value on "becoming an educated person" or "developing a philosophy of life." A minority deemed "making a lot of money" as the main reason to attend college. Beginning in the 1990s, a majority of students say that "making a lot of money" has become the most important reason to go to college, outranking both the reasons above, as well as "becoming an authority in my field," or "helping others in difficulty." This shift in values among college students takes place at the same time that rates of depression, suicide, and other psychological problems have risen dramatically among this group.

Armand Hammer, the self-promoting industrialist once said, "Money is my first, last, and only love."[16] Aside from the obvious misperception that money can somehow serve the same psychological function as love, connection, and reciprocity, there is also the suggestion that all energy—psychological, physical, sexual, and emotional—should be devoted to this illusory pursuit. When money becomes overly important, it crowds out other goals, endeavors, and interests; work, friendship, marriage, hobbies, parenting, spiritual development, and intellectual challenges can all fall by the wayside.

While few among us believe that money is our "first, last, and only love," the UCLA study results highlight the fact that more and more young people feel that the pursuit of money takes precedence over personal, moral, and intellectual development. As we saw in Allison's story, materialism is both a cause and a symptom of impaired self-development. Materialism is not only about having shallow values; it is also about how easy it can be to choose the simple seduction of objects over the complex substance of relationships. Materialism sucks the life out of purpose and altruism as kids become increasingly self-centered and indifferent to the needs of others.

Most psychologists are in agreement as to the fundamental needs of people. First and foremost are basic biological needs for food, shelter, and clothing. In addition, humans are believed to have "higher-order" but still fundamental needs for authentic self-expression, intimate relationships, contributions to the community, and a sense of being able to master challenging tasks.[17]

Money can, but does not necessarily, make a contribution to the fulfillment of "higher-order" needs. We have all known happy, fulfilled people with little in the way of money or material goods, and miserable, destructive people who have "everything money can buy." Clearly, money can help the development of "higher-order" needs by providing educational opportunities that lead to a sense of mastery, or travel opportunities that contribute to interests or relationships. We don't necessarily contribute to our children's emotional problems when we buy them cars or expensive clothes or high-end vacations; we contribute when they believe, either by observing our behavior or our values, that these are the things that matter most in life.

At its worst, materialism turns even our most valuable relationships into commodities. A Citicorp billboard claims "Your most important asset is the one who is asking you when you are going to raise his allowance." Examples of blatant materialism can be easy to spot, but when they suffuse our culture they can be difficult to recognize. Parents need to be alert to how both they and their children can have their attitudes shaped by advertising messages that subtly or humorously suggest that things and people are of equivalent value.

Research clearly shows that our own levels of materialism profoundly affect our children's levels of materialism. When parents—mothers in particular—value financial success more than affiliation, community, or self-acceptance, they are likely to have children who share these values.[18] Alternately, prosocial moms turn out prosocial kids. Materialism and prosocial values work in opposition to each other. Materialism is disproportionately focused on individualism, acquisition, and competition. Prosocial values promote the idea that the needs of the group are at least as important as the needs of the individual, that those who are more fortunate have a responsibility to help those who are less fortunate, and that progress is often best accomplished by communal effort. Not only does a materialistic value orientation bode poorly for our society—materialists are unlikely to be philanthropists—it also bodes poorly for kids themselves. Materialistic kids have lower grades and higher rates of both depression and substance abuse than nonmaterialistic kids.[19]

Transmitting values is one of the most important parenting jobs we have. Instead of talking about your next purchase, consider sharing with your children your enthusiasm for activities that make you feel productive and engaged—your work, your book group, a volunteer job or community-education class you're considering. Talk about how to make moral choices, whether at home or out in the world. Help your kid understand the difference between healthy and unhealthy competition. When a subculture is heading in the wrong direction, it is up to the adults of the larger culture to steer it back in the right direction. If the adolescent subculture pushes crime, then parents need to push safety; if it pushes materialism and self-absorption, then parents need to push altruism and generosity.

THE FALSE PROMISES OF MATERIALISM

It is likely that almost all Americans are materialistic to some degree. After all, we live in one of the most affluent countries in the world and have at our disposal a dazzling array of fun, aesthetically pleasing, status-enhancing toys to choose from. With the exception of small pockets of individuals who have chosen to separate themselves from the cultural mainstream, most of us are constantly bombarded by messages implying or insisting that our lives would be so much happier if we just had whatever it is that is being sold. A foldout Macy's ad asks "What Makes You Happy?" and when we open the flap we find out that the answer is "Shoes, Bags and Jewelry."

Capitalism needs consumers, and as President Bush told us after September 11, we are doing our patriotic duty when we shop. But dabbling in material goods is far different from having materialism as a central value in one's life. While occasionally parents transmit materialistic values openly, more often the ways in which we encourage materialism in our children are subtle and unintentional.

Why "Retail Therapy" Is an Oxymoron

Most of us have heard the term "retail therapy," or "shopping therapy." We live in a complex and frightening world, one in which many people feel they have little control. Without a robust sense of self, and in the absence of family, community, or religious support, the world can seem overwhelming and frightening. Shopping is one way to control our environment. It puts us in charge of transactions and confers a sense of power on the buyer. This type of power is illusory, of course. The real power is being exerted by large corporations and their advertisers, who are paid to suggest that consumer goods confer magical and protective powers on buyers. Advertising directed at women, who are responsible for the majority of consumer decisions in this country, plays to our emotional, physical, sexual, and financial insecurities. Hair-color products promise to make us "sexier," douches promise to make us "cleaner," cars promise to give us "power," and in the most compromised advertising on this planet, cigarettes promise to give us "freedom" instead of cancer, heart disease, and emphysema.

Because advertising is designed to first make us feel insecure and then solve our insecurity by offering products, it is particularly problematic for adolescents, who already feel terribly insecure. Adolescent girls in particular are vulnerable to the siren song of materialism and consumerism because they are more likely to be in the marketplace than boys. Magazines, popular among pre-teens and teens, distort developing concepts of relationships by presenting images of female perfection possible only through the wonders of airbrushing and computer manipulation. Researchers and clinicians such as Jean Kilbourne and Mary Pipher have done an excellent job of exposing the ways in which advertisers target girls and women in an effort to make them feel bad about themselves in order to encourage consumerism.

Can it be fun to shop with our kids? Sure, if you're going shopping for things that are needed, for a special event, to look around, or just to hang out together for a few hours. Young adolescent girls shop together as a way of developing relationships and gaining competence out in the marketplace. Shopping becomes problematic when it is regularly used as a way to reduce distress. Both boys and girls use this poor solution, but it is a particularly popular strategy shared by mothers and daughters. Taking your daughter shopping to "chase away the blues," or because "she brightens up whenever we go shopping," not only teaches materialistic values, it also prevents the development of skills for dealing with sad feelings. Throwing material goods at problems is a notoriously unsuccessful solution; problems need to be addressed with thought, insight, and empathy, not shoes and purses.

It is a short hop from thinking that external "stuff" will alleviate emotional distress to thinking that drugs or sex will do the same thing. Parents need to reinforce with their children the reality that it is not external things that help them to handle difficult feelings; rather, it is the development of internal resources that provide a safety net when they are struggling. Helping your child understand and manage her distressing feelings, and finding ways to cope with them, are life-long gifts; designer jeans are only good for a season.

Materialism and Unhealthy Competition

Materialism and competition go hand in hand. Consumer goods have magical, curative powers only when they are not possessed by too many others. Louis Vuitton bags lose their cachet when you can buy replicas for $35 on Third Avenue. Materialism needs an aura of exclusivity in order to lessen the insecurity that drives people to become materialistic in the first place. An outgrowth of materialism is the notion that there are "winners" and "losers," the "haves" and the "have-nots." Parents need to check in with themselves regularly and avoid endorsing values that pit children against each other or suggest that resources are so scarce that children must be in constant competition. In general, it is better for kids to see each other as potential sources of cooperation than as competitors.

The excessive focus on competition found in many affluent homes comes from diverse sources—anxiety, narcissism, and insecurity, as well as materialism. But the link between materialism and competition is particularly strong. In a fascinating study that looks at who chooses to cooperate with friends and who chooses to "get ahead," researchers find that college students who rate high on materialism are far more likely to choose "getting ahead" over cooperating with their friends.[20]

For your kid to get into Princeton or Yale or Stanford, twenty similar kids have to fail in their attempts. Getting into top schools is a terrific achievement. It helps when parents emphasize integrity along with achievement. Without this balance, kids find themselves competing and even cheating against their best friends.

At the prestigious private high school in my community, the SAT scores of some 300 students had to be thrown out because a handful of kids were found to be cheating. One of the cheaters was a patient of mine. I can vouch for the fact that this young, frightened girl is not without a conscience. On the contrary, she talked about feeling keenly responsible for "making my parents happy after all they've done for me." A bright enough, but not stellar, student, she felt compelled to cheat so that she did not run the risk of disappointing her parents or being seen as a failure by her friends. Pressure to excel was so intense that moral issues were swept aside, and this ordinarily thoughtful girl lost sight of the fact that her actions could negatively affect many other students.

HAPPINESS IS AN INSIDE JOB

We want to avoid training our children to believe that it is external rewards that are responsible for personal happiness. This is not to say that external things never soothe us. We all have times when something we buy gives us a bit of a lift. But we also need to recognize that whatever was troubling us was simply Band-Aided by our acquisition. Sometimes cuts are superficial and all they need is a Band-Aid to heal. But deeper wounds are not cured by Band-Aids; as a matter of fact, Band-Aids can temporarily hide wounds that are festering and in need of more serious attention. To effectively deal with the deeper cuts in life children need to be able to turn inward and find a reliable repertoire of skills that will help them navigate life's inevitable challenges.

Having money can make it easy to externalize problems, which in turn can cultivate materialism. Affluent teens buy their English essays online, pay other kids to wait on long lines at movie openings, and cajole their tutors into completing homework assignments that have been neglected. They come to see the outside world, and the "stuff" that can be bought there, as a dependable (if temporary) source of relief and satisfaction.

Money can also act as a powerful disincentive for children to step into the real world of work. Dr. Donna Mehregany, a child and adolescent psychiatrist, and a clinical faculty member at Case Western Reserve in Cleveland, Ohio, has a large practice of adolescents drawn largely from the affluent suburbs of Shaker Heights and Pepper Pike. She points out that children with unlimited resources at their disposal are unlikely to appreciate the kinds of work opportunities that have traditionally been valued by youngsters. She experienced this lack of appreciation firsthand while baby-sitting a nine-year-old boy and his five-year-old sister, the children of a neighborhood friend. Toward the end of the day, when Dr. Mehregany had to attend to some work, she asked her own nine-year-old son and her friend's son if they could watch his sister briefly. As incentive, she offered them two dollars each. Her friend's son was taken aback and then contemptuous. "I have two million dollars in my trust fund, why would I work for two dollars?" Aside from exhibiting a *really* bad attitude, this young man missed the opportunity to learn the importance of taking responsibility seriously, and the satisfaction of being a contributing community member.

Children need work experiences to develop a sense that success is a function of their own efforts. Some of the wisest, and most successful wealthy parents I know are extremely careful about how much money their children have. These parents have their kids participate in family chores and neighborhood jobs and do not discuss family wealth with their kids—after all, none of it was earned by the child! Every affluent community has a couple of insufferable youngsters who are only too happy to let everyone know exactly what is in their bank accounts and what their parents are worth. While they may be temporarily cultivated as friends for the goodies they provide, they are never genuinely well-liked kids. Parents are role models, and when they use money to manipulate behavior, they teach their children to be manipulative as well.

A mother sits in my office and offers her son a new car if he will just stop taking drugs, another mother unabashedly offers her daughter a hundred dollars for every pound she loses. Because money and material objects are plentiful in comfortable families, they often become the default motivator when parents want to change their child's behavior. This is a disastrous approach on two counts. First, it models materialism to the child. Second, it can be very seductive to teens who are still shoring up their judgment and impulse control. It schools them in a strategy of relying on others rather than on themselves to make changes in their lives. The more desperate we feel about needing to use rewards to enforce compliance, the less likely it is to be successful. The very fact that we are trying to buy our children off with material goods should tell us that we are feeling overwhelmed and ineffective. Products can never substitute for parental interest, presence, and guidance. My office carpet has seen a steady stream of Versace sunglasses, Prada bags, and BMW keys thrown down in disgust by teenagers who know that their parents have gotten off cheap when they resort to materialism and external rewards as a parenting strategy.

I have seen this kind of brokered deal made over and over in my office. "Do this, or don't do this, and I will buy you whatever." *It is a strategy bound to fail, and while it may produce some short-term behavioral change, I have never seen it produce long-term effective change in a child.* Buying children off is a parenting strategy that only leads to a lessening of parental power and a fortifying of childish greed. It is a particularly damaging approach with adolescents who need every opportunity they can get to further the development of internal resources like independence, self-control, and the ability to disregard peer pressure. Kids quit smoking, lose weight, and stay off drugs when they see the benefit of those behaviors *for themselves*. Unfortunately, a lifetime of shaping behavior by using material rewards makes it difficult for children to turn inwards with any confidence in their own ability to make reasonable decisions in the absence of external, seductive direction.

Internal motivation is the generator that propels children to figure out their particular interests, abilities, and passions. Internal motivation is not tied to rewards; it is what drives kids to engage in activities that are satisfying for their own sake. It is the basis of all true learning. Think of the child who pores over history books, skateboards for hours on end, or works diligently in the garage fixing his bike. Think of the experience we have all had of "getting lost"—what researchers call "flow"—in something we found compelling and challenging.[21]

External motivation, on the other hand, drives kids to participate in activities not *primarily* because of the activity itself but because of some associated gain—a grade, a trophy, a mention in the local newspaper. It strips learning of excitement, since what is most valuable is not the learning experience per se but whatever perks accompany it. Externally motivated kids tend to confuse performance with learning and as a result have lower grades, lower achievement scores, less interest in learning, less ability to think creatively, and greater psychological impairment than children who are internally motivated.[22]

One of the most capable teachers in my school district tells the following story. It was the end of a long week, and her class was so preoccupied with their upcoming math test that she found her lesson constantly interrupted by anxious kids wanting to know more about the test, the grading, how much of their final grade would rest on this test, and so on. Unable to get her kids to focus on the day's lesson, she told them to put away their binders and that they would spend the rest of the period drawing. A dozen hands shot up, all wanting to know how she would grade their artwork. "That's when I knew I was through with teaching," she said.

When external measures of success are all that kids can think about, their ability to find meaning in their work is diminished. Being passionate about grades is not the same as being passionate about Faulkner, calculus, or the periodic table of the elements. Admissions counselors at some of the most prestigious universities in this country have commented on the lack of enthusiasm about learning among their bright and accomplished incoming students. William Caskey, former admissions officer for Brown University, comments: "I see many teens of means with few interests or passions. Ironically, many are academically successful. Rarely, though, is their success driven by a quest for knowledge. Rather, they tie academic achievement to an eventual lifestyle of luxury."[23]

Matt Stone, one of the talented creators of *South Park*, summarized the irrationality of our excessive focus on performance. Describing the anxiety he faced in sixth grade when he took a math exam, Matt remembers: "Everyone said don't screw up because if you screw up you won't get into honors math in the seventh grade and if you don't get into honors math in the seventh grade then you won't get into it in the eighth or ninth or tenth or eleventh and you'll die poor and lonely." Parents need to reassure their children that they will not "die poor and lonely" if they don't get into honors math, or become school valedictorian, or go to Harvard. Kids are bombarded with messages about the importance of high performance at school, at home, and in the media. What they really need is to be educated about the values of perseverance and perspective, and to understand that learning and performance are not always the same thing. They need to see that their parents value effort, curiosity, and intellectual courage.

Internal and external motivation are not mutually exclusive. Young children are driven both by their innate curiosity and their strong desire to please their parents. External motivation morphs into internal motivation as children take in the ideas, interests, and values of their parents, sort through them to find the ones that are a good fit, and tailor them to their own particular temperament, level of development, interests, and abilities. The point is not to stop valuing high grades or outstanding performance but to help our children internalize *for themselves* a desire to be capable and interested in learning. We do this by valuing the process more than the end result. Studies show that children who are internally motivated not only learn more and perform better, but, perhaps most important, they *enjoy* their work more, making it more likely that they will be willing and eager to try their hand at increasingly difficult challenges.[24]

Parents do nothing but get in the way when they insist on replicating their own interests, values, and even professions in their children. "Of course you'll go to law school. All the men in our family have been lawyers." Much better for your son to find out early on that he's not suited to being a lawyer before wasting ten years in a profession he hates and relying on Prozac to get him through the day. We need to always deal with the child in front of us, not the child of our fantasies. You may love getting up and speaking to the PTA, but your child may find public speaking downright painful, preferring instead nonverbal, spatial tasks like drawing or building. We need to help our children find those activities that suit their particular strengths and interests. Your enthusiasm and pleasure in these activities will help nurture your child's sense of competence.

I once conducted an entire psychotherapy with a twelve-year-old self-proclaimed "geek" by talking almost exclusively about tropical fish. No one in his family shared his passion for marine life, and his parents were concerned about his mediocre grades in spite of his high IQ. I'm still in occasional touch with this remarkable young man, who is healthy, happy, and working on a Ph.D. in marine biology at a major university. Try to take pleasure in your child's idiosyncratic interests. It is at this intersection of internal motivation, parental support, and developing interests that the child's sense of self is taking shape.

Money is not the culprit. Money does not contribute to emotional problems in our children. It does not foster depression, anxiety disorders, or substance abuse. It is the culture of affluence—a culture that embraces materialism, that values performance over learning and external motivation over internal motivation, that overemphasizes competition and offers a dearth of opportunities to see adults behave with compassion and integrity—that is sickening our children. In order to correct these deficits we need to teach our children that objects can never replace relationships. We need to encourage the development of internal motivation and downplay the importance of external motivation. And, finally, we need to model altruism and reciprocity, both within our families and our communities.

While this book is certainly aimed at understanding and remedying the emotional problems faced by an increasingly large percentage of privileged adolescents, it is not only for the parents of kids who are at odds with themselves. Much has been learned about child and adolescent development in the last decade. Many of the "theories" that once drove our understanding of child development have been debunked. For example, for many years competitive parents bombarded their squirming toddlers and preschoolers with flash cards to help them become early readers. We now know that children who learn to read in preschool are no more likely to be academically successful than children who learn to read a couple of years later, in elementary school. Time, money, and energy were all wasted on an effort that was out of synch with how children develop. We could all benefit from reacquainting ourselves with the basic tenets of child development. We need to understand what a child's healthy sense of self looks like and be alert to failures in the development of the self. Finally, understanding the challenges that children face at different stages of development makes it more likely that we can help them with their most important task—developing a sense of self that, regardless of the vagaries of life, will always offer a place to come home to.

PART TWO

HOW THE CULTURE OF
AFFLUENCE WORKS AGAINST
THE DEVELOPMENT
OF THE SELF

· CHAPTER 4 ·

What Is a Healthy "Self"?

Years ago when I greeted a new adolescent patient and said, "Tell me about yourself," I was typically met either with oppositional silence or a feisty, "You're the doctor, *you* tell *me* what's wrong." This opening interchange was a prelude to therapeutic work. It suggested my interest, and it gave my wary young patients an ambiguous opening to answer as they saw fit. A few plunged right in, talking about their problems at home or their feelings of depression, but the majority waited me out a bit, testing to see if I was trustworthy before revealing vulnerable parts of themselves.

More recently, the well-off teenagers I see seem confused by this same question. They tend to respond with a list of accomplishments: "Things aren't too bad. I'm in three honors classes and I'm a starter on varsity basketball." Or failures: "My life sucks. I hate the way I look. My butt is way too big and my boobs are way too small." Typically, this type of factual description of the self is common among young children. Ask a six-year-old to tell you about herself and she's apt to say, "I can run fast, my eyes are brown, and I hate broccoli." A decade later, this same child is expected to communicate about her "self" with more insight and awareness. My current crop of patients has difficulty "fleshing out" their inner lives. In spite of often being personable, they seem surprisingly immature. Over the course of treatment, it becomes clear that, for many of these teenagers, the development of a sense of self stalled somewhere back in childhood.

Developing a "self" is an inspiring, complex, creative, and some-times unpredictable developmental process. A young child's sense of self is formed largely by the opinions of his parents. Their approval or disapproval provides the foundation upon which a child begins to have a sense of who he is and whether or not he is lovable. **A sense of lovability is the core of all healthy self-development.**

Remember how in the early months of your child's life you could spend extraordinary amounts of time simply gazing at your infant, awestruck by the unique and precious being that lay in your arms. Remember how your child gazed back at you, mirroring your seriousness or delight, your smile or your laughter. The profound feelings of love that parents feel for their new son or daughter provide a working model for children of how the world will value them, as well as how they will value themselves. A child who consistently gazes into loving eyes, into eyes that notice and take pleasure in his *uniqueness,* is being helped to develop a healthy sense of self.

Given consistent parental love and support, children feel brave enough to enter the beckoning world on their own. They feel loved and valued both for the mere fact of their existence as well as for their particular endowments—curiosity, charm, thoughtfulness, adventurousness, generosity. At this intersection of a child's inborn predispositions and a parent's loving acceptance a sense of self takes form and flourishes.

Clearly, a child cannot remain dependent for a sense of self on his parents or other important adults in his life for too long. Not only is this unrealistic, it's unhealthy as well. A child needs to become increasingly independent, capable of drawing on his own *internal* resources as he moves forward. Parents, coaches, teachers—all have other interests and preoccupations; they move away, they die. The reason that a well-developed sense of self is so critical is that, in the desirable and inevitable absence of external support, a sense of self provides both a comfortable home base and an internal compass for navigating through life. Lives are never perfect—not our own, not our children's—but a healthy sense of self helps insure that life will be interesting, satisfying, and manageable.

Kids need to be encouraged to "think for themselves," to incorporate the point of view of parents and teachers and peers, and then be able to formulate their *own* point of view. As children become increasingly comfortable with a sense of who they are, with their particular strengths and weaknesses, they are able to develop a reliable repertoire for meeting challenges, as well as for recovering from failures. "I always go for a run when I'm feeling down," says a teen who has found, *within herself,* a reliable and effective way of dealing with distressing feelings. While this solution may have begun as a parent's suggestion to "walk it off," the teen who takes it in and makes it uniquely her own—in this case a run, not a walk—has developed a dependable strategy for dealing with upset. Her sense of self is fortified as she has repeated experiences of successfully figuring out ways to handle difficult feelings. Kids carry their "selves," not their parents, around with them at all times.

Children of privilege often run into trouble with self-development when parents are hesitant to encourage this transition from reliance on adults to self-reliance. The danger of the culture of affluence is not simply that it is superficial or materialistic; what is far more dangerous are the ways in which it interferes with the development of a sense of self. For many children in this culture, parents' demands for achievement have all but crowded out kids' internal push toward autonomy. It is hard to develop an authentic sense of self when there is constant pressure to adopt a socially facile, highly competitive, performance-oriented, unblemished "self" that is promoted by omnipresent adults. This may encourage *some* children to perform at high levels, but, more important, it also encourages dependency, depression, and a truncated sense of self in *most* children.

Parents pressure their children to be outstanding, while neglecting the very process by which outstanding children are formed. "Outstanding" is not about grades, trophies, high status, or recognition by others, although it certainly may include these things. In and of themselves, these things tell us nothing about a person's psychological health. Wealthy, powerful people can be desolate and lead miserable lives. They commit suicide at the same rate as people from less-fortunate economic circumstances. From a psychologist's point of view, outstanding children are those who have developed a "self" that is authentic, capable, loving, creative, in control of itself, and moral. These components of a healthy sense of self—what they are and how they are developed—deserve a closer look. If kids can look so good on the surface but still suffer from significant deficits in their sense of self, how can we tell the difference between the healthy and the impaired child?

Kate is sixteen years old. She is shy but personable once she feels comfortable. Her grades are mostly B's with an occasional C and an infrequent A. While she likes school, she is only modestly motivated and prefers devoting time to her long-standing interest in classical guitar. Other musical classmates have tried to interest her in playing electric guitar in their popular heavy metal band. Her lack of enthusiasm for this project disappointed her classmates, and eventually she came to be seen as a "dork" because of her idiosyncratic musical interests and her avoidance of the spotlight. Nevertheless, Kate has a small group of close friends, some of whom share her interests while others simply appreciate her quiet and kind manner.

Kate is one of those kids who you have to pay attention to in order to see; otherwise she tends to blend into the background. A mild learning disability makes eye contact difficult for her, and as a result Kate can seem disinterested when someone is talking to her. On the other hand, she has a quick, dry wit and is eager to talk about her adolescent dilemmas. She smokes pot occasionally, enjoys it, but worries about whether or not this could be a problem. She has a moderate amount of conflict with her parents, who believe that she should be more attentive to her schoolwork, but she looks to them for advice on subjects other than academics. She does not have a boyfriend, but she volunteers once a week at a soup kitchen and has her eye on one of the boys there. She is hesitant to get involved with him, however, because she does not feel ready for a sexual relationship. She keeps a supply of birth-control pills in her drawer but has not begun to use them.

When asked to describe her level of happiness, Kate says she is "pretty happy."

• • •

Marissa is also sixteen years old. She is an outstanding student and has one of the highest GPAs in her class. She does particularly well in English and is considering a career in journalism. She is stylish and immaculately groomed, and several of her teachers have suggested that she consider broadcast journalism because of her writing skills and her striking appearance. Although she clearly has strengths in a number of academic areas, she seems to have settled on broadcast journalism, largely because "everyone" says she would be so good at it.

Marissa has a large group of popular friends and works hard to maintain her status with these boys and girls. She can at times be dismissive of other students and understands that in order to maintain her high standing she needs to be clear about the values of her "in" group: academic excellence, physical attractiveness, and high social visibility. Marissa doesn't like it when she is "mean" to other girls, but she is not particularly troubled by this behavior since "that's the way it is in high school."

In spite of all her accomplishments, Marissa's relationship with her parents is quite strained, as they are relentless in their insistence that their daughter excel in all areas, academic and extracurricular. There are predictable fights every Saturday morning as Marissa tries to avoid the soccer matches she dislikes and her parents insist that she participate. In response, Marissa smokes a bit of marijuana, just enough to "get her through the game." Once soccer is over, she quickly returns to her group of friends, happy to be free of her parents' pressure and looking forward to a weekend that includes partying and a fair amount of alcohol use.

When asked to describe her level of happiness, Marissa says she is "quite happy."

Kate and Marissa are not unusual kids in my affluent community. Marissa has been a patient of mine for two years. Her initial depression has lifted although her frequent substance use still concerns me. In spite of her extraordinary grades and impressive physical appearance, Marissa's adolescence is not going well. Marissa's life is about surfaces and not about mining her inner life. She is overly dependent on others, she can be quite cruel to other girls, and rather than assert her independence she avoids conflict by self-medicating with illegal drugs. She is unable to talk to her parents about her problems, partly because they are so demanding, and partly because she has so little empathy for their anxiety.

Marissa's parents have overlooked the warning signs of trouble—the red eyes before soccer games, the mints on her breath when she comes home after weekend parties. This only reinforces Marissa's view that she is uncared for, that her parents are not committed to her well-being. While she appears to have many friends, in fact she feels quite alone and empty. She takes solace in her academic performance, and this is an area of strength for her. Hopefully, she will use her intelligence in a way that feels exciting and authentic to her, as opposed to predictable. With two years left before Marissa leaves for college, her work will be to dismantle her façade and begin to confront the issues of adolescence head on. She will need to shore up self-control so that she is not so vulnerable to substance use, and she will need to become interested in and curious about her internal life. If she can do this, she will be able to fortify her weak sense of self; if not, she is unlikely to successfully manage the challenges of being on her own over the college years.

Kate is not a patient but rather the daughter of a neighborhood friend. She helps me occasionally with filing or going to the library and finding articles I need. She seems to like chatting with me, because "You know a lot about kids." I enjoy Kate, she's a bit of a relief from the often terribly unhappy girls I spend my days with. To my knowledge she's never been in therapy, nor does she appear to have any need for psychotherapeutic intervention.

Kate doesn't fret about her looks or particularly care about how she is viewed by others. While this could be a way of defending herself from rejection, I suspect the more accurate explanation is that Kate is at ease with herself and feels enough concern and support from her few good friends that she sees no need to capitulate to the demands of the more popular kids. She confides that she doesn't much like those kids anyway and is content to practice her guitar and hang out with her own circle of friends.

Her lack of motivation about schoolwork is of concern. This is different from saying that her grades are of concern. Her parents are right to encourage more effort from her, although it would be better if there was less conflict and more emphasis on challenging Kate to think about what is preventing her from working to her full capacity. She can appear somewhat inhibited, but this is likely to be a combination of her predisposition to shyness and perhaps her learning disability.

Fortunately Kate has loving and supportive parents, and as a result she feels generally good about herself, although she has typical adolescent worries about drug experimentation and boys. Since her drug use is not for the purposes of self-medication, it is of less concern than Marissa's drug use; also, Kate is reflective about her use. Her work in the community is notable and shows compassion and generosity. The biggest concern I have about Kate is how little value the community places on kids like her. Even though she has played classical guitar at several concerts locally, this never shows up in the school newspaper. She says that sometimes she feels "invisible." Kate will probably attend a reasonable but not outstanding college and make a good adjustment there, preferring the diverse student population she is likely to encounter to the rather homogenous, frequently superficial group of kids in her current high school. She has a well developed sense of self—authentic, compassionate, and capable—and is likely to continue to develop into an emotionally healthy young adult.

I have presented these two examples to highlight the difference between surface and substance in healthy self-development. All kids are different, and there is no single "profile" of a child with an impaired sense of self or a child with a robust sense of self. It is important to know that a teenager with a healthy sense of self may slam doors, or experiment with drugs, or clam up when her parents want to talk. Alternately, there are kids with an impaired sense of self who successfully fly under the radar because they are so exquisitely attuned to what is expected of them that they can pass off an inauthentic and fabricated sense of self as real. Understanding what a healthy sense of self is in our children means that we are willing to look past the obvious and evaluate whether or not our children are making progress along a number of dimensions. Do they feel effective out in the world? Do they have a sense that they are in control of their lives? Are they able to form deep and enduring relationships with others? Do they have hobbies and interests? Do they value and accept themselves? Do they know how to take care of themselves? These critical qualities, while they certainly will wax and wane, are shared by children who are making good progress toward healthy adulthood.

KIDS WITH HEALTHY SELVES ARE READY AND ABLE TO "OWN" THEIR LIVES

One of the constant themes of childhood and adolescence is the desire to feel that actions originate from within: "I can do it myself," "I can handle it myself," "I can figure it out myself." This is not to say that children don't need, and even want, outside help at times. They certainly do. But the drive, the general direction in life, is toward feeling internally capable. Children are rightfully proud of their abilities to manage on their own and are eager to expand their repertoire of self-directed activities. Kids want to crawl and then walk and then run and then ride their bikes and finally drive their cars. Psychologists agree that this push toward activity, curiosity, and exploration is innate. The only time an infant lies still in his crib is when he is sick or sleeping. Otherwise he is busy looking, gnawing, laughing, crying, kicking, and flailing in his early attempts to explore and influence the world around him.

The need to experience a sense of control over things that affect our lives is universal. Whether it is a primitive society appealing to rain gods to help assure good crops or upper-middle-class families appealing to Princeton Review to assure good SAT scores, human beings strive to control, predict, understand, and influence what happens to them. By successfully influencing events, we can increase the odds of good outcomes, while decreasing the odds of poor ones.

We all prefer to feel that our choices in life are authentic, that they come from within, as opposed to being dictated to us by others. When children are denied the opportunity to figure out their own values, desires, and interests, the outcome is often a despairing dependency, the antithesis of healthy autonomy. Autonomy means that we are independent, capable, and loving and that we are *free to choose* how we use these qualities. We may write well but choose to study medicine, believing it to be a more altruistic profession; we may prefer solitude but willingly take in a disabled parent to live with us, feeling that it is the right thing to do. It is this ability to choose that helps us feel not simply that we were born with certain qualities but that we also have some control over how much these qualities will dictate the course of our lives.

Self-efficacy is the belief that we can successfully impact our world. Unlike self-esteem, which is concerned with judgments of self-worth, self-efficacy is concerned with judgments of personal capability. While self-efficacy often overlaps with self-esteem, it is not the same thing. And unlike self-esteem, which has very little relation to academic, personal, or interpersonal success, self-efficacy has a strong correlation with positive outcomes for children.[1] When children are high in self-efficacy they find it easy to act on their own behalf. **This ability to act appropriately in one's best interest is termed: agency.** Self-efficacy refers to beliefs; agency refers to actions; but they both refer to a sense of personal control. Clearly, efficacy and agency are interrelated; the more we *feel* that we are able to exert control effectively in the world, the more likely we are to *act* effectively. High levels of agency are found in proactive people, "go-getters" who "know how to get things done." While the term "self-efficacy" may not yet trip off the tongue quite as easily as "self-esteem," it is far more likely to contribute to healthy emotional development.

Two twelve-year-old boys in the same class receive a poor mark on a book report that they feel was undeserved. The first child does nothing; the second child speaks to the teacher. It is the second child who is exhibiting a sense of agency. If I am active in what happens to me, there is an increased chance that I will have an effect. The child who feels helpless to change anything about his situation is liable to feel apathetic or even depressed. Clearly, the child who speaks to the teacher has a better chance of having his grade reconsidered. But even if his grade remains the same, he is more likely to feel that he "gave it a shot." The worst, and unfortunately frequent scenario in competitive homes is that the parent calls up and demands to know from the teacher why the grade was low. Certainly there are times when children, particularly young children, need parental intervention. But these times are fewer than we think, and the goal should always be to help the child learn about how to act on his own behalf

A sense of agency begins in infancy. The infant who squeezes a rattle and finds that she makes a novel sound is having an early lesson in how her actions impact her environment. Imagine if that same baby didn't get to squeeze the rattle, but had her parent always squeezing it for her. The infant would come to feel at the whim of the environment, that actions did not arise from within her. While a perpetually rattle-squeezing parent is unlikely, it illustrates how even at the youngest ages children benefit from the experience of exploring independently and of not being interfered with by overzealous parents.

Play experiences are among the child's earliest internally driven experiences. Kids play because they are driven to touch, taste, manipulate, explore, and confront their environment. Parental involvement for safety reasons is essential. However, when parents become overly involved, play no longer retains its function as an activity where children develop independence, competence, and a sense of control, and instead becomes another arena in which children become overly dependent. Many of the affluent kids I see in my practice have made it clear that they much prefer organized sports activities to spontaneous play. When asked if they ever go down to the schoolyard for a pick-up game, they look sincerely puzzled, and ask, "Who would referee?" The very notion that twelve- and thirteen-year-olds could rely on themselves to organize and set standards for a simple ball game is foreign to many upper-middle-class kids who have had adults directing their athletic activities for as long as they can remember. While these kids may be good athletes because of their willingness to practice and take direction, the sphere in which they feel a sense of control and competence is unwittingly diminished by adult overinvolvement.

Amid all the expensive, educationally correct toys that my three sons had when they were toddlers, it was the pots, pans, and spoons they loved best. They could produce sounds with their own hands, gentle rhythms, or, more often, cacophonous riots. And because the racket usually sent me fleeing to the next room, they were able to explore with a minimum of parental intervention, usually until my nerves or my eardrums became frayed. This simple example serves as a model for the kind of experiences that are valuable for kids, regardless of age. Provide a safe environment, give your kid a few tools, and get out of the way. The delight that my sons experienced while pounding on those pots needed no encouragement from me. It would have been ridiculous to go in and tell them how musical or capable or good they were. It was clear that the very experience of being able to have an impact, of learning something about how the world works, was pleasure enough. Bang on the pot, I make a noise, don't bang and there is no sound—my actions have an effect on the world. Expanding the arena of cause and effect—I practice, my soccer skills improve; I study hard, my grades get better; I listen well, my friends seek me out—is how youngsters come to develop a sense of agency. Parents can help by focusing on the effort ("You really put a lot of work into learning the chords for that song"), not the end result.

Researchers have found that helping infants and toddlers build a sense of agency increases cognitive and intellectual development.[2] While financially comfortable parents are able to provide a wide range of opportunities and experiences for their children, the fact is, they are no more likely to provide the kinds of psychological experiences that nurture autonomy and self-efficacy than parents who are less financially secure. Therefore "socioeconomic level makes little unique contribution to cognitive development."[3] As a matter of fact, the kind of anxious, overprotective, oversolicitous, intrusive parenting that has become commonplace in affluent communities actually diminishes a child's sense of efficacy and autonomy. **Anxiety and its frequent companions, overinvolvement and intrusion, combine to make a particularly lethal combination.** This parenting style makes children hesitant to actively approach a world that the parent portrays as dangerous, and, as a consequence, it limits children's natural eagerness to try out new and challenging experiences.

As I write these lines, I have just waved goodbye to my youngest son, who is off for a week of rock climbing in Yosemite National Park. My own anxiety level is high. After all, Jeremy has never gone rock climbing out of doors, he is asthmatic, and the camp is far from a hospital. I am in the middle of one of those experiences where I have to put my money where my mouth is. I know that this experience will be good for his developing sense of self, although it will be demanding for me. I was raised in an anxious household and as a result have always been hypervigilant about my own children's safety. But I also know that Jeremy is excited about this new experience, that his asthma is under control, that he carries medication, and that I have entrusted him to competent, experienced people. Not letting him go would certainly have been far easier for me; I know that I face many moments of worry in the following week. But depriving him (because of my worries) of the opportunity to learn something valuable—not just how to rock-climb but how to respect the environment, how to enjoy things that are outside of the competitive suburban life he leads, and how to manage on his own in a challenging environment—would be harmful to both of us. So I grit my teeth and let him go. Letting go is necessary; it is sometimes extremely difficult. By allowing my son this new experience, and by forcing myself to tolerate anxiety and separation, we both get the opportunity to discover and develop new skills for dealing effectively with challenge. He learns to belay, I learn to deep-breathe. We both feel more in control of our respective worlds.

The issue of self-efficacy becomes particularly critical in adolescence, as teens begin to address the looming issues of adulthood: friendships, romance, work interests, and the ability to function on their own. Adolescents increasingly have to choose between healthy and self-defeating behaviors and activities. The success of teens in dealing with these issues depends in large part on a firm sense of autonomy developed throughout childhood. Peer pressure becomes an increasingly potent force. Youngsters who enter adolescence with a compromised sense of personal efficacy are far more likely to fall victim to self-defeating behaviors: substance abuse, promiscuity, eating disorders, and self-mutilation.[4]

Children who don't feel that they "own" their lives, children for whom feelings, thoughts, and actions come from outside as much as they come from inside, are at risk for being easily manipulated by others. You may have your child's best interests at heart, but the world is unlikely to be so generous. In addition to the fact that a sense of personal control is essential for your child's healthy self-development, it is also a thrill for us when we realize that the totally dependent infant we once held, guided by our love and good sense, has matured into a person who feels capable of making his way out in the world.

KIDS WITH HEALTHY SELVES CAN CONTROL THEIR IMPULSES: "I'M THE BOSS OF ME"

Self-management is what allows the kindergartner to raise his hand before going to the bathroom, the ten-year-old not to slug the kid at first base who misses a game-winning catch, and the sixteen-year-old to finish at least part of her homework before partying with her friends. No accounting of the self can be complete without understanding self-management or how the self makes the adjustments necessary to maintain harmony both within itself and with others. Self-management includes such skills as self-control, impulse control, frustration tolerance, the capacity to delay gratification, and the ability to pay attention. It differs from self-efficacy and agency because it is a specific set of skills that allow children to regulate their internal states as well as their relationships with others.

It is those outside the child, typically parents, who initially encourage the development of self-management. By transforming external demands ("*You* need to sit still in class") into internal self-management skills ("*I* need to sit still in class"), children come to experience an increasingly reliable sense of personal control. Initially, children are driven to internalize the restrictions and values of their parents because they want their parents' love and approval. Over time, the fact that friends, teachers, and other adults reward good self-management skills reinforces its value. But ultimately the ability to control one's self becomes its own reward as children come to feel authentic and capable.

By definition, learning frustration tolerance means that our children have to be frustrated, learning impulse control means that some impulses must be denied, and learning to delay gratification means that kids can't have everything they want. My own experience with kids is not so much that they are spoiled (though, yes, many of them are) but that they are immature. Many children from affluent homes have not had enough opportunity to work on self-management skills because parents are quick to limit their child's frustration and distress. Parents who are harried and preoccupied can be too willing to reduce consequences and capitulate to demands rather than stand their ground. It is difficult to deny our children their wants and desires, whether it's the toddler desperate for candy at the supermarket checkout or the teen insisting that her life is over if she can't buy the latest fashion accessory. However—and this is a painful psychological truth—our primary responsibility is not to gratify our children (which of course we do often, and happily) but to make certain that they develop a repertoire of skills that will help them meet life's inevitable challenges and disappointments.

Dr. David Fassler, a child and adolescent psychiatrist and a clinical professor of psychiatry at the University of Vermont practices in Burlington. He is insightful and succinct when he says that the affluent kids he treats "haven't had enough bad things happen to them." Clearly, Dr. Fassler is not suggesting that we encourage our children to participate in unsafe activities. Rather, his point is "that in order to learn how to cope with normal frustrations, with ups and downs, we have to first experience them." Affluent kids are often so protected from even the most minor disappointments and frustrations that they are unable to develop critical coping skills.

Dr. Fassler tells of several of his affluent (not to mention highly anxious) parents who have talked with him about the possibility of attending summer camp, or even college, with their children. General MacArthur's mother may have set up camp right outside the gates of West Point, but for the rest of us, it's a *very* bad idea. Resilience is the outcome of many factors in a child's life. As adults we know that it is one of the most powerful allies we have in making it through the inevitable tough times. A child cannot possibly develop resilience when his parents are constantly at his side, interfering with the development of autonomy, self-management, and coping skills.

Many of the patients in my practice attend the same high school, several in the same grade. One night, the electricity went out in my community, shutting down all computers for several hours. Two of my patients had the same assignment to complete, a ten-page history paper. When the electricity came back on, both of them had lost a large part of their work. One spent the better part of the night reconstructing his paper, the other handed his mother his notes and went to bed while she stayed up and rewrote his paper. The adolescent who reaches inside himself and finds that he is capable of working through a difficult problem is at a tremendous advantage, both psychologically and practically, over the adolescent who depends on others to "fix" things for him. It was undoubtedly tough for the mother of the boy who chose to rework his paper to go to sleep knowing that her son would be up most of the night; but by allowing him to come up with his own solution, she let her son know that she trusted his judgment and admired his initiative. This, in turn, furthers his self-confidence, making it more likely that he will continue to make good decisions in the future.

Parents help their children develop self-management skills by setting limits, modeling self-control, and being clear about the value of tolerating frustration, delaying gratification, and controlling impulses. **The ability to self-manage effectively is a great predictor of both psychological adjustment and academic achievement.** Researchers have shown that children as young as four years old who can control their impulse to eat sweets placed in front of them are more likely to be both academically and socially successful a decade later![5]

Parents also have to be able to tolerate their children's disappointment, resentment, and even anger when their wishes aren't granted, when they are pushed to work out problems on their own, or when they are frustrated. A routine theme among the parents of my distressed teens is their inability to tolerate their children's unhappiness. There is not a parent who doesn't understand that self-control is critical to success in life. But if we can't tolerate seeing our children "unhappy," if we feel we have to give them "everything," then we become incapable of teaching the very self-management skills that our children need to stay out of trouble.

There is a natural progression to the kinds of frustrations children are likely to encounter. For the most part, kids are handed the kinds of challenges that they are capable of managing. Sometimes I use the metaphor of children climbing stairs to illustrate the value of allowing them to experience incremental increases in frustration. For example, when a toddler trips on the first set of stairs, we would do well to let him pick himself up. His fall, after all, is only a matter of inches. If we intervene too quickly ("Oh, he's so young, he could get hurt so easily"), we make it harder for him to climb up the next flight of stairs. When we are anxious, he becomes anxious, and he loses the opportunity to practice the self-management skill of perseverance. But say he's managed to climb up a flight or two and now finds himself frustrated by a "time-out" at preschool for grabbing another kid's toy. If we swoop in and tell the teacher to "be gentle because he's going through a stage," we make his next set of stairs even more difficult. Now he's both anxious and looking outside himself to maintain equilibrium. He's also lost an opportunity to learn the real-world consequences of poor self-control.

Every stage in a child's life delivers frustrations, disappointments, challenges, and opportunities. Parents who have difficulty tolerating their child's distress, who are quick to step in and take over, hamper their child's ability to continue climbing. Kids who have not had repeated experiences of finding ways to manage frustration may give the appearance of moving forward, but they have not accumulated the necessary self-management skills of self-control, perseverance, frustration tolerance, and anxiety management that will allow them to address the more complex challenges they will encounter as they climb higher. Kids who have found that they have within themselves the ability to pick themselves up and keep going develop a repertoire of self-management skills and a sense of resilience.

Risk taking is inevitable and even desirable in life. Paraphrasing Dr. Spock, the famous author and pediatrician, any child who has not been bandaged has not been well parented. Difficult as it can be for parents, it is imperative that we allow our children to go out in the world, to try their hand, to bang up against difficulties, to learn how to fall down and then get up again. We must understand that when we allow our children these kinds of opportunities, we are actually helping them develop both the internal regulation and the sense of agency that ultimately will allow them to make good choices about themselves, their health and their relationships. By allowing them to get occasionally bruised in childhood we are helping to make certain that they don't get broken in adolescence. And by allowing them their failures in adolescence, we are helping to lay the groundwork for success in adulthood.

Compromised self-management skills put children at risk. Car accidents are the most common cause of death among adolescents. Kids who drink and drive, who submit to outrageous fraternity hazings, who overdose on drugs or alcohol—these are kids who are unable to self-regulate, who don't know when enough is enough. In healthy development, the self develops in tandem with self-management skills, and choices are increasingly experienced as coming from within. Without this internal touchstone, kids are vulnerable to peer pressure and their own confusion about whose values are actually driving their life choices. Younger teens may stay away from drugs because of fear of parental sanctions, but I can assure you that this is rarely the case in middle and late adolescence. Teens need to feel that *their* self-definition does not include being a drug user. And while many teens may experiment briefly with drugs and alcohol, the teen who has learned to self-regulate is at much less risk of substance abuse than the teen who still depends on others for regulation.

Thankfully, the vast majority of teens make it through adolescence relatively unscathed. From time to time many of them will do some stupid things; things that a more fully developed brain would understand to be against their self-interest. But, self-regulation is not an all-or-nothing deal; we all work on these skills as new and seductive opportunities present themselves. The piece of cake we should have passed up; the gym bag lying in the corner as we settle back into our novel; zipping up our kid's jacket when we know they are perfectly capable because we don't want to miss the beginning of the movie. Part of the human condition appears to be the successful resolution of conflicting desires, both within ourselves and between ourselves and others. Nobody "grows out of" the need to self-regulate; most of us just get a lot better at it.

Being alert to major failures in self-regulation—the youngster who consistently bites and hits other kids in frustration, the grade school student who obsessively rewrites his papers well into the night, the teen who comes home regularly drunk on the weekends— is a critical part of successful parenting. We need to keep our eyes wide open and act on failures in self-regulation without delay. Particularly in adolescence, these failures can have tragic consequences.

KIDS WITH HEALTHY SELVES
CAN BE GENEROUS AND LOVING

If it was possible to choose a single breathtaking story about human psychology, it would surely be the progression from the total dependence and "narcissism" of the infant through attachment to parents and peers in childhood and ultimately to the capacity of the teenager or young adult to form a reciprocal, relatively selfless, loving relationship with another human being. While love certainly does not begin with the adolescent's "first love," the underpinnings have been there since birth, all the work that parents have done to love, encourage, teach, and discipline reaches fruition when their children move out into the world and have the capacity to both maintain their independence and merge their desires, needs, and goals with another.

The capacity to love—as well as the impairment of this capacity—begins in the earliest interactions between mother (or primary caretaker) and child. Infants come into this world with a partial template of the person they are likely to become: quiet or active, easygoing or temperamental, anxious or laid-back. But this is just a beginning, and the child, and ultimately the adult he or she becomes, depends largely on social experiences. The latest research in brain development demonstrates that the infant's brain is *neurologically* altered by the quality of the mother-child relationship.[6] Our brains are constantly being shaped by experience, but babies in particular "outsource" much of their physiological and emotional governance to their caregivers.[7]

The child who is well loved in infancy, who develops a secure attachment to his mother, is being helped to develop a capable brain. Both mother and child "tune in" to each other in an early form of reciprocal communication. **This reciprocal form of communication, called *attunement*, is aided by the mother who is sensitive to both the internal and external feelings and experiences of her child.** Every child's first love is his mother. For the infant, the mother acts as a "looking glass," mirroring back to the child, through her words, facial expressions, and gestures an image of who he is. As she reflects interest and delight in her child's very existence, along with his ever-increasing abilities and independence, her child begins to define himself as someone worthy of interest, appreciation, and love.

By contrast, the uninvolved or depressed mother who lacks zest while interacting with her child is likely to hinder his sense of lovability. The consequences of parental involvement or disengagement will follow the child throughout his life, either promoting connection with others or making the child inhibited and wary about close relationships. There will always be other mirrors to gaze into as children grow into young adults, and what they expect to find there plays a large role determining their choice of partners. While a parent's accurate attunement is a critical part of priming children for healthy relationships, other factors (traumas such as divorce, the sudden death of a parent, sexual abuse) can exact a toll on a child's developing capacity for connection.

Twenty-year-old Jessica considers herself "lucky" to have found Adam. They have been dating for two years and enjoy a loving, respectful, and honest relationship. While it's unclear whether they will ultimately end up together—they both have career goals that might force a prolonged separation—they feel excited and secure in their relationship. Jessica's roommate, Claire, on the other hand, considers herself "unlucky" to have fallen in love with Chris, a good-looking, charming, but dishonest and unreliable boyfriend. Chris regularly cheats on Claire, but she finds him irresistibly exciting and always takes him back. While Claire doesn't consider Chris "husband material," she hopes that eventually he will settle down and want to marry her. Luck and timing may play some role in how relationships develop. But the real good luck for Jessica were her stable, caring, secure parents; parents who reflected back to Jessica a lovable, worthy self, exactly what she saw reflected in Adam's eyes. Alternately, Claire's choice of Chris was not simply a case of bad luck. Chris reflected back to Claire the sense of unpredictability and inattentiveness that she had seen in the mirror of her own unhappy, distracted, insecure parents' gaze.

While it may be harder for a child to form a secure, loving relationship with his parents when they themselves did not receive good parenting, it is not impossible. Dr. Mary Main, whose pioneering work on attachment has spanned decades, has found suggestions that even when parents have had marked difficulties with their own parents, they can still raise securely attached children *if* they are able to focus on and make sense out of their early disturbing experiences.[8] Other researchers are beginning to find that a good marriage—and other supportive relationships, with friends or counselors, for example—may offer the love and emotional safety that encourages honest self-examination and self-development.[9] This helps parents who originally had insecure attachments to their own parents to develop secure attachments to friends and partners as well as to their children.

Many researchers are currently working on how people with insecure beginnings can develop secure attachments. Those who can are said to have "earned attachment."[10] The greatest predictor of a child's secure attachment is a parent who has achieved, whether from their own secure childhood or from later positive experiences, what Main, Hesse, and their colleagues call a "secure-autonomous" state of mind with respect to attachment.[11] It is then on the foundation of secure attachment that connection and the capacity to love are built. It should be quite reassuring for parents to know that they do not have to repeat the same unsatisfying relationships they had with their parent with their own children. Attachment, like almost all aspects of human development is dynamic and open to change.

Children love their parents and then other important adults. They experience the precursors of intimacy with their peers, their friends, and in their early dating experiences. Love can take many forms; it can be spiritual, platonic, and humanistic as well as romantic. Children who can love can set aside their own needs, their own natural greediness, and attend to the needs of someone outside themselves. This can be a boyfriend or girlfriend, but it can also be a grandparent, a younger sibling, a good friend, a pet, or a down-on-his-luck individual at the local homeless shelter.

Parents tend to worry if their child isn't popular in elementary school, isn't socially in demand in high school, isn't dating in college. Kids have different timetables for intimacy, particularly romantic intimacy. Parents should be paying attention to the openness of their own relationship with their child as well as to their child's capacity to have close friendships. These two factors are predictive of the capacity for a loving romantic relationship. Modeling kindness and generosity helps children become more prosocial and therefore more capable of understanding the needs of others outside the walls of their house, and beyond the fence of their schoolyard.

Children with poor early parenting experiences are notably reluctant to enter into intimate relationships, but, interestingly, so are children who have been indulged and overprotected when they were young. One of the problems of the zealous overinvolvement of affluent parents is not only that it tends to create immature children, it also creates children who are hesitant to move into the challenging territory of intimacy because it means relinquishing their childish dependence on others for a sense of self. A healthy romantic relationship is characterized by both the need for security and the need for self-growth. Hovered-over children grow up to choose security needs at the expense of expanding self-development. The outcome of this is the frequent complaints of the partners of insecure teens: "She's too dependent" or "He makes me feel guilty whenever I want to be with my girlfriends." For a loving relationship to endure, there has to be a safe space for both partners to retreat to together, as well as an equally safe space in which they are both free to develop their particular interests. After the initial stage of "falling in love," when security needs are likely to outweigh needs for self-development, relationships are likely to flounder if both sets of needs are not met.

The culture of affluence does not foster the development of reciprocity, a critical part of being a kind and loving partner. In order to love healthily, a child cannot believe that the moon and stars revolve around him. Spotlights are blinding, and the child who is constantly told how special he is will have difficulty seeing other people clearly. He is bound to be disappointed when his partner doesn't show the same unbridled enthusiasm his parents once showed for his every effort. I see a steady stream of kids who are profoundly angry and disappointed when their girlfriend or boyfriend dumps them, usually because of their wearisome narcissism. It is hard for these kids to understand that healthy relationships are based on reciprocity, not hero worship.

In addition, the culture of affluence, with its emphasis on appearances, keeps already insecure adolescents in a perpetual state of worry about their clothes, skin, and, most of all, their bodies. Half of all adolescent girls in America are dieting at any one time and one-third will go on to have some form of an eating disorder in college. Dr. Ernie Cowger, a practicing psychologist and a professor at Louisiana Tech University, in Shreveport, lost a sister to anorexia. He rates eating disorders as "the most underrated problem" among affluent girls. Being so intensely preoccupied with body image takes energy and attention away from the task of developing empathy and focusing on the needs of others. Finally, the emphasis on materialism keeps kids involved in consumerism as opposed to philanthropy. Healthy relationships always include a generosity of spirit. Affluent kids are particularly ungenerous when compared to less-affluent kids. Meanness of spirit, hoarding, and self-preoccupation all bode poorly for the development of loving relationships.

The child who is well loved, and well schooled in the importance of empathy, who can respect his own needs while being sensitive to the needs of others, and who is eager to share his well-developed internal life has a much better chance of forming satisfying and enduring relationships than someone who has trouble seeing beyond themselves.

KIDS WITH HEALTHY SELVES
ARE GOOD ARCHITECTS OF
THEIR INTERNAL "HOMES"

What is an "internal home"? It clearly is not built of bricks and mortar, but of the psychological building blocks of self-liking, self-acceptance, and self-management. It is the welcoming and restorative psychological structure that children need to construct in order to be at ease internally as well as out in the world. It is where kids—where all of us—retreat to when we need to "pull it together," "think it over," or just take care of ourselves.

In many ways this internal home is a reproduction of what was once a reassuring transaction between mother and child. The warmth and love that are part of a good parent-child relationship provide the architectural drawings from which a child can later design his own internal place of comfort. A child who has been well loved—who has experienced high levels of unconditional support, has been soothed, has been helped to navigate difficult waters, and has been reassured that his value does not rest on his performance or his ability to please others—develops a sense of lovability and value. He is *worth* caring about, and so he comes to care about himself.

For many of the kids I see in my practice, this internal place of comfort and respite is dangerously underdeveloped. These kids have been so successfully taught to train their vision outward that they have difficulty turning inward, being reflective, or simply taking the time out from their driven lives to check in with themselves, to give themselves a break. Often these kids seem confused by the concept of an internal home. They need lots of examples to begin to get a sense of the value of something that is unseen and unappreciated by others, but vital to their own healthy self-development.

For me, this internal place looks and feels very much like the big oak tree I used to climb up in my backyard when I was a child and needed to savor an experience or work out a problem on my own. In my mind I have spent countless hours sitting on the sturdy branches of this oak as I continue to face both the extraordinary and the ordinary challenges of living. Every child I see needs help constructing a place that offers them the same pleasure and solace that my internal oak tree offers me. Creating this space is highly personal, and kids, once they get the hang of it, can be quite creative in figuring out a place that feels authentically their own. For some it's the beach, a favorite park, a spot under a bridge, grandma's kitchen table, or simply an internal feeling of peace and quiet.

Many younger children are quite adept at turning inward to some "special place." Unfortunately, this ability is often lost in adolescence, just when kids are in desperate need of a place of retreat to help them gain perspective on the inevitable conflicts of this stage. The normal adolescent tendency toward overstimulation—the music blaring loud enough to be downright painful to adult ears, the homework that is done with the television, the radio, and the computer all turned on—is an adaptive measure for the teenager who would otherwise be overwhelmed by the rapid demands, changes, and conflicts at this stage. They actively pull themselves out of their heads so that they don't feel the distress of lingering too long in uncomfortable psychological territory.

Teens need to be reassured that by constructing an internal "home," they will not be opening themselves up to additional demands. When I tried to explain this concept to one of my skeptical young patients, he blurted out, "You mean a place where it's all cool." Indeed, a place where it's "all cool," where kids can put aside the multiple demands placed on them and either reflect or simply "chill out." We should not be dismissive of "chilling out." The expression, so popular among kids, is a reflection of the need to free oneself psychologically from immediate problems and recharge one's batteries. Worn-out batteries are useless, and kids need an abundant source of energy for the many challenges they face.

Throughout this book there is an emphasis on "internal resources" and the necessity of their development in order to produce a child with a healthy sense of self. Self-control, the ability to delay gratification, frustration tolerance, a sense of competency, self-efficacy, the ability to act in one's best interest, all of these have been shown to develop out of a mix of genetic endowment and good parenting. Together they combine to form an internal landscape that is healthy, independent, and skilled. The reason that a welcoming internal home is of such great importance is because it provides the psychological space, the opportunity, and the stage upon which children try out, practice, and fortify these "internal resources."

It can be difficult for parents to evaluate whether or not their child is having success constructing this internal home base. After all, the point of it is that it *is* internal and not available for public scrutiny. Conclusions about whether or not your child is developing an internal capacity for reflection and self-comfort are inferred, rather than seen directly. The child who says, "I need to think it over," or, "I'm working on it," can be assumed to be developing internal skills. Parents would do well to respect such statements and not push too much, while being clear about their availability. "I'm glad you're thinking about it. Let me know if you want some help," both acknowledges your child's developing capabilities and reassures her that you care about her and are available on an as-needed basis.

This chapter has not addressed every aspect of what a healthy self looks like. That would take a book of its own. But it has addressed what I consider to be some of the most important components of a healthy self. The next story illustrates how even good, attentive parents can neglect the warning signs of an impaired sense of self in their child, and how, with courage and honesty, they can help their child (and themselves) back onto a healthier track.

TYLER'S STORY: WHOSE LIFE IS IT ANYWAY?

Tyler is a seventeen-year-old, extremely appealing young patient of mine. Good-looking, bright, and soft-spoken, his slight Southern drawl and extreme politeness are reminders of his early childhood in South Carolina. Tyler's father is a high-powered corporate executive; his mom is a homemaker. Tyler is the oldest child, and has two younger sisters. The family is tight-knit, loving, and competitive. Tyler's parents have high expectations for all three of their children, often failing to notice the significant differences in temperament among them.

I began seeing Tyler when he was sixteen because his parents were concerned about his lack of motivation. They were worried that he might be depressed, particularly since depression ran in the family. Tyler was maintaining reasonably good grades and was an outstanding soccer player, but he agreed that he often felt depressed. An early note from one of my sessions reads: "I have everything a kid could ask for, but I'm not really interested in much of anything. I'm just kind of going through the motions, trying to make my parents proud." Although Tyler was well-spoken, he had difficulty articulating things that were meaningful to him. While his parents were genuinely concerned, they both felt that if he just worked harder and gained admission to his father's prestigious alma mater, then he would get "back on track." Mom spent hours every night reading and rereading his school reports, and grilling him before major tests in order to insure that his grades remained high. He was criticized for minor academic lapses, while regular episodes of heavy drinking were dismissed as the "hijincks" of teenage boys. An attractive athlete, he had little trouble "hooking up" with girls, but felt no emotional connection during these experiences.

In spite of Tyler's growing unhappiness during his senior year, his father worked behind the scenes of his alma mater and was able to secure Tyler's admission. When Tyler left for the East Coast, both parents breathed a sigh of relief. I had been unable to convince them that Tyler was really not prepared for the intensity of a high-pressure school, and that he was likely to find the 3,000-mile separation from home daunting.

For several months after Tyler left I would run into one of his parents from time to time and they would give glowing reports about how much Tyler "loved" his school. This was in stark contrast to the teary boy who was still calling me several times a week, his depression escalating, his substance abuse increasing, and his ability to attend classes becoming virtually nonexistent. After three months of charade, Tyler agreed to come home and, with my help, talk to his parents about how miserable he was.

Like many of the children I see from affluent, high-powered families, Tyler was stuck between a rock and a hard place. Not wanting to disappoint his parents who poured time, attention, and resources into him, he unwittingly had sacrificed his own self-development under the pressure of his parents' hopes and anxieties. His dad, a self-made man, had to "claw" his way to the top. He wanted an easier life for his son. Unfortunately, in the process, he neglected to notice that his son was quite different from him—softer, more introspective, and far less driven. Mom, in the meantime, often neglected by her hardworking husband, and bright, but with no intellectual outlets, had poured all of her unrealized ambitions into her oldest, compliant son. Her overinvolvement with Tyler kept at bay her anger at her husband and her boredom. When Tyler looked into the "looking glass," he saw only what his parents hoped he would be: tough, competitive, and high-achieving. Bright and psychologically astute, Tyler was aware that what his parents reflected back to him had little to do with his as yet undeveloped authentic self.

As Tyler became increasingly able to unfold his experience to his parents, they were confused and angry. Hadn't they done everything possible to make their son a success? Helping Tyler's parents understand their own needs and histories made them aware that, while they poured so much of themselves into their son, they had neglected the equally important parental task of stepping back and allowing a safe space in which Tyler could develop his own likes, dislikes, interests, and priorities. Tyler had become very adept at *appearing* to be a good student, a good athlete, a good son, a good brother, but he had hardly a clue as to what kind of person he really was meant to be. Tyler felt that he was "a fake." Gradually Tyler came to see how much he resented his parents for their inability to love and accept the person he actually was—kind, thoughtful, quiet, and cooperative. The drugs, depression, and refusal to attend classes were all outgrowths of

Tyler's anger at his authentic self being rejected by the very people who claimed to love him so much.

Drawing on the genuine love and good intentions of Tyler's parents, I was able to bring this case to a successful outcome. I continued to see Tyler for another year while he attended a local community college. Much of our time was spent on building up the self-management skills that Tyler lacked. He learned to do his own work, to experience frustration without turning to drugs or alcohol, and to honor the parts of himself that were quite different from his parents. He was able to develop within himself a place of quiet retreat when he wanted to turn inward and work on problems. He often visualized himself on a soccer field, a place where he felt relaxed and in control, "kicking around" the issues that troubled him.

Occasional sessions with his parents helped them to learn to tolerate Tyler's increasing independence, while reinforcing their ability to love him without dictating to him. Mom took a part-time job so that her needs for stimulation and connection were no longer solely focused on her children. Through several grueling sessions, Dad came to accept the fact that his son, although like him in some ways, was quite different in others. While Dad's intentions were to provide Tyler with all the opportunities that he himself had been deprived of as a child, he was unwittingly depriving his son in other ways. Tyler craved his father's approval, but felt that his real self would be a disappointment to his father. In spite of all the attention focused on him, Tyler did not feel he had the support or encouragement that he needed to pursue his own path.

Tyler moved out of his house at the end of his freshman year, continued his therapy, and at the end of his sophomore year transferred to a well-regarded school in California with an outstanding program in physical therapy. Tyler's love of sports, combined with his gentle manner and sincere interest in people, made this an excellent, but, more important, an authentic choice for this special young man. He has been seriously dating a young woman who is both supportive and respectful of his occasional need to withdraw and figure things out on his own.

Tyler's depression, confusion, substance abuse, promiscuity, deception, and inability to stand up for himself were all failures in self-regulation, an outgrowth of his impaired sense of self. In spite of his well-honed capacity to give the impression that he had things under control, internally Tyler felt neither capable nor in charge of his own life. His parents' criticism and pressure made him feel unlovable and contributed to his depression. Tyler's ability to move forward and build a healthier foundation depended on many factors: his motivation to change, his psychological curiosity, and his ability to examine both his love and his anger towards his parents. He was aided by his parent's willingness to take a closer look at their own histories and motivations. Because Tyler's parents had the courage to examine the roles that their own unresolved issues of loneliness and insecurity played in creating problems for their son, this family emerged out of crisis stronger, healthier, and with the ability to truly "see" and appreciate each other.

Every time we are willing to honestly confront our own parenting difficulties, to work on mending our own problems with anxiety or depression or substance abuse or marital problems, we help both our children and ourselves. Children, particularly teenagers can be helped to emotionally separate from unhappy, intrusive parents, but the far better outcome, as we saw in Tyler's case, is to have both parents and children work on problems together.

Every child and every family is different. Had Tyler been born into a less competitive, less critical household he might have avoided the depression and substance abuse that plagued his adolescence. On the other hand, his sisters, fiercely competitive and reasonably at ease with their parents' high expectations evidenced no significant emotional problems. There is no single factor that predicts emotional difficulties for children. Certainly some parenting styles, some types of problems in parents themselves, and some social and economic circumstances make it more likely that children will experience difficulties in adjustment. But as we know, kids with a strong sense of self can come out of dismal economic circumstances and kids with an impaired sense of self can come out of the most fortunate economic circumstances.

KNOWING WHAT REALLY MATTERS
AND WHAT DOESN'T

In this discussion on how a healthy self develops, it is important to note what has not been included. Most of the trappings of the culture of affluence are markedly missing. Status, money, possessions, achievement, the school your child goes to, or the grades he gets, are not factors that contribute to the development of a healthy sense of self.

My husband and I both come from working class backgrounds and, of necessity, worked our way through both college and postgraduate education. As our kids grew up they regularly heard stories about my flipping burgers with one hand and reading Steinbeck with the other, or my husband dressed in jacket and tie waiting tables at the local girls' finishing school in Boston. These stories were told with humor and perhaps a bit more pride than we realized. As our children grew up and the older ones were off to college, we were delighted that they would not have to show up bleary-eyed to class in the morning after a late night-shift. We told all three of our sons we would pay for their education for as long as they pursued it, and after that they were expected to be self-sufficient. It was a point of pride for us both that we could "provide" for our children.

Midway through law school our oldest son, asked us to stop paying for his education. He wanted to take out loans and re-pay them when he was done with school. My husband was delighted—I wasn't. "Why make it harder on yourself? This way you start out without any debt," I practically begged. My son's answer was clear and to the point; "I want to *own* some part of my education." He reminded us of the stories we had told, and how proud we both seemed of our ability to make it on our own. The mom in me wanted to protect him, to make his life easier, to insure that he got the break I never had. But he had spent months listening to me go over the fine points of self-development for this book, and decided that at age 24 it made sense for him to be more financially responsible, to feel more in control of his life. I read and re-read my own words, knowing that he was right and also knowing that sometimes it is much easier to give advice than to take it.

The self is born in the crucible of interaction between parent and child. Every time we encourage exploration, applaud independence, and require self-control we help our children grow into their best selves. The "stuff" we buy our kids, the "advantages" we insist on providing say more about our own needs than our children's. I wanted so much to pay for my son's education because I had lost my father as a teenager and never wanted my own child to feel the desperation I had once felt about whether or not I could manage. But my past loss could not be made up, certainly not by creating another set of problems for my son who was aching to fully launch himself. Most of us know the nagging feeling when we are too invested in some part of our children's lives. That feeling should alert us to take stock of our own needs. Children do not have the market cornered on development; we also need to make sure that we are moving forward in our development, just as we are encouraging our children to move forward.

If this all sounds like an awfully demanding job, it is. But the job is made easier if we understand and take care of our own needs and understand the evolving needs of our children as they pass through different stages of development. While large parts of how we parent remain constant—our love, our support, and our willingness to discipline—the form they take varies according to the intellectual, emotional, and psychological needs and capacities of our children. Now that we have a general overview of what a healthy self looks like in kids, we can turn to the more specific needs and challenges of children at different ages.

· CHAPTER 5 ·

Different Ages, Different Parenting Strategies

- Your three-year-old comes home from preschool and collapses on the floor wailing. "I won't go back. Everyone is s-o-o-o mean." A note tucked into his backpack from his teacher explains that he was given a "time-out" for refusing to wait his turn on line at the water fountain.

- Your ten-year-old comes home from baseball practice, tosses his mitt on the kitchen floor, and explodes. "I'm quitting the team. Coach stuck me in the outfield again. He's so mean." He runs out of the room in a fit of indignation and slams his bedroom door shut.

- Your fifteen-year-old skulks into the kitchen after cheerleading practice. She rolls her eyes when you ask how her day was and angrily says, "I've had it with those bitches on the squad. I'm quitting. They're so mean." Refusing any further discussion, she flips open her cell phone and begins recounting the day's trauma in great detail to her best friend as she huffs off in the direction of her room.

In each of these situations would you . . .

(a) ask for more information?

(b) sympathize with how badly your child feels?

(c) say, "I'm sure you're upset, but it's unacceptable for you to act/speak this way"?

(d) call the teacher or coach to find out why your child is so upset?

(e) say, "I'm sure you'll work it out"?

Answer: It all depends.

How we help our children effectively handle inevitable personal and interpersonal problems depends largely on how we understand the normal progression of child development. The study of child development includes how thinking skills and social skills advance as children move from infancy through adolescence. While some parenting interventions, like showing empathy, for example, are helpful regardless of your child's age, the helpfulness of other interventions, like calling a teacher or perhaps not intervening at all, depend heavily on age and stage of development. While age is not always an accurate indicator of where any *particular* child is in his development, it is a reasonably good proxy for child development *in general*.

The anecdotes above portray children confronted with similar conflicts at three very different stages of development. Parents' responses should be directed at helping each child develop the skills that will help them to manage the particular challenges of their stage of development. For example, preschoolers need to develop skills like self-control and frustration tolerance, school-age children need to learn how to accurately assess their abilities, and teenagers need to resolve issues of identity and independence. Knowing this, we might call the teacher for our preschool child, trying to find out how persistent a problem is our youngster's lack of self-control. We would do well not to call the coach for our ten-year-old, helping him instead to assess what his skill level actually is, how he might improve it, and how to talk to his coach about his frustration. And we most certainly should not be calling the captain of the cheerleading squad. By mid-adolescence, we are most helpful when we explore alternatives with our teenagers, leaving the final decision in their hands as often as is safe and appropriate, in order to encourage their confidence and decision-making skills.

Children wrestle with the major developmental issues of their age, reach adequate but not complete resolution, and move on to the next set of challenges. Getting stuck at a particular point in development throws children off course. The youngster who is unable to master enough self-control early in elementary school to stay in his seat, raise his hand, and wait to be called on, is certain to run into trouble later in elementary school. Parents who make excuses for their youngster's bad behavior, who don't allow him to experience the consequences of his impulsivity hinder his forward progress. His next set of developmental tasks—figuring out interests and abilities, building close, loyal friendships, and participating in organized activities with peers—will be interfered with as he is repeatedly called to account for his impulsive behavior. Socially and psychologically he will fall farther and farther behind, until he masters enough self-control so that this issue is no longer front and center in his life. Only when he develops adequate self-control, can he begin to turn his attention to the issues that are central to preadolescents and get back on track.

Understanding normal child development is an exciting and generally intuitive process. Parents raised children successfully long before the parenting sections of bookstores were full of books on bonding, toilet training, self-esteem, child development, and the renegade adolescent. Because of our high, and frequently unwarranted, levels of worry about our children, many parents are losing touch with the intuitive side of parenting. We need to remember that parenting is an art, not a science, and that decades of "expert" (often conflicting) advice have challenged even the most capable parents' confidence. Mothers, in particular, have been frightened into believing that missteps on their part will inevitably lead to "messed up" kids. Certainly there are parenting styles that can be damaging, constant criticism, for example. But, in general, most parents should respect their intuitive understanding of what is likely to be beneficial to their child. For example, intuition (coupled with our own memories of what we craved when we were teenagers) tells most of us that adolescence is a time for working on independent living skills, refining a sense of self, and expanding interests and abilities free from parental intrusion while certain of parental oversight, concern, and availability.

Instead of being in tune with the developmental challenges of adolescence, competitive parents' anxiety about "success" gets in the way of intuition, leading parents to poke their noses into what is rightfully their teenager's business. "If you quit the baseball team now you'll never make varsity in high school." "You *have* to take honors math and physics—what a boost that would be to your college application." As we've seen, when anxiety drives parenting decisions, those decisions tend to be suboptimal. Whether your child should quit baseball or take honors classes are perfectly reasonable questions when they are addressed in ways that correspond to your child's needs and abilities, not to *your* anxiety. In order to understand what *should* drive parenting decisions we need to take a close look at the capacities and conflicts that are typical at different ages and let our common sense, along with our children's developmental level drive our parenting decisions.

One caveat with regard to relying heavily on a point of view that stresses parenting as the critical variable in child development: we all know great kids who have come out of trying home circumstances and impossible kids with loving, attuned parents. There is a revolution going on in the field of modern neuroscience. As scientists are increasingly able to peer inside not just the gross anatomy of the brain but inside specific regions as they are activated, using imaging devices such as PET scans and functional MRIs, our understanding of how the environment and genetics interact is increasing exponentially. We must bear in mind that human behavior is astonishingly complicated and that researchers are just beginning to look at the brain sequences that lead to behavior. When it comes to the brain, we know very little about cause and effect. Your child may be fearful because a dog bit him when he was two, because you were not empathic with his fear and trivialized the incident, or he may be fearful for a million other reasons. We need to be humble about the connections we draw between cause and effect.

Scientists are uncovering very subtle differences in characteristics such as risk taking, pessimism/optimism, introversion/extroversion, and anxiety. Interestingly, while we don't generally think of these characteristics as "genetic," researchers are now able to pinpoint particular regions on the human genome as being linked with a host of psychological characteristics. We've become accustomed to thinking of bipolar illness as having a genetic basis; it's a little tougher to think of our child's contrariness as genetically based. But if we understand how much of our children's behavior comes genetically encoded, it may make it easier for us to be sympathetic with their particular challenges. Some children are more negative than others. We can make a negative child more contrary by turning every discussion into a power struggle, or we can finesse some of these discussions by suggesting that sometimes people just see things differently. It helps if we don't take our children's particular characteristics personally or feel that we are responsible for every aspect of our child's personality.

The next section looks at the progression of *cognitive development* (how a child thinks,) *social development* (how a child relates to others), and proposes parenting strategies that are most likely to facilitate development at different ages. The kinds of parenting pitfalls associated with affluence will be highlighted. By understanding our children's capacities and challenges at different stages of development, we are better positioned to parent in ways that advance their moves toward autonomy and a healthy sense of self.

THE MAGIC YEARS—AGES 2 TO 4

Cognitive Development It is quite a stretch for an adult to "get into" the mind of a preschooler. Young children do not think, act, or experience the world the same way adults do. The way preschoolers think about the world is quite magical and certainly not bound by logic. They do not understand cause and effect the way an adult, or even an older child, does, they tend to see things in physical terms; and they do not appreciate complex or changing relationships. For example:

- Allow a three-year-old to play with a red car. In view of the child, place the car behind a green filter that makes the car appear to be black. Ask the child what color the car "really" is and she will say black.

- Show a four-year-old two identical tall glasses of water. As the child watches, pour the water from one into a wide, shallow glass. The child will believe that the tall glass has more water in it than the wide, shallow glass.

- Ask a three-year-old to tell you where he lives and he assumes you have information about his neighborhood. "Well, you go there and then you turn and then walk and that's it."

What the first two examples share is the fact that the young child sees only what is in front of him. The fact that he saw the red car or two equal amounts of water only a moment ago is lost to the immediacy of the black car in front of him and the difference in appearance of the water in the new glass. Psychologists term this kind of thinking "concrete." Concrete thinking is bound to the physical, to what is easily observable.

In the third example the young child's "egocentric" thinking is evident. He knows where he lives from his point of view only and assumes that you know where "there" and "it" is. Children this age can only see things through their own eyes and have great difficulty imagining anyone else's point of view. Their thinking is black and white. Accuracy doesn't count for much.

The young child's growing ability to express himself in language has tremendous impact on the development of the self. Language gives young children the ability to label and begin to define themselves. "Good boy," repeats the two-year-old after hearing it for the millionth time. He can begin to hang his embryonic self-concept on this simple phrase. Language also helps youngsters to remember in the present what happened in the past. The preschooler who becomes anxious when his mother is gone is comforted when he can remember and say to himself, "Mommy come home yesterday." Memory and language combine to give the young child a beginning sense of continuity that can be called on to combat moments of anger or fear.

Social Development While parents remain the most important people in young children's lives, their world is beginning to expand. Preschool and play dates offer youngsters opportunities to work on emerging social skills.

At this stage, because the child's thinking is black-and-white, his social relationships can be either very loving or quite hateful (for the moment, at least). The child who one day throws his arms around you, declaring his undying love for you, can be found the next day telling you that you are the "worst mommy in the world." For many young children, love affairs—with teachers, siblings, or peers—begin and end in a single day, only to start all over again the next.

Just before age two, children begin to understand that their behavior influences the adults around them, and they begin to actively seek adult approval, while avoiding adult disapproval. **This nascent ability to appreciate adult standards sets the groundwork for young children to begin experiencing feelings of accomplishment as well as feelings of shame or guilt.** "Remember how good you felt when Johnnie shared his snack with you yesterday? He seems sad today. I think it would be nice if you helped him feel better by sharing your snack." Young children are motivated to be generous because it makes *you* happy. Alternatively, when you express disappointment, young children are apt to feel guilty or ashamed. An exasperated "How could you wet your pants again?" shames your child, making her feel criticized and guilty. It also fails to teach your youngster skills for developing self-control. Better to matter-of-factly go over recognizing the sensations of a full bladder and how to respond to it. Having control over basic bodily functions lays the groundwork for a feeling of control in one's life.

Use the young child's desire to please you to encourage self-management skills and generous behavior. While children at this age cannot show true empathy—they do not yet have the ability to "stand in someone else's shoes"—parents can certainly encourage their children to show kindness and sympathy.

Parenting Strategies The changes in thinking and social development taking place at this young age are astonishing. Children with only the most rudimentary self-control skills are being called on to "sit still," "share," "wait your turn," and "play nice." As they get closer to entering elementary school, most kids are able to master these feats of self-control. Parents help their children see the value of self-control as they express pleasure or displeasure with their actions. This is not the age for long discussions about behavior. Parents need to be clear and brief about what pleases them and what doesn't. Many of us who value verbal skills end up explaining our reactions in ways that are beyond our child's capacity to understand. A simple "Mommy doesn't like it when you are mean to your sister," coupled with a consequence for bad behavior, is infinitely more useful to your child at this age than a treatise on sibling rivalry.

Make certain that you speak to your child firmly but respectfully. Children of this age imitate their parents endlessly. They will practice walking in your shoes, the way you hold your pocketbook or briefcase, your posture, and your style of speech. Make sure that they see you showing respect and consideration when dealing with others. Affluent parents who are often used to directing others can develop an incipient tone of arrogance; woe to the child who talks to his teacher in this tone of voice. Bossy children are generally shunned on the playground.

Another critical teaching tool for young children is play. Play is a way of miniaturizing the world so that children can try their hand at different situations and strategies. It is a mistake to constantly be managing your child's playtime. Children do not need to be "taught" how to play. Bring a young child to a playground or a toy store, and if she feels secure she will play. No one ever had to teach a child how to "use" a sandbox. Forget about the latest gadget that supposedly teaches your child how to quantify time, computers for two-year-olds and any toy that promises to raise your child's IQ. Give your child a safe environment; join her on the floor with simple toys like blocks and trucks and dolls. Make sure that she has plenty of unstructured playtime. When you invite her friends over, intervene as necessary, but set yourself up at a distance where you can observe. Then put up your feet, pay the bills, or call a friend.

Children's controls at this time are fragile and easily challenged by fatigue, hunger, and frustration. One day your four-year-old is able to resolve a fight with a friend, offer her sister half of her cookie, and put away her toys; the next day she may throw herself in a screaming heap on the floor when her mother suggests that it is bath time. This is normal. Child development never, ever proceeds in a straight line. It's best to resist comparing your child with other children at this stage. Development is rapid and uneven, and comparisons only serve to raise anxiety for parents.

When I was a preschool consultant, unless the presenting problem seemed truly worrisome, I would always set appointments with parents at least a couple of weeks after their initial phone call. I knew, from experience, that time would take care of most parental concerns and behavioral problems. Be patient; most childhood problems blow over.

Don't worry about your child's missteps at this stage—these missteps are critical to learning. When your child hits another child on a play date, use the opportunity to teach him about acceptable behavior and consequences for bad behavior. "You may not hit. Because you did not control yourself, we have to go home now. But you can try and play with Dylan again tomorrow."

Remember that one of our most important parenting jobs is helping our children develop self-control. We do not advance their ability to control their impulses when we regularly soften consequences for bad behavior.

For several years, the parents I saw in my practice were under the impression that the child who hits needs just as much attention and reassurance as the child who gets hit. As a result there was a huge increase in bullying, as parents tried to "get to the root" of why their child was so angry as opposed to disciplining their child. Notions about child development come and go, and parents need to remain thoughtful and sensible. Young kids hit because they are easily frustrated and don't have adequate self-control. Children need firm limits and swift consequences to help them develop internal controls. Kids want to please their parents; your approval is the most important thing in their life. Coddling a child who is smacking other children deprives him of the opportunity to learn the importance of self-control and the real-world consequences of unprovoked aggression.

When bad behavior is chronic, despite repeated attempts to help your child learn self-control, speak to your pediatrician or your child's teacher. They have seen hundreds of children, not one or two, and will help you evaluate whether any further help is needed.

MASTERS OF THE UNIVERSE—AGES 5 TO 7

Cognitive Development Children in early and middle childhood are having a love affair with the world. Enormous strides in thinking, as well as physical development, enable children in this group to do things that were inconceivable just a year or two before. They can ride a bike, read simple words, and understand that 2 plus 2 equals 4. Their horizons are expanding with dazzling speed; they are enchanted by their families, their neighborhoods, their schools, other children, other countries, and outer space. The world has become their oyster.

Typically, children in this age group describe themselves in exuberant terms. They still think in black and white and overestimate their abilities. "I'm the best runner in my class. I'm happy and excited when my dad sees me run because I'm faster than everyone."

Younger children can describe their emotional state with a single adjective: "I'm happy," or "I'm excited." It is not until ages five to seven that children can express two feelings *that are similar* about themselves at the same time: "I'm happy and excited when my dad sees me run." However, they cannot acknowledge both favorable and unfavorable parts of themselves at the same time. "Sometimes I'm a good runner and sometimes I'm not," is still beyond them. This is very important, since it means that children this age think about themselves as "all bad" or "all good." This makes them vulnerable to taking in unrealistically negative or positive views of themselves. Parents need to help their children gain perspective on their abilities. "I know you feel pretty bad about math today, but remember last week when you really understood your math homework," helps children to remember past successes and protects them from "all-or-nothing" thinking.

Social Development Children in this age group *really* care about what adults think. They know that they are being evaluated and care about how positive that evaluation is. Because children at this stage are not yet reliably capable of either self-evaluation or self-control, their behavior is still primarily controlled externally, by reinforcement, punishment, and instruction. What is bad is what gets punished. Don't be disappointed when your five-year-old is caught with her hand in the cookie jar despite repeated injunctions against cookie grabbing. "You should know better," sighs Mom. But the child cannot fully appreciate the notion that taking delicious cookies is ever really a bad idea. What she does know is that you don't like it. Parents and teachers who are clear about what is expected and what is acceptable do children a great favor at this age. We may wish that our children were more internally motivated to do the right thing, but they simply don't have the capacity yet. Parents still need to act as an auxiliary ego, reminding children of house rules and acceptable social behavior.

Interestingly, in countries throughout the world, most children enter school full-time between ages five and six. This is not coincidental but reflects the fact that by five or six a child can reliably respond to adult requests for self-control. Once a child crosses the threshold into a kindergarten or first-grade classroom, life is irrevocably changed. Throughout the day, new rules, new tasks, and new expectations challenge the youngster at every turn. The smallest details of behavior are now prescribed in new and exacting ways; where to sit, when to sit, even how to sit. Fortunately the child cares very much about how he does, and in his quest to be "good" he tries hard to comply with adult requests.

Because school brings children into a far more diverse social environment than home or preschool, the opportunities for developing friendships expand. Children begin navigating a social world on their own out in the school playground. While the parent-child power gradient is always weighted in favor of the adult's power; on the playground children meet as equals and begin to negotiate with other kids in order to have their needs met. Lifelong patterns of dominance or submission can be formed as a child's temperament leads him to be inclined to lead or to follow. Being liked by other children offers the five- to seven-year-old a strong incentive to learn how to regulate aggression, treat other kids fairly, and offer support and loyalty. There is still considerable unevenness in how children navigate their friendships, and your child's "best friend in the whole world" one day may be discarded the next. Still, the general direction is toward stability in friendships.

Parenting Strategies Because children this age see themselves as "all good" or "all bad," they are extremely vulnerable to criticism. Since kids still need considerable help honing self-regulation skills, parents need to develop a working alliance based on warm collaboration rather than criticism. The child who still has difficulty sharing at this age needs to be reminded of how good he feels when his friends share with him, rather than being told that he is "selfish." Negative accusations ("Why were you so mean to your brother?" "You're a bad friend if you don't invite Sasha to your birthday." "You must be hyper, the teacher says you're always squirming around.") can lead children to overgeneralize and feel that they are completely selfish or mean or difficult. Being mean, selfish, unpredictable, or restless are normal parts of being a young child. Because children this age cannot hold two concepts of themselves together at the same time—"sometimes I'm generous and sometimes I'm selfish"—they need to be corrected in ways that are not about their worth as a person but about their behavior. "I know it's really hard to sit still in class sometimes, but it's important for you to keep practicing this so that you can learn more and not distract other kids," does the job without labeling the child as difficult or hyperactive or selfish. **Once a child forms a negative impression of himself, it is very difficult to change.**

Once their children are in school, affluent, competitive parents often begin in earnest their decades-long overinvolvement in their child's academic career. Anxious parents regularly show up at back-to-school night for their kindergarteners, wanting to know how their children will be "evaluated" in math and language arts. Children this young do not benefit from grades. Fortunately they are unlikely to compare their performance to other kids, and so parents would do well to follow their lead and not ask how they or other kids are "doing" in class. There is a wide range in academic readiness at this age, with some kids eager for complex academic adventures while others are just hoping to remember to bring their pencil and notebook to school. Be interested in those things that excite your child; that might be reading, but it might also be his rock collection or the salamander he found at the creek. Kids who are "turned on," whether to a school project, their pet rat, or Captain Underpants, are likely to become good students because they are curious. Never bribe children to learn; it sets the stage for them to depend on rewards of one kind or another to learn. This sets them up to be good performers and poor learners.

The kinds of "special" services that people with money come to enjoy are often unnoticed by everyone except the young child. If you're used to cutting to the front of the line at your favorite restaurant because you're a regular, don't be surprised when your child zips past her classmates to hand in her paper rather than waiting in line. Rather than being welcomed, she will be properly chastised. When we want our children to follow the rules, we need to make sure that we're following them ourselves.

Be kind to your child; her beginning sense of self is still largely dependent on your opinion of her. You will need to set limits and define expectations since your child is not yet capable of this. Stay focused on the fact that your child is eager to please you and take advantage of her enthusiastic pursuit of your approval. As the parent of any teenager can attest, this will not always be the case!

HOW AM I DOING?—AGES 8 TO 11

Cognitive Development During this period, children's thinking abilities advance by leaps and bounds. **A great revolution in thinking takes place as children develop the ability to think logically and to appreciate cause and effect.** A joke used by researchers illustrates the difference in thinking between a younger and an older child.

> Mr. Jones went to a restaurant and ordered a whole pizza for dinner. When the waiter asked if he wanted it cut into six or eight pieces, Mr. Jones said: "You'd better make it six. I could never eat eight."[1]

This doesn't seem like a joke to a young child, who understands it as a reasonable request by a not-so-hungry Mr. Jones. The younger child's thinking is not yet guided by logic, and so six pieces of pizza is less than eight pieces. The older child, whose thinking is informed by logic, "gets" the joke, understanding that the total amount of pizza is the same no matter how you cut it.

The world becomes a much more manageable place as children are now able to make predictions based on past information and experiences. They know, more or less, what to expect from teachers, parents, and friends. This gives middle-age kids a period of balance sandwiched between the rapid changes of toddlerhood and the tumult of adolescence. In the words of two of the best-known developmental psychologists, Louise Bates Ames and Francis Ilg: "There's nobody nicer than a ten-year-old."[2] Children this age can be relatively free of conflict and, as a result, are able to turn their attention to schoolwork and advancing their thinking skills. This is the time of boy scouts and girl scouts, of piano lessons and horseback lessons, of soccer, baseball, and basketball, 4-H club and chess club. Children this age are propelled to learn about the world and try out their newly acquired thinking skills.

A hallmark of this age is that children can now understand that opposites can coexist. "Yesterday I was sad, but I'm feeling much better today," is the kind of leap in thinking that allows older children to see gray, not just black and white. They understand that all kinds of feelings can be part of a single person. As older children understand that the same person can behave differently under different circumstances, they begin to grasp the concept of motivation. "Chris never seems to try hard in class, but boy does he work his tail off being captain of the volleyball team." Chris is no longer just a poor student or a good athlete; he has become, in the eyes of the older child, an individual with different, sometimes opposing, attributes.

Because children at this stage can hold multiple concepts of themselves and others, their own self-evaluations become more realistic. "I'm the best" is pretty much gone at this age, as children begin developing a realistic picture of their abilities. "I'm really good in language arts, but I have trouble with math," can be a realistic appraisal of strengths and weaknesses. While this is an important advance, it also opens the door for children to become increasingly critical about themselves. Children this age are anxious to know if they are "really" good at something. They know that their parents may crow over their uninspired piano playing, but the outside world is not likely to be so generous.

Parents are most helpful when they are supportive and realistic. This doesn't mean letting your child give up on schoolwork or activities that are challenging for her, but it does mean acknowledging that she will have to put in extra time and effort. Point out that we all have strengths and weaknesses. Use examples from your own life about how you deal with things that don't come easy. All my sons know that the only way I can tell left from right is by consulting the scar on my right knee. Help your child develop compensatory strategies for things that are hard for them. Remember that development is still very uneven, and the child who has trouble stringing a sentence together at age eight may be on the debate team in high school. Parents need to help their child maintain a sense of perspective and not cut off interests prematurely.

Social Development As children move through elementary school, they become aware of themselves not only as individuals but also as group members. As a result of this emerging "social self," children at this age increasingly evaluate their performance in comparison to that of others. "My best friend and I both draw really well. But she's better at portraits and I'm better at landscapes." These social comparisons help children appreciate their uniqueness and differentiate themselves from others. They deal in comparisons not because they are anxious to crow over their abilities (many children at this age do not like to be singled out, even for excellence) but because comparisons help them know where they stand. It is part of the ongoing task of this age to begin to evaluate oneself realistically.

Another major social task of this age is the development of friendships. Children now actively choose their friends based on shared interests and attitudes. Some remarkably enduring friendships are forged at this stage of development. Children can now see things from a friend's point of view as well as their own. This newly emerging capacity to truly see things from another perspective can have some interesting twists for children at the end of this developmental stage. "I'm having a party and you can't come," says your ten-year-old daughter to a friend she's mad at. "You are such a retard," says your eleven-year-old son out of frustration when his younger brother makes off with his iPod again. As disturbing as such cruelty may be to parents, it actually represents a step forward in psychological development. Unlike the younger child who hit out of frustration or anger, older children have the capacity to stand in someone else's shoes and know how painful exclusion and insults can be. It is this ability to stand in another's shoes that parents need to harness in prosocial ways to help their children control the psychological damage they are now capable of inflicting when they behave in antisocial ways.

Research shows that parents who encourage and model prosocial and altruistic behavior tend to have children who are also prosocial. This is a time when kids should have chores, and should be expected to contribute to the family. Worrying that kids won't be able to maintain their grades if they are expected to straighten their room, set the table, take out the garbage, and do whatever else is appropriate for their age and needed by the family (wash the car, walk the dog, mow the lawn) is a sign of misplaced priorities. Certainly grades are important, and particularly so for affluent, competitive parents, but academic competence is only one part of what children need to learn in order to be productive, emotionally healthy, good people.

These years are important for instilling character into our children. Parents might involve themselves in some community/religious/spiritual activity, and bring their child along with them. There is more to be learned from becoming a contributing member of a group (the ability to cooperate, the value of good deeds, the satisfaction of contribution, the advancement of daily living skills) than from another hour of cramming. Also, becoming competent at everyday tasks makes children proud of their emerging abilities. My middle son started cooking at this stage, and soon we all looked forward to his tasty concoctions, which usually included smoothies made from every fruit in the house and pizza topped with happy faces of assorted cheese strips. Our appreciation, coupled with his own motivation, helped fuel his interest. To this day, he's still the family member who can throw a meal together in a pinch.

Parenting Challenges Children at this stage are becoming critical and competitive. "I'm the worst player on the team, I'm quitting," is a typical complaint of a ten-year-old who sees temporary challenges as insurmountable. In reality, he has several options: he can quit the team, practice harder, enjoy playing regardless of skill level, or find another activity that is more suited to his skills and temperament. As a tonic to the older child's relentless comparison of himself to others, it is important that parents model self-acceptance and courage in facing personal challenges. Parents need to be careful not to overemphasize competition and performance. Unfortunately, the opposite is often the case, as affluent, competitive parents throw themselves into monitoring their child's academic and athletic progress with vigor now that letter grades have become standard and teams have become "select." Parents' overinvolvement in their children's academic progress has become legend, driving some of the most talented and capable teachers out of the profession in the process. Children need to see that we value their character first, their effort second, and then their grades.

This is not to suggest that parents should be uninvolved or unconcerned about their child's academic progress. The difference between involvement (which aids academic achievement) and overinvolvement and intrusion (which lessens academic achievement) has to do with how highly parents are invested in their child's performance.[3] If you feel awful (or worse yet, angry) about an occasional low grade or elated about a high grade, then you are probably overinvolved or intrusive. Resist the temptation to monitor every inch of your child's progress. We all know that some of our best work is done when no one is watching, when we feel free to be flexible and creative. Make sure your child has time to explore and create and learn without the pressure of constant scrutiny and the threat of constant evaluation.

An important research finding for children during this developmental stage is that girls are given more negative feedback than boys, both at home and in the classroom.[4] Girls who perform poorly are characterized as being less smart, while low-performing boys are characterized as putting out less effort.[5] Intelligence is generally considered to be one of those things we have little control over, whereas effort is seen as something the child can choose to change. As a result, girls begin to have more negative feelings about themselves than boys as they head into adolescence. It is likely that the high levels of depression seen in girls in the next age group are a result of the subtle, but nonetheless persistent denigration of girls that begins in middle to late childhood.

WHAT HAPPENED TO MY KID?
—AGES 12 TO 14

Cognitive Development A revolution in thinking takes place in early adolescence. **In addition to the ability to think logically, young adolescents can now also think abstractly.** While it may come as a surprise to dazed and confused parents, their young adolescents actually think pretty much like adults. Young teenagers can think about past, present, and future; they understand that people have motives that are often not readily apparent; and they understand the function of symbols. They can make formal, logical arguments, and the fact that this may be about their need to have a 2:00 A.M. curfew or to be allowed to smoke marijuana doesn't diminish their ability to put forth a well-thought-out argument. Judgment and experience lag behind formal thinking skills at this age.

Since thinking is now nuanced, young teens can take positions contrary to their own. True empathy becomes evident as teens are able to look at issues from different points of view and understand that many different factors determine a person's motivation. As a result, the severe moral judgment of younger children is now tempered by understanding: "I'm mad that Brooke copied my test, but I understand because things are pretty tough for her at home. Her parents are getting divorced." Granted, this understanding rarely seems to extend to parents and siblings, but it will eventually. In the meantime, teens should be encouraged to think about moral dilemmas as preparation for the many decisions they will face over the next few years.

Because of the rapid advance in cognitive skills, young teens find social, moral, and personal issues fascinating. One of my young adolescent patients comes in with a weekly moral dilemma: "Would you eat human flesh if you were starving?" "Would you kill an evil person to save an innocent person?" "Could you kill an innocent person to save your family?" This parade of moral questions reflects advances in thinking, empathy, and moral judgment. It is also a way for this bright and sensitive young girl to plumb my thinking process and my values as she strives to develop her own sense of right and wrong.

Dinnertime is a good time for children this age to float their different and sometimes startling opinions—everything from condoms in the nurse's office to gangsta rap to the invasion of Iraq. Parents need to listen respectfully as they play to the developmental strengths of this age—intellectual curiosity, thinking skills that can handle increasingly abstract information, and a desire to clarify moral positions. This is not to say that parents need to agree with their inexperienced teens' views on drugs or sex or parental nonintervention; but it is a great time to model thoughtfulness. Look for opportunities to share ideas with your kids: driving to events, a quiet evening at home, a special outing together. Your genuine interest in their burgeoning intellectual skills helps young teens feel loved and worthwhile at a time when they are generally feeling insecure and vulnerable.

The phenomenon of "plasticity" has received a great deal of attention recently. Plasticity refers to changes that occur in the brain in response to any one of a number of factors in the environment: drugs, toxins, nutrients, parenting, and other relationships. Any of these can heighten or lessen a child's vulnerability to emotional illness.[6] The child who has had many stressful family experiences will have higher levels of the stress hormone cortisol. Too much cortisol impacts the brain, and can damage neurons in specific brain regions; with these effects most profound during early childhood when brain plasticity is high.[7]

Another critical period in terms of how parents impact the structure of their child's developing brain is during adolescence. Beginning at about age twelve there are dramatic changes in both sex and stress hormones, both of which affect impulse control and psychological adjustment. In fact, the portion of the brain that is responsible for controlling impulses does not fully mature until the early twenties. Research has established that the teen's capacities for self-regulation are strongly shaped by the quality of their relationships with their parents.[8] Because brain plasticity remains high in adolescence, it is an opportune time for parents to help their children master self-regulation skills. Encouraging independence while monitoring behavior helps teens to develop a more capable brain.

Social Development Being a young teenager is not easy. Neither, for that matter, is living with one. No other period of development generates as much fear and anxiety in parents as the new adolescent. Surly, confused, oppositional, and often withdrawn, the early adolescent often seems an unfortunate replacement for the easygoing and cooperative child of the previous developmental stage.

Kids who just a couple of years earlier were quite comfortable that they were generally good people now question every aspect of themselves. There can be a lot of conflict at this age as kids struggle with identity issues and parents run out of patience. Your fourteen-year-old daughter may attack you for your lack of social consciousness because you don't recycle the garbage, while leaving a trail of straws, wrappers, and cardboard behind her at the fast-food restaurant. Contradictions in thinking and action seem to escape the notice of the young teenager. Annoying as this may be to parents, it spares the already overwhelmed young teenager some of the emotional distress of having to make sense out of emerging contradictory parts of the self.

Peers typically supplant parents as the arbiter of all things "cool" in early adolescence. Because the drive toward separation is great at this time, kids who used to love to engage in activities with their parents are now appalled at the very suggestion. When my own sons hit this age and we were forced out into unbearable shopping expeditions, I noticed that they would walk several feet ahead of me in order to make it clear to all involved—other shoppers, myself, but most of all themselves—that we were not related. Humor can be a great tonic to the sense of rejection we are likely to experience as our kids suddenly act as if disowning us could quite possibly be the single best solution to all their problems.

Just as the young child crafted a sense of self out of the "mirror" of the mother, teens this age craft a sense of self out of the mirror of their peers. The shifting allegiances of teens at this age make the reliability of this mirror quite poor, only adding to the young teen's confusions about how she measures up in the world. It is critical that parents bear in mind that this is a temporary state of affairs and that in spite of appearances to the contrary, kids this age are still very dependent on their parents for a sense of well-being.

Many parents at this stage feel that they've done their job and their children are old enough to manage on their own. Parents back off in all areas except academics, leaving their kids home alone after school or even on occasional weekends. Kids this age are in need of adult supervision because too much freedom leaves them vulnerable to their own underdeveloped judgment. We know that kids who start experimenting with drugs or alcohol in early adolescence are at heightened risk for substance abuse later. It is important for parents to work at maintaining connection with their young teens in spite of the protest, and even rejection, typical of this age. Eye rolling passes, but the protection that parental involvement confers lasts a lifetime.

Parenting Challenges One of my favorite moments as an adolescent therapist came when a fourteen-year-old patient of mine was trying desperately to explain to his mother why he was having trouble in his advanced math class. He worked hard; he did his homework; but he just was "not getting it." Mom kept interrupting, telling him how smart he was, if he just tried harder, if he wasn't so lazy, if he didn't have such poor study habits, then he wouldn't find the class so difficult. She reminded him that for years he had done very well in the high math group and she just couldn't imagine where his bad attitude came from. He used to be the first kid up to the board, she explains, and now his teacher could barely get him to move when called on. Wiping away tears of frustration, he yelled, "Yeah, well that was before I had a boner most of the time!"

It was a gutsy and realistic answer to a mother who was in the dark about the self-consciousness of adolescent boys. A quick reminder of some of her own experiences of embarrassment in early adolescence helped her understand her son's mortification. The physical changes that accompany puberty, the social self-consciousness, the uncertainty about who one is, and the need to separate from family make this one of the most, if not the most, challenging developmental period for both parent and child. Navigated well, it puts young teens on a path that will help them manage the physical, emotional, and psychological demands that adolescence and adulthood invariably bring. Managed poorly, it sets kids up for a host of difficulties at a time when they are exceedingly vulnerable to peer pressure and making unhealthy choices.

Parents need to have a good grasp of the enormous tasks that are being worked on in early adolescence. In addition to the three principal tasks that kids have been working on for some time—sense of self, academic success, and friendships—young teens are now engaging in another monumental task: they are in the process of separating and individuating from their parents. They are taking on the challenge of navigating out in the world under their own steam. In the process of developing an independent sense of self, many young adolescents find it necessary to challenge, ignore, reject, and criticize their parents. While this can be incredibly painful for parents, coming often as it does just as middle age and even menopause exact their own toll, it serves a necessary function for young adolescents. The young teen who finds fault with her parents and then finds that her parents can tolerate this fault-finding has learned an important lesson: no one is perfect. And no one feels *less* perfect than the young adolescent. So parents who can tolerate *some* criticism from their teens are imparting a valuable lesson: that one does not have to be perfect to be okay. For the youngster who feels like he is under a microscope, whose every pimple is magnified, whose hair and teeth and body are scrutinized constantly for imperfections, a parent's good-natured response to criticism can be a tonic to the teen's ruthless self-criticism.

The need to have some "psychological space" as well as physical space from parents is critical during early adolescence. It is interesting to me that kids at this age often respond to my questions about their parents with a kind of physical revulsion. Parents would be astounded to see that the children they insist are "so close" to them, gag or shudder or close their eyes when I ask them to describe their relationship with their parents. When pressed about the meaning of these gestures, many kids will say, "She gets under my skin," or "I just wish they would get out of my head." Teens naturally are engaged in a kind of psychological skirmish with the parent they have internalized, as they struggle to replace their parents' attitudes and values with their own. As parents have become increasingly involved not just with the traditional roles of parenting, but have become *über*-parents, participating in all domains of their child's life, the skirmishes have turned into outright warfare as the young teen struggles to maintain a sense of self separate from his parents.

Kids need plenty of opportunities to dream about and work out the details of their future selves. Too many kids from comfortable families seem to be bypassing this process as they adopt a manufactured self promoted by schools, parents, and the media. These "selves" are well received by adults and the community, but they bypass the mandatory work and messiness of early adolescence. Waiting on line at the deli counter of the local supermarket confirms that everyone's kid is on the traveling team, gets straight A's, has been chosen to be part of some special program at some special school, and gets along "fabulously" with their siblings and parents. Yet my office tells quite a different story, where kids in various states of disrepair talk about how "fake" they feel, and how angry they are at their well-meaning but intrusive and critical parents who insist on micromanaging their lives.

Kids will always find a way to escape adult intrusion; they will take drugs, sneak out at night, have promiscuous sex, cut themselves, stop eating, or adopt any one of a thousand self-defeating behaviors that proclaim "This is *my* life." A parent's job is to welcome the separation that their young teenager needs while they continue to address issues of safety and provide a warm nest to return to. Not unlike the toddler, the adolescent needs a few good friends, a safe environment, and parents who are willing to get out of the way. We need to say "yes" when we can, and "no" when we have to. We need to be just as interested in the child who is trying to fly on her own as we were in the child who needed a copilot.

Just recently my husband and our fourteen-year-old son were discussing what to do over spring break. My husband was pushing skiing, an activity he loves and has enjoyed with all three of our sons over many years. Our fourteen-year-old was not interested, for whatever reason, this year. Seemingly out of nowhere he decided that he wanted to learn archery. On cue, my husband said, "Don't you want to get good at skiing?" and my son responded, "I'd rather learn something new." I realized as I listened to this exchange that the unspoken part of their conversation was my husband's sense of loss at not being able to continue an activity he loves with our youngest son, and my son's desire to choose an activity that no one else in our family is likely to be interested in, one that would define him as separate from the rest of us.

Being aware of the subtext in conversations with our teenagers is important. So much of the conflict of this stage has to do with issues of loss, identity, independence, and control. My husband is right that practice matters; our son is right that new experiences are important. But, more important, they are navigating a radically new relationship between them. As our children move through adolescence we need to welcome their emerging identities. There is sure to be a sense of loss for us as the child we had fantasized about raising becomes a flesh-and-blood reality, often quite unlike our fantasies. Our children cannot be assumed to follow in our footsteps, assuage our losses, or compensate for our inadequacies. Their adolescence is a very good time to take psychological stock of ourselves and make sure that our own lives are rich enough, so that when our children leave home in a few short years, we are not bereft.

WORKING ON THE "REAL ME"
—AGES 15 TO 17

Cognitive Development The proliferation of "selves" and concern over "who is the real me?" ratchets up in middle adolescence. Kids this age are very aware of contradictions in their sense of self. This makes them confused about how they will ever integrate the curious kid at school, the rowdy kid with friends, the quiet kid in new situations, and the crabby kid at home into a single comfortable person. Their internal landscape is cluttered with multiple selves, some in contradiction with each other. "I really don't know anymore if I'm a good person or not. I love my friends, but sometimes I just hate my parents." While there have been many advances in their thinking, it is still just beyond their reach to integrate opposing characteristics. This makes for a very unsettled sense of self.

Unlike the younger teen who often ignores contradictions in the self, the older teen has to struggle to resolve whether she's intelligent or an airhead, introverted or extroverted, a slut or a prude. At this age, teens begin to understand that different characteristics may become more or less evident in different situations. A common dilemma for girls can be the wish to perform well in school, both for their own sense of competence and for their parents' approval, and the wish not to be seen as a "brain" by the boys they're interested in. They may study hard at home and seem nonchalant in the classroom. Boys often struggle to hide their more sensitive feelings, fearful that they might be ostracized by the predominantly macho culture of high school boys. A teenage boy may be quite capable of talking with a girlfriend about his distress over his parents' fighting, yet pass her in the school corridor with hardly a word. Trying to resolve these opposing parts of the self results in the common adolescent experience of feeling conflicted. One of my patients described this dilemma particularly well when she said, "I feel like a puzzle, only I can't get all the parts to fit." The adolescent mind works overtime to put the pieces together so that a cogent, predictable, and comfortable image of the self can emerge.

Social Development As teenagers move through adolescence, they are confronted with major psychological and social issues probably paralleled only by those encountered in toddlerhood (an age that has much in common with adolescence). While the toddler's "I do it myself" has been replaced by the adolescent's "It's my life, don't tell me what to do," the battle for self-definition and autonomy are comparable. Now, however, the adolescent has acquired thinking skills and the ability to realistically gauge his performance in a way that was not possible for the youngster. And while the mother of the toddler was able to reflect back a fairly consistent image of her young child, the multiple mirrors that teenagers gaze into reflect back bewilderingly different images: a good friend, a difficult kid, a competitive athlete, an unenthusiastic student, an envied sibling. All this leads to the inevitable "moodiness" of adolescence, as self-worth swings back and forth, depending on which mirror the teenager is looking into.

The world of adolescence is filled with seemingly unsolvable contradictions. Although some teenagers may continue to pursue long-standing interests, others seem eager to disassociate themselves from earlier interests. One day the teenager is a Democrat and the next he's a Republican. Jocks become poets, and poets become jocks. Good girls become fast girls, and fast girls become nuns. Great romantic passions well up and just as frequently dry up.

Because the teenager is busy differentiating the many roles he plays, he also begins to differentiate his relationships with his mother and father. Younger children tend to see their parents as a unit, teens are aware that they can have very different feelings toward each parent. "I don't get it, it's so easy just hanging out with my dad, but my mom makes me crazy," complains a fifteen-year-old boy. This can be a particularly tough time for moms, as they generally spend more time with their children than fathers and have typically been more involved with their children's emotional lives. In general, teenagers have more conflicts with their mothers than with their fathers. They can be particularly cruel toward their mothers as they flail about trying to effect the separation they need. A beleaguered mother sits in my office, begging for an explanation of why her teenage daughter still wants to be tucked in but will not allow Mom to sit on her bed because "you have such a fat ass." Letting go of the reassuring dependency of childhood is hard for us and harder for our children. While we should not tolerate cruelty or real disrespect, we should expect some rather bumbling attempts at separation.

Parenting Challenges Self-regulation is a pressing issue for the adolescent, just like it was for the toddler. Countless teens have sat in my office, swearing that they wouldn't drink at the upcoming weekend party—only to beg my intervention the following session after they had been grounded for coming home drunk. "I don't know why I got trashed. I was sure I could handle it." While parents absolutely have to have clear standards about issues like drinking, the fact is that teens will, at times, be unsuccessful at juggling their multiple selves. The teen who drank too much had every intention of being a "good kid," but the internal push to "try things out" and the social demand to be a "party girl," turned good intentions into a muddle.

Parents need to have clear expectations and appropriate consequences as they help their teenager learn how to manage difficult situations. In a year or two, these same teens will be at college or out in the world, where temptations will be greater and supervision less. Teens need all the practice they can get learning how to benefit from their disappointments and failures as well as from their successes. This is not the time to get a lawyer for your kid's DUI, to have a professional write the essay for your daughter's college application, or to confront the coach who isn't giving your son enough playing time. During this critical period of time, kids can, will, and must make mistakes, suffer the consequences, and dig deep within themselves to find better solutions and alternative strategies while they are still under your roof. Teens tend to live "in the moment" and have difficulty anticipating when things may take a turn for the worse. A license suspension today is difficult for a teenager, but nowhere near as difficult as a vehicular manslaughter charge tomorrow. **We should never, ever, allow our kids to buy**

their way out of trouble. When we mitigate natural consequences for our kids we deprive them of one of life's most important lessons: that we are held accountable for our actions.

In my practice, adolescents are constantly asking questions about my own history. Did I take drugs? What kind? How often? How old was I when I had sex? Did I tell my own mother? Adolescents are desperate to obtain information, to know what is "normal," and to have the opportunity to collaborate with a nonjudgmental adult about the pressing and confusing issues they face as they transition from childhood into young adulthood. Treating our teens like inexperienced adults ("That was a new experience for you, what do you think your options might be next time?") rather than as recalcitrant children ("I knew you weren't mature enough to handle this.") helps to keep channels of communication open.

While parents are often telling their teenager to "play the field" when it comes to dating, because they recognize the hazards of cutting off social options too early, so do teenagers need to "play the field" when it comes to political ideas, moral choices, academic interests, and outside activities. Hounding teens about the benefits of "sticking with" long-standing interests, insisting that they remain on the soccer team because "colleges are interested in kids who stick with things," is only partially true and may get in the way of their developing more appropriate and authentic interests. Parents need to support their teenagers' dizzying profusion of "selves." At the same time, parents also need to promote the values of hard work, patience, and persistence—the kinds of self-management skills that are necessary for psychological, interpersonal, and academic development. You're not imagining it when it feels like life with a teenager is a lot like walking a tightrope.

Embedded within every section of this chapter is the belief that a child's emotional development is aided by parents who understand that kids at different ages have different capacities and different needs. Most of us intuitively know that we can't control a fifteen-year-old in the same way we control a five-year-old. This is not to say that both the fifteen-year-old and the five-year-old don't need parental control; they do. Similarly they both need love and attention, and even this takes different forms as our children grow. The bear hug of childhood may give way to the adolescent "pyramid" hug, where shoulders can touch but other body parts are scrupulously avoided, but all kids need frequent and genuine expressions of love and goodwill from their parents.

While the particular manifestations of good parenting may morph and shift over the course of raising a child, the same two dimensions remain critical: how we connect with our children, and how we discipline them.

Affluent parents face particular challenges in both these regards. For example, our well-documented tendency to pressure our children to perform at the highest levels certainly affects the quality of our connection with them, and our pressured and fast-paced lifestyle often results in our physical or emotional exhaustion, making thoughtful discipline decisions impossible. In order to approximate the parenting style considered optimal for children of all ages, we need to understand that both connection and discipline exist along a continuum, and that where we fall on this continuum significantly impacts our child's emotional development.

PART THREE

PARENTING FOR AUTONOMY

· CHAPTER 6 ·

How We Connect
Makes All the Difference

Somewhere back in college, if we took an introductory child-development course, we were introduced to the work of Diana Baumrind. A research psychologist at the University of California, Berkeley, Dr. Baumrind has investigated the impact of different parenting styles on child development for over forty years. Her work, which has been tested and reproduced at research centers throughout the country, has been presented in almost every book written about parenting in recent memory. Her central concern has always been to identify those parenting strategies that are most likely to turn out autonomous children, children who are independent, capable, and loving.

In her original research, Dr. Baumrind identified three styles of parenting—authoritarian, permissive, and authoritative—and their outcomes in terms of child development.[1] Dr. Baumrind and other researchers have since refined and added to her findings, but her work remains the "gold standard." Embedded within each of Dr. Baumrind's parenting styles are very different approaches to connection (researchers tend to use the words "warmth" and "connection" interchangeably) and discipline (how parents control their children).

The most current research on parenting has moved beyond simple categories into a more complex understanding of the factors that predict healthy or poor adjustment in children. While both connection and discipline on their own are important parenting factors, what is really predictive of how well kids do is the *interaction* of these two factors. Warm connection is a good predictor of healthy child development—but it's a much better predictor when paired with appropriate discipline than when paired with either harsh or lax discipline. In affluent households parents typically believe that they have a warm relationship with their child but worry that their kids "get away with too much." This is a legitimate (not to mention accurate) concern. Holding kids to their responsibilities is just as important as cozy late-night talks.

We all understand that parenting is about connecting with our kids and providing boundaries. We want to establish a loving connection so that our kids have a solid base from which to launch their adulthood and we want to discipline our children so that we keep them safe enough to develop the skills they need to take care of themselves. But, as this chapter and the next will illustrate, these well-intended goals are far more nuanced than many parents realize.

We all want our children to be able to love and be loved, to go out into the world and lead meaningful and reasonably happy lives of their own. While many things are beyond our control, ranging from our child's genetics to the pervasiveness of the consumer culture peddled by the media, the one thing we do have control over is how we parent. In hoping to move our children in the direction of autonomy, competence, and connection, the direction that makes it more likely that they will have the kinds of lives we hope for them, we need to be willing to consider and sometimes reconsider the ways in which we parent.

Caveat: As we look closely at parenting styles and the factors that advance healthy child development, we need to retain compassion for ourselves as we stumble upon some of our less desirable parenting strategies. Having the courage to honestly evaluate our own parenting makes it likely that we will discover unintended mistakes and long-standing vulnerabilities that have either regularly, or from time to time, compromised our parenting efforts. Parents, like children, grow and change; parenting styles are not written in stone. Avoid feeling guilty about what you have or haven't done (frankly, it's water under the bridge) and move forward enthusiastically with new insights about those things you can do.

KNOW YOUR PARENTING STYLE

Do As You're Told: The Authoritarian Parent

Authoritarian parents, while typically engaged with their children, rely on a strict and inflexible set of rules for running their households. They are not interested in hashing out differences with their child, nor are they particularly interested in their child's point of view. They believe that discipline, enforced swiftly and without discussion, is the most effective way to parent, and are very controlling. Authoritarian parents are more demanding of their children than they are responsive to their needs. They are often disinclined to support their child's growing autonomy since this is likely to change the balance of power between them.

"Because I said so" is the mantra of those who subscribe to this parenting style. Children from authoritarian households are regularly punished for failing to conform to parents' demands and expectations. While engaged with their children, authoritarian parents are more cold than warm. They demand compliance, tend to have high expectations, and when their children are young can have relatively conflict-free and orderly homes. In adolescence, however, their homes can become war zones as rebellious teens are severely penalized for engaging in the kinds of healthy risk taking that are not sanctioned by authoritarian parents. This includes everything from divergent political views to occasional drug or alcohol experimentation.

Unfortunately, many children from authoritarian homes, while reasonably conforming and obedient, have low self-esteem, poor social skills, and high rates of depression. In addition, they lack curiosity, which makes sense when you consider how "thinking outside the box" is not encouraged in their homes. These children often remain overly dependent on others for guidance and control.[2] Of particular concern is the fact that studies show that children from authoritarian households are more aggressive than children from families with other parenting styles.[3] Authoritarian homes, with their one-way emphasis on power, can provide a breeding ground for bullies.

Do Your Own Thing: The Permissive Parent

Permissive parents tend to be "friends" with their children. They see parenting as a collaborative effort between parent and child, and their relationships with their children are warm. Permissive parents are more responsive than demanding and they are reluctant to exercise control over their children

Permissive parents are extremely involved with their children, but they often do not insist on appropriate behavior. Their response to criticism of their child's poor behavior is likely to be "It's just a stage she's going through." Teachers, coaches, other adults, and kids all come in for their share of criticism as permissive parents try to protect their children from the consequences of their bad behavior or disappointing run-ins with reality. A low grade is because the "teacher didn't present the material well," not because their child didn't study hard enough. Minimal playing time on the field is because the coach "plays his own kid," not because their child has limited athletic skills.

These parents avoid confrontation with their children and have trouble tolerating their children's unhappiness. Permissive parents, in addition to having difficulty with discipline, shy away from confrontation and are hesitant to curb their child's impulses. Rules are enforced erratically and children in these households have few responsibilities. The children of permissive parents have little sense that the adults in the house are the ones who are in charge.

On a more positive note, the permissive parent is likely to encourage creativity and individuality. Children of permissive parents tend to be likable, social, and to enjoy high self-esteem. On the other hand, they tend to be impulsive, immature, and to have difficulty understanding the consequences of their actions. These children tend to be manipulative and have lower rates of academic achievement and higher rates of substance abuse than children from either authoritarian or authoritative homes.[4] This is a particularly worrisome outcome of permissive parenting, given the disproportionately high rates of substance abuse among affluent teens.

We Can Work It Out: The Authoritative Parent

Authoritative parents are warm and accepting, but at the same time they set clearly defined limits and expectations. They are both demanding and responsive and in general feel they are in control of their households. Support, rather than criticism or punishment, is typically used to encourage children to meet expectations.

Authoritative parents are concerned with things other than simple compliance or being "pals" with their kids. They place a high value on cooperation, social responsibility, and self-regulation, and their children tend to be socially adept and responsible. They also value achievement and self-motivation but do not overly emphasize competition. Authoritative parents promote autonomy by encouraging their children to figure out how to approach challenges on their own, rather than prematurely stepping in and problem-solving for them.

Because authoritative parents are clear about their parenting role and don't look to their children to make up for a lack of connection or friendship in their own lives, they are able to do a good job of meeting the needs of their children. This in turn frees their children from being preoccupied with finding ways to get their own needs met, allowing them instead to pay attention to the needs of others. When kids are interested in others, friendships and deep connections are more likely to develop. This type of parenting supports the child's growing autonomy by focusing both on independence *and* connection.

Authoritative parenting is not simply "middle-of-the-road" parenting; rather, it is a highly committed and unique parenting style. Dr. Baumrind believes that it is the authoritative parent, the parent who is warm but also capable of appropriate discipline, and who is committed to supporting a high degree of autonomy with equally high demands for maturity and achievement, who stands to have the best-adjusted child. **Her research shows that children from authoritative families have more balanced attitudes about achievement, better social skills, higher grades, lower rates of substance abuse, and less depression than children from either permissive or authoritarian households.**[5] In other words, these are the children who are most likely to have a healthy sense of self, to have developed the skills that comprise the trinity of healthy child development: the ability to lead independent lives, to maintain loving interpersonal relationships, and to enjoy a sense of competence.

CULTIVATE WARMTH TO PROTECT EMOTIONAL DEVELOPMENT

What does being a "warm," connected parent mean? Is parental warmth simply a feeling of goodwill between parent and child? Is the touchy-feely mom always "warmer" than the mom who is more physically restrained? Is warmth invariably salutary, or can there be too much of a good thing? Is it really possible to maintain warmth in the face of disappointment or anger at our children?

Researchers always talk about "operationalizing" their terms. This is a fancy way of saying that to understand a word like "warmth" we not only have to define it but have to know what it looks like out in the real world. **Warmth is the quality of involvement, understanding, acceptance, and love that parents communicate on different levels and in ever-evolving ways as their children grow.** With infants, a warm parent is attuned to the unspoken needs of the baby and willingly meets these needs quickly and without resentment. As infants grow into children, warm parents maintain their interest and empathy even as they lessen their involvement in the child's basic tasks of self-care, such as taking a bath or getting dressed for school. And in adolescence, parents convey warmth by letting their teens advance their independence secure in the knowledge that their parents are standing by on an "as-needed" basis.

Yet even though it is clear that children with warm, connected parents are better adjusted, the way parents connect to their children exists on a continuum. At one end of the spectrum is over involvement, intrusion, and enmeshment; at the other is criticism, and rejection. Optimal connection lies somewhere in the middle, and being able to keep our parenting in this territory is one of the most critical skills we can develop.

Good Warmth: Acceptance, Understanding, and Investment

Think about someone in your own life who treats you warmly—a spouse, a coworker, or a friend perhaps. Try to separate out the feeling of warmth from other parts of your relationship, like shared purpose or shared interest. For most of us, warmth has a very specific quality of acceptance. "He likes me, warts and all." "She accepts me for who I am." These are the kinds of statements we make about people with whom we have warm relationships. Acceptance is a very important part of warmth. It is also the part of warmth that is easily tested when our children behave in ways that we disapprove of. Acceptance doesn't mean, that you have to like your son's pierced nose or your daughter's tattoo. It does mean, however, that in spite of inevitable disagreements and disappointments, the essence of your child remains dear to you.

Loving an infant or small child is easy. They soak up our love and delight in our attention. We can accept their missteps and mistakes because they are easily remedied, usually with a little elbow grease and a good cleaning product. We can maintain our warmth, our acceptance, because, while our preschooler may swat our hand away as she tries to put on her own mittens, we still typically feel a profound sense of connection, of being needed by our young children.

Maintaining a warm, accepting stance toward our teenagers is one of the most protective factors in their development, and one of the most challenging in ours. We have to tolerate their attempts at separation, their muddling around in ambivalent feelings toward us, and even their defiance. Our children are always a work in progress, and part of true acceptance is our ability to love our children even as they swing back and forth between attachment and separation, between alienation and commitment. We can't possibly love every minute of this process. It can be extremely trying. But every teenager knows the difference between the parent who is temporarily put out and the one who is permanently put out. Good parents always try to come back to a position of acceptance.

Acceptance, however, is not the whole of warmth. We all have people in our own lives who are accepting but with whom we don't feel particularly close. Warmth goes deeper than just acceptance. A truly warm relationship is characterized by a sense not only of acceptance but of deep understanding as well. Whether I'm working with adolescents or adults, the theme of being misunderstood, the longing to be connected to someone who can see clearly, without distortion or projection, is universal. Over and over patients talk about the relief they experience when they feel truly "seen" or "heard."

Think about the way you listen to a close friend and then think about how you listen to your children. When we listen to our friends it is usually with the purpose of understanding their dilemmas, of helping them clarify how they feel, and of letting them know that we care. We listen long enough to know what it feels like to be in their shoes. Too often with our children, we rush in and offer suggestions, propose alternatives, or solve problems. While well-intentioned, this kind of premature cutting off of communication is often a result of our anxiety about letting our kids struggle. It can also be the most expedient solution when our own demands are great and our time is short. Unfortunately, when we intervene prematurely, we lose the opportunity to understand a bit more about who our particular child is, and how developed her skills for approaching a challenging situation. Teenagers in particular complain that their parents don't "get me" because they don't take the time to really listen. We can't understand our children unless we take a few steps back, follow their lead, and listen to their stories openly and with curiosity. There is nothing more reassuring or more likely to encourage connection and communication with our children than our inviting, listening, presence.

Current research has uncovered another aspect of connection that has to do with a child's sense that their parents are committed to them.[6] Our children need to feel protected; that they will not be emotionally abandoned in times of fear or distress. Children need to feel protected, not simply comforted. Remember your relief when someone turned the lights on (either literally or figuratively) and you were no longer afraid? Even within a warm child-parent relationship, the child's belief that his parents are both committed and protective of him confers additional psychological advantages.

While most research has focused on the value of maternal warmth, there is a growing body of evidence indicating that the warmth and acceptance shown by fathers, who are generally less involved in daily childcare, make a significant contribution to their children's (especially their teenagers') well-being. Feeling accepted by Dad appears to be particularly important when it comes to grades and conduct.[7] This may be because a child has fewer interactions with Dad, so that each one takes on a heightened meaning, or because father's approval tends to be more conditional, depending on how well the adolescent has performed. In any event, a father's warmth and acceptance are strong predictors of academic success, social competence, and a low incidence of conduct problems in adolescence.[8]

Children need our time, our understanding, our acceptance, our protection, and our love. Taken together, these things add up to a healthy parent-child relationship. Of course, no parent can be perfectly in sync with their child; we have needs of our own, and are subject to multiple demands on our time and energies. When it is not possible to be warm, either because you are too pressured, too angry, or too depleted, it is important to model emotional responsibility by letting your child know that you are working on whatever problem has put you temporarily out of commission. "I had a difficult day at the office today, but tomorrow, I'm going to talk with my boss and clear the air. Sorry, I'm feeling kind of low tonight, but I should be fine tomorrow and then we can talk about your fight with Katie."

There are no shortcuts to knowing our children well. Warmth is cultivated when we take time, when we linger with our children, when we get to know them in the most intimate and specific ways we can. Know what delights *your particular child* and what disappoints her; know what engages her and what turns her off. Does your daughter love poetry and hate science fiction? Does your son keep the television on all night because he likes the background noise or because he's afraid of the dark? Being truly connected with our children means knowing and valuing the unique, idiosyncratic, one-in-a-trillion child who stands in front of us. Reinforce your love and appreciation as often as you can. Make sure your child knows that, if given a choice of all the children in the world, he or she is the one you would choose.

Bad Warmth: Overinvolvement, Intrusion, and Parental Neediness

If warm connection has been shown to be the silver bullet of effective parenting, how can it possibly damage children or impair their development? The hard-to-face answer is that warmth and connection easily can slide into overinvolvement, enmeshment, and intrusion. That's when parents are likely to hear: "Get off my back," "It's my problem, not yours," or "Stay out of my business." Sometimes our children's unsafe behavior dictates that we have no choice but to fully insert ourselves into their lives, but more frequently we have drifted into overinvolvement out of our own fear of uncertainty or anxiety about loss of connection. At times it can be difficult to know whether we are being appropriately loving, or intrusive. But listen to your instincts, and your children; they will usually be only too happy to help you with this distinction.

Parents are genetically programmed to protect their children from threats. When our early ancestors sensed the presence of a predator, heightened anxiety would release a flood of hormones that raised awareness and produced a fight-or-flight response, increasing the odds of successfully protecting their young. Thankfully, the more recent historical threats to our children's well being—malnutrition and devastating childhood illnesses—have been eradicated, or greatly reduced. Yet levels of parental anxiety remain extraordinarily high.

In less financially secure households, many parents are busy trying to keep the wolf from the door, putting time and energy into second jobs and making certain that they can make ends meet. Affluent parents, who are relatively free from the concerns of sustaining their household economically, have more psychological space; they can "afford" to spend more time worrying about their children's performance and sizing up the competition. While many affluent parents have extremely demanding and pressured schedules, others are relatively free of demands outside the family. Higher-income families also typically have fewer children, giving parents more time to obsess about the details of each child's life and to devote time, energy, and money to polishing their "star" qualities.

The perceived threats of contemporary society—competition for grades, well-known schools, prestigious job offers—should not elicit the same kinds of hypervigilant, controlling responses that, say, exposure to polio once elicited. Persistent worry about how well one's child stacks up against other children inevitably leads to parents who are overinvolved and emotionally exhausted as well as to children who are impaired in their ability to function independently. The affluent parents of even the youngest children anxiously compare notes on developmental milestones, social progress, and academic achievement, ratcheting up their involvement when they fear their children are slipping behind the competition.

In spite of good intentions, the levels of adult overinvolvement that have become typical in so many comfortable homes and communities are startling and counterproductive. Mothers and fathers spend whole weekends for months on end shuttling their children to athletic events, ignoring the fact that friendships and marriages suffer under the barrage of child-centered activities. Open house nights at school features the assorted talents of parent architects, engineers, and interior designers, as grade school dioramas resemble corporate prototypes. Parents willingly pay thousands of dollars for tutors, coaches, and preparatory courses in the hope that their child will outperform his friends and classmates and win an advantage in the classroom, the playing field, or the admissions process. We seem to believe that if involvement is good, then overinvolvement must be better.

I want to be clear that children do need a great deal of involvement from their parents. High levels of parental involvement are shown to be an important predictor of success for children in many areas. But appropriately involved parents know the importance of stepping back as soon as practical, and of respecting their child's strivings toward independence. It is this capacity to know when your involvement is moving your child forward and when it is holding her back that distinguishes the appropriately involved parent from the overinvolved or intrusive parent.

Overinvolvement is not simply "more" healthy involvement; rather it is involvement that can get in the way of child development. It is an umbrella term, often used to cover a wide range of overzealous parenting activities, ranging from the relatively benign to the downright disastrous. Overinvolvement refers to unnecessary involvement. It is usually, but not always, ill advised, and *some* children can be remarkably forgiving about this sort of behavior. I tend to think of overinvolvement as the things we do *for* our kids—the forgotten dishes we wash, the unmade beds we straighten, the editing we do on our child's writing assignments. The overinvolved parent may linger too long after her son's lacrosse game, cajoling the coach in the hope that he will pay closer attention to her son's skills and perhaps give him more playing time in the next game. But overinvolvement stops short of psychologically manipulating the child. It is more likely to slow progress than to damage children.

Intrusion, on the other hand, is always unhelpful, if not damaging. It invades the child's developing psychological space, and blurs the appropriate and necessary boundaries between parent and child, invariably to the child's disadvantage. Listening in on our child's phone calls; repeating a complaint about a classmate that our child made to us in confidence; "encouraging" our child to take an honors class by making him feel guilty or ashamed—these are examples of intrusion. "I know you tried hard, but I can't understand why you're not ashamed to hand in a paper that still has errors," says the intrusive parent, mistakenly believing that shame will motivate her child to try harder. **Promoting guilt and shame invariably works *against* progress—and, more importantly, they weaken the ties between child and parent.**

Both intrusion and overinvolvement prevent the development of the kinds of skills that children need to be successful: the ability to be a self-starter, the willingness to engage in trial-and-error learning, the ability to delay gratification, to tolerate frustration, to show self control, to learn from mistakes, and to be a flexible and creative thinker. Kids who develop these skills have a large toolbox to dig into, both to enrich their lives and to help them problem-solve.

Little has been written about the falling off of creativity among kids; it is, however, an ominous trend. Creativity, the ability to look at things from a fresh perspective, is an underrated but critical life skill. It prevents us from getting "stuck" in nonproductive ways. If your kid is withdrawn or your spouse is distant or your job requirements are changing, you need a repertoire of solutions. One solution rarely fits all, and we end up feeling like we're banging our head against the wall when we keep using the same ineffective solutions over and over again. Creative thinking gives us a range of tools to try when problems don't respond to the usual corrections. Your kid may typically respond to gentle humor when he's feeling down, but not always. If you also know how to invite him to talk, how to leave him alone, how to suggest activities, how to hug, how to allow distance, then your chances of helping him are greatly increased. The larger our toolbox, the more we can be creative and "think outside the box," and the more likely we are to come up with effective solutions.

Kids need this same ability to think flexibly and creatively when they find themselves having social, academic, family, and personal issues—which of course is practically every day when you're a kid! The falling off of creativity should alert us to the fact that kids have a smaller and smaller toolbox to dig into when they are unhappy, conflicted, or perplexed. Whenever we prematurely solve problems for our children, we deprive them of the opportunity to come up with the novel solutions that allow them to add another tool to their arsenal. We also deprive them of the sense of competence that comes with figuring things out on one's own.

Warmth often slides into unhealthy dependency when we turn to our children for the loving connections missing in our adult relationships. Affluent communities are tough places to form intimate connections. Our lives tend to be busy; and gates, large lawns, and thick walls separate us from each other. Growing up, I can remember the parade of neighbors who stopped by our house for a cup of sugar, a bit of cream, or an extra potato. The idea of trekking over to a neighbor's house when the pantry is short an item or two seems almost laughable now. The easy camaraderie that existed among working-class women, a function of both desire and necessity, has been lost to take-out food, housekeepers, and a fear that revealing our problems, no matter how incidental, will result not in support but in embarrassment.

Many affluent women have active social lives but few real friends. Rates of marital dissatisfaction are high, affected by the same forces that burden our kids: too much pressure and too little real intimacy. Without a close friend to share our problems with, we are likely to turn to our children for solace. This leads to "enmeshment," when the boundaries between parent and child have collapsed. When we "bleed" onto our children, share our hurt and disappointment and anger, often about their other parent, then we make it impossible for them to get on with the business of growing up. Supporting an unhappy parent, being our confidants and advisors, saps children of the emotional energy and the sense of security they need to work on their own development. Know the difference between warmth and enmeshment or intrusion. Warmth protects our children from psychological trouble; enmeshment and intrusion invite trouble into our homes.

Children can read the needs of their parents remarkably well. They know that the mother who spends a disproportionate amount of time and energy inserting herself into her child's life is likely to be fending off her own unhappiness. She needs to be overinvolved, and, in an unfortunately common psychological drama, her child is willing to sacrifice his own needs to meet hers. Parental overinvolvement and intrusion are typically indications that a parent's own needs are not being adequately met. When a marriage is cold, a child's bed is a warm place to be.

The more we pour ourselves, our talents, concerns, and aspirations into our children, the less room they have to develop their own, talents, concerns, and aspirations. **Autonomy, not dependency, is always the goal of good parenting**. Mother birds know the value of nudging their fledglings out of the nest so that they learn how to soar on their own wings. Overinvolved parents are clipping their children's wings.

Understanding Why Praise Is Often "Bad" Warmth

The self-esteem movement, which had an extensive and undeserved run in this country, blurred the boundaries between encouragement, praise, and warmth. In spite of refrigerator doors covered in badges and ribbons, and gold stars awarded for even the slightest effort, kids today are not only *not* better adjusted than they were thirty or forty years ago, they are in fact more emotionally troubled and less academically successful by most measures.[9] Meta-analysis—the merging of hundreds of studies to enable researchers to make overarching conclusions—shows that "raising self-esteem will not by itself make young people perform better in school, obey the law, stay out of trouble, get along better with their fellows; respect the right of others, or produce many other desirable outcomes."[10] **In actuality, self-esteem has a very limited relationship to either accomplishment or deviance.**

Serious researchers in the field of self-esteem have suggested that while our overly broad focus on self-esteem has not been productive, there is value in boosting our children's self-esteem when they work hard and show good moral character.[11] However, praise for ethical behavior, sincere effort, and worthy achievements needs to be balanced with expressions of disappointment and correction for hurtful behavior and lazy effort. Children need a realistic sense of self, not an inflated sense of self. Indiscriminate praise makes it hard for children to evaluate themselves realistically.

We all tend to praise our children reflexively, and it's hard to imagine that this can have negative effects on their development. If warmth is such a desirable quality in a parent, how can praise, which seems to convey interest, appreciation, *and* warmth, be a bad idea? While perhaps it's reasonable to question excessive praise, the idea of questioning everyday praise—"Good job," "I'm so proud of you"— seems unreasonable. For many parents, warmth and praise seem inseparable. But they are not the same thing, and appreciating this fact is important to understanding how some children come to be appreciative and others come to be entitled.

The disturbing sense of entitlement so often observed in affluent kids is partly an outgrowth of parents' efforts to elevate their child's sense of self with persistent praise. The difference between high self-esteem and narcissism can be hard to distinguish in privileged kids who have been repeatedly told that they are special. As one of my patients said, "If I'm so special, then why do I have to set the table or take out the garbage?" She was slyly taking to its logical conclusion her parents' single-minded focus on individualism and self-esteem—and, likewise, their failure to stress kindness and reciprocity. Self-absorption may have few personal costs. However, its costs often accrue to others: an exhausted mom cleans up the dinner dishes for her son; an overworked dad takes out the trash for his daughter.

Praise is a transaction between two people and as a result has an impact on both the giver and the receiver. This should be obvious when we notice the reaction of our child after telling her for the tenth or hundredth or thousandth time how "smart" or how "good" she is. After about the age of five, such rote praise is typically met with indifference or, more commonly, the astute "You're just saying that because you're my mom."

The truth is, we often praise as much to bolster our own needs as to bolster the needs of our children. Praise is well intended, and we hope it makes our kids feel good, but it makes us feel good as well. It keeps us attached to our children, involved in their efforts, and provides us with leverage. While superficially praise seems to be about warmth and connection, on a deeper level it is about control and compliance.

Many of my patients have commented on how each and every grade seems more important to their parents than it does to them. "Great job," "I'm so proud," "You're so smart, good, talented"— these are ways to keep our children invested in the things that matter to us. "I'm so proud of you for getting an A on that vocabulary test" carries the embedded suggestion that we are less than proud about the B in spelling or the C in math. But it may be the B in spelling, or even the C in math, that represents the greater effort, the truly higher achievement. Although well intended, our praise for the higher grade actually works against real learning. It teaches that our love and acceptance are conditional on outstanding performance. **It ignores the most critical aspect of learning: effort and improvement.**

The child who is constantly admired for a particular skill frequently becomes less interested in trying out new things. One of the costs of such an attitude is that children begin to play it safe and in the process lose their willingness to experiment and challenge themselves. It is disturbing to see children as young as ten or eleven decide that it is "too late" to learn a new sport or take on a new challenge. Seduced by the praise they have received for their tennis or chess or math or dance skills, they shy away from exploring other interests. This constriction of thinking and activity works against one of the main tasks of childhood and adolescence—exploring a range of interests and abilities in order to find those that are a good fit. Sometimes we follow our strengths and sometimes we follow our interests. They are not always the same.

High-strung Emma, an accomplished thirteen-year-old tennis

player, cries in my office because she is exhausted from her rigorous work-outs and secretly pines to join her friends, who spend frequent weekends at Lake Tahoe, skiing. Under the Lindsay Davenport poster in her bedroom is a concealed picture of a wildly flailing Bode Miller. She is certain her parents will not support her change of heart because she is already nationally ranked in tennis. She is right. Her parents sit in my office stunned that "After all the work *we've* put in, how could she want to throw it all away?"

Bolstered by my support, their daughter tells them that being with her friends matters more to her right now than being a tennis player, that she thinks she could be a good skier, too; and, besides, competitive sports simply isn't that much "fun." Her parents go to work on her quickly, reminding her that she is "one of the most talented young players in America." They compliment and cajole her, pointing out that her name has already been mentioned in several prestigious sports magazines. This may look like praise; it is in fact manipulation. Praise easily becomes a wolf in sheep's clothing.

I watch Emma's resolve dissolve in front of my eyes as she sinks down into my couch, resigned to sacrificing her autonomy to the pressure her parents are exerting. Emma's parents are torn between their high hopes for their daughter and their recognition that their hopes are out of sync with their daughters' needs and her stage of development. Emma's parents may be right when they insist that they have the "big picture," that they, not Emma, can see the benefits of being an outstanding athlete when it comes to Olympic development teams or college admissions. I'd like to say that this kind of insistence is always born out of good intentions and not parental narcissism. Unfortunately, I have seen my share of parents who fill up their own brittle selves with their children's accomplishments.

But the vast majority of parents I see, like Emma's, are insistent because they believe that their child will have a more exciting, interesting, and fulfilling life; that the opportunities that outstanding performance bring will be well worth the temporary sacrifices that their child needs to make. Certainly it makes sense to encourage our kids to stick with activities they are good at long enough to know whether or not *they* become passionate about the activity. If they've agreed to sign up for a team activity, in general, they need to complete the season even if they've decided that "basketball is just a waste of time." In addition to skill-building, group activities also teach the importance of persistence, committment, and selflessness. But once a child starts having symptoms, is teary, anxious, or suffering from a raft of somatic symptoms like stomachaches or headaches, then we have pushed too far.

Emma's parents came to see how their constant praise was a way to keep Emma "on track," on the track that they considered most promising for their talented daughter. As they came to understand the developmental importance of her exploring a range of interests and skills, they softened their resistance to Emma's new interest. Emma ultimately became a skier, an ordinary one at that, but thrilled to have her childhood back, and to be free of the burden of her parents' praise and expectations. Her well-intentioned parents took solace in the fact that their angry and anxious daughter was now happier and calmer.

Praise does not make us a warm parent. Neither when we use it to push our accomplished children to greater achievements nor when we use it to bolster their flagging sense of self. A warm parent is accepting of accomplishments as well as mistakes and failures. Often we are so pained by our child's unhappiness that we rush to make them feel better without considering that the better parenting strategy might be to allow them to experience our love regardless of how well they are performing. These kinds of experiences teach children that our love and acceptance are not conditional on their performance. True warmth and acceptance have nothing to do with how your child does and everything to do with who your child is. Unconditional love means that our hearts are full enough and open enough to accept our children as the startling, unique creatures that they are, even as we work to polish their rough edges, help them cultivate interests and talents, and encourage them to be good, responsible, and productive people.

Parenting is for better and for worse. Just as our children thrill us, they are also bound to let us down. How we handle this task—

parenting our children when they fall short, when they disappoint us, when they take us away from our feeling of warmth and love and into darker and more unhappy feelings—is one of the greatest challenges parents face. While it is tempting to deal with our disappointment and anger by being critical, research is very clear that, just as warmth and connection are the silver bullets of parenting, criticism and rejection are the deadly ones.

AVOID THE DAMAGE INFLICTED BY CRITICISM AND REJECTION

In affluent, educated families, criticism is often covert rather than overt. We all understand how damaging harsh, rejecting comments like "I wish you were never born" can be to a child's sense of self. But over and over in my office I see criticism sugarcoated and disguised and damaging nonetheless. Typically such criticism is directed at a child about some area that the parent himself or herself is uneasy about.

- "You would be so cute if you just lost ten pounds so you could wear those little tank tops all the girls are wearing." (Said by a size-four mother with eating problems herself who can't bear the idea that her daughter's body type is stocky not svelte.)

- "I know you love theater, but all the popular boys seem to be going out for sports—why don't you give it a try?" (Said by a social-butterfly mom who is fearful that her son's interest in theater means he is gay, or at least that he will be perceived by others as being gay, and therefore less socially desirable.)

- "Why in the world would you think about taking physiology instead of AP chemistry? You're smarter than that." (Said by a physician dad who is struggling to acknowledge that his son is average-bright, not superior.)

No matter how delicate or oblique you think you are being, statements like these are clear declarations that your child is "not good enough." But what is behind these types of criticisms? None of the kids in the examples above were involved in antisocial or self-destructive activities. They were all simply being the child they were meant to be. Trying to turn each of them into a different child is typically not possible, and even if it were, the cost, in terms of damaged sense of self, is way too high. When we criticize we make clear our difficulty tolerating imperfection, and we express our dislike, and even loathing, for the child in front of us. Criticism is a way to divert us from our own disappointments and project them instead onto our children. It is a place where parenting can turn truly ugly.

The issue of parental criticism deserves special attention because it is such a virulent form of communication between parent and child. **Criticism is a particular communication from parent to child about the *value* of the child himself.** Not everything that is a "no," or that expresses displeasure or even disappointment, is criticism. We certainly have times when expressing our disappointment is a necessary part of teaching good values. (For example, "I'm really disappointed in the way you treated your friend.") But our disappointment should be directed at our child's behavior or choices, not at their existence. "You're such a disappointment to me" is the type of sentiment that catapults children into a tailspin of depression or acting out.

Similarly, correction is an important and necessary part of parenting. But correction should be informational, not personal. For example, let's say your twelve-year-old gets a poor grade on a math test that he didn't study for. You have several options:

1. *Ignore it.*—Often acceptable, but it can also signal parental disengagement, which is not a good thing. Kids whose parents monitor (not do) their child's homework tend to have kids who perform well in school.

2. *Follow through on consequences.*—"We agreed that if you did poorly, your television time would be limited to the weekends, giving you more time to study during the week."

3. *Try to help identify the reason for lack of success.*—This involves talking with your kid about how *he's* feeling about *his* work. "I know you usually do pretty well in math class. Was there some reason that you blew this test off? Do you need some help?" Don't just pepper your kid with questions; listen to what he says.

4. *Express disappointment about the effort.*—"My guess is that you could have done better if you put in more effort. I'm disappointed that you decided not to try your best, but it's your grade and it's up to you to decide whether you want to try harder next time."

5. *Respond critically or with rejection.*—"I knew that you were going to get a lousy grade. You just can't pull it off, can you!"

While the first four responses are all legitimate (and vary, depending on parenting style and where your child is at any particular moment), the critical response is only damaging. It is damaging because it does nothing to address the problem, and in fact only heightens the problem by making your child feel defective. Repeated attacks, rejections, and criticisms lead children to the unfortunate conclusion that they are essentially unworthy of love. Children who believe that they are unworthy of love are at high risk for depression and suicide. Cutting, an increasingly common form of adolescent acting out, frequently begins in the face of relentless parental criticism. A patient of mine made the following chilling comment: "I take in all my parents' contempt and then I let it out with my blood." **Whenever we attack our child's developing self we feed feelings of self-hatred, perhaps the most dangerous feelings kids can have.**

While most of the stories in this book have focused on compliant children who become depressed in the face of parental pressure, overinvolvement, and intrusion, parents who are unremittingly critical tend to turn out children with a very different set of problems. These kids are often "in-your-face," acting-out, even antisocial, and their pain can be much harder to see.

Sixteen-year-old Dylan saunters into my office, cigarette in hand, and tells me that my office "sucks." I can't help but ask him if he begins all his relationships by being so charming. Disarmed, he smiles for a split second before regaining his aggressive indifference. I know that as long as he can still smile at me, we've got a shot together.

Dylan's parents are both intellectuals. Mom is a professor and Dad a successful writer. They have two other children who seem more or less in tune with the family values of academic excellence and intellectual curiosity. Dylan, on the other hand, is a mediocre student. Testing reveals that he is bright enough but that his real talents are "visual-spatial." He is the kind of kid who would make a great mechanic, and in fact he spends much of his time working on old cars that he buys with the money he makes working at the local auto shop. His parents cannot even begin to relate to his interests and criticize him constantly for "wasting his time" and for his "lack of ambition" warning that he will be a "nothing" in life unless he starts digging into his schoolwork. In fact, Dylan has areas of real expertise and is ambitious; he is one of the few kids in my practice who is actually willing to work a job after school. I settle in for a long psychotherapy with Dylan, and learn how to change the oil in my car and fix a flat tire. It is easy to see how in a less affluent and less competitive household, Dylan's contributions would be greatly valued.

Dylan reacts to the relentless barrage of criticism by opting out of his family. He is one of those kids who is so angry at his parents, who feels so unloved by them, that he is willing to drill a hole in the boat, knowing that he'll drown as well. He is heavily involved in drugs and has been in quite a few fights that necessitated police intervention. He seems to take some pleasure from the distress this causes his parents, proud of his ability to "kick some ass in this fucking family." At this point he is quite a handful, and his drug problem in particular has me considering whether placement in a treatment facility is the best option for him. There are days in my office when he is reasonable, even sweet, and other days when he is impossible, angry, and vulgar.

Over time Dylan and I are able to develop a warm relationship, at least partly because I find much to admire in him: his skills, his perseverance, even his anger, which is a reasonable defense against the depression he would feel if he really allowed his parents' disappointment in him to fully sink in. Little by little he reveals his sense of inadequacy and defectiveness. Dylan hangs out with equally dysfunctional boys, and keeps his distance from girls, saying, "Who could love a punk like me?" These revelations are usually followed by some acting-out behavior resulting in late-night phone calls or visits to juvenile hall. After twice-a-week sessions over the course of six or seven months, I feel I have enough leverage with Dylan to insist that we deal with his drug and alcohol problem. When faced with the possibility of being sent to rehab and not being able to be in contact with me, he opts to quit using drugs and drinking and to attend AA sessions five times a week.

Without drugs and alcohol to mask his depression, Dylan becomes sad and teary in my office. He reveals the ways in which he feels "I'll never be anything but a screw-up." Working with his parents helps to clarify the extent of their disappointment, but also their worry about Dylan's future. They are helped to imagine a life that is quite different from their own but satisfying nonetheless. We talk about how to set appropriate limits on Dylan without attacking his character. Dylan's parents begin to understand how toxic their criticism has been to their son's developing sense of self. Like most parents, no matter how disappointed or angry, Dylan's parents harbor hope that they can find a way back to loving their child. Undoing the damage of years of criticism is not easy, and Dylan backslides from time to time, particularly when he feels rejected. Ultimately, however, after several years, Dylan makes a good recovery and his parents not only accept, but find value in, their son.

One of the reasons that Dylan, in spite of his panoply of serious symptoms, was ultimately able to do well was because the criticism didn't begin in earnest until his adolescence, so he had already developed a kernel of "self" that was relatively uninjured. That was the smile, the brief moment of connection that I saw in our first session. But for kids who are subject to criticism from early on, the chances of success in outpatient psychotherapy are greatly reduced, because their sense of self is so impaired and their feelings of self-hatred are so intense that self-destruction becomes a very real possibility.

Criticism has been found to have such a profound negative effect on child development that some of our most cherished notions need to be reexamined in light of what we now know about it. For example, one popular notion about why children from comfortable homes are showing such high rates of emotional problems holds that it is because they are "overscheduled." It is assumed that affluent parents are pushy about everything, including their kids' after-school activities, and are exhausting their children in the process. This particular theory has been well publicized by the media, causing many parents to be concerned about whether their child's extracurricular athletic, art, academic, or volunteer experiences are really healthy or damaging. Overscheduling has become a catch-all term, encompassing many different levels of activity. If your child has no time to breathe, think, or eat, if she is unhappy and having somatic symptoms, then she *is* overscheduled. But many kids are robust and energetic and can engage in a wide range of activities without any ill effects.

Recent research exposes the core issue behind "overscheduling," and, for younger teens at least, it is not the after-school activities per se. In a study of affluent suburban fourteen-year-olds, the most common reason for participating in these activities was for "fun"; only a minority said they participated because of adult pressure. While being involved in after-school activities was good for most children, parental criticism about their performance in these activities was damaging. Girls in particular were susceptible to both emotional and academic problems when their parents were critical about their extracurricular performance.[12] There is a world of difference between the experience of having a parent who is happy when you are chosen for the chorus of a show and the parent who says, "Aren't you even good enough for a small speaking role?" Holding out high standards for our children is not the problem, but humiliating and disparaging them when they fail to meet expectations is.

Listen to how you speak to yourself. If you've forgotten to do something, do you think "What an idiot I am," or are you more likely to use a gentler voice—"It was a busy day, guess I can't remember everything"? Is the voice that runs commentary on your day a harsh and critical one, or does it treat you kindly? This is the same voice that our children hear every day of their lives. Were your own parents critical of you, and if they were, do you continue to "hear" them talking to you in denigrating, belittling ways? If so, then you need to work on developing a new and softer voice to guide you through the day, and also to talk to your children. Effective parenting is much more than being a perpetually warm and welcoming presence (although that's an excellent start!). You will need to mold, guide, correct, punish, inform, monitor, and model. All of these can be accomplished without attacking your child at his core. Before you criticize your child, think about how it would feel if the criticism were directed at you. If it stings, find another way to say it.

While finding the optimal level of connection can be challenging, the fact is, most of us do a pretty good job. Connection is how we began our relationship with our child, it is the yummy, gratifying part of being a parent. This may be part of the reason why younger affluent children do not appear to have the disproportionately high rates of emotional problems seen in their preadolescent and adolescent counterparts. Most of us "do" connection pretty well. Connection nurtures us at the same time that it nurtures our children. Done properly, it is the "win-win" of effective parenting.

Discipline, on the other hand, has an entirely different feel. While we know that punishing a child for bad behavior or enforcing consequences for irresponsibility is the right thing to do, emotionally it's a hard job. We are not greeted with smiles or hugs or "I love you" when we discipline. On the contrary, we are most likely to be treated with withdrawal, anger, even contempt. Nevertheless, discipline has been shown to be a crucial part of parenting even if it's a lot less fun than connection. It helps if we understand its critically important protective function for our children, and learn to take pleasure in our skilled ability to discipline effectively.

· CHAPTER 7 ·

Discipline and Control: The Tough Job of Being the "Bad Cop"

Discipline often takes a backseat in affluent families. When time, not money, is the most valuable commodity in a household, then tasks that take a lot of time and effort with little apparent payback are often swept aside. So what if your son didn't clear his breakfast dishes from the table, the housekeeper will; or if your daughter is "too tired" to go back to the soccer field and retrieve her abandoned sweatshirt, it's easy to buy another one. Busy parents already feel guilty about the little time they have to spend with their children. Few of them want to "waste time" in conflict and anger and as a result are often only too happy to sidestep discipline issues. The unfortunate result is that children do not learn how to take responsibility, control their impulses, or be thoughtful. This is a particularly dangerous state of affairs for teenagers because it makes it less likely that they will be able to recognize when they are being taken advantage of or even preyed upon.

Discipline and control, like warmth and connection run along a continuum from one extreme to the other, with the middle ground being the most effective. At one unfortunate end of the discipline continuum lies physical abuse; at the other, lax and indifferent discipline. It's clear that both physical and psychological abuse, or letting one's children "run wild," are both bound to be ineffective and traumatizing discipline strategies. Most of us try to discipline with moderation. Parents are always curious about what kinds of infractions merit disciplinary action. Should my child be punished for rudeness, for not doing his homework, for not emptying the dishwasher, for forgetting to feed the dog, for lying about a test grade, for coming in past curfew, for drinking alcohol or smoking pot? While these questions certainly are important individually, few parents have the energy for a daily evaluation of their child's misdemeanors. It's easier on both parents and kids when parents have developed a general discipline strategy, one that is clear, firm, and fair and that eliminates endless discussions about what is and isn't okay in your particular household.

Most important, remember that discipline takes place within a parent-child relationship that has a particular "feel" to it. As we saw, warm connection forms the foundation and provides the ballast to help our children manage life's ups and downs, including ups and downs in their relationship with us. It also makes it much easier for us to be effective disciplinarians. **We can learn all kinds of "techniques" for disciplining, but they are bound to fail unless, at heart, we have a loving relationship with our child.** This is not to say we won't have moments of profound disappointment, or anger. We most certainly will. We will also have moments of absolutely hating our role as "bad cop," as the parent who is paying attention, setting limits, defining consequences, and, in the process, incurring our children's anger. But this is part of the job and the price of parenting; and it is mandatory, for our own sanity, to acknowledge how demanding and difficult it can be.

FIRMNESS:
BEING CLEAR ABOUT
YOUR AUTHORITY

Various studies have found that firm parental control is associated with children who can take care of themselves, who are academically successful, who are emotionally well developed, and who are happier.[1] It may be that parents who are able to maintain firm control are less conflicted about exercising their parental authority and are better able to keep the boundaries between parent and child clear and unambiguous. This clarity of roles, expectations, and consequences is extremely helpful as impressionable children and teens are called upon to make decisions about unfamiliar experiences. In spite of the seemingly endless capacity of adolescents to be contrary, when parents are clear about expectations and set up consequences for noncompliance, then teens are actually much more capable of adhering to parental standards. For example, research shows that when parents were clear with their young teens about the unacceptability of marijuana use, only 5 percent of their children used marijuana at any time in the previous month. However, among those teens who perceive their parents as less clear in their objections, parents who "somewhat disapprove" or "neither approve nor disapprove," 20 percent of those teens used marijuana in the same time period.[2]

Firm control needs to be established early in a child's life. If you say, "You can't bike ride with your friends today because you were reckless on your bike yesterday," you need to mean it. There is nothing to be gained by idle threats and everything to lose. Week after week, one of my adolescent patients or another is hatching some plan that is an exercise in bad judgment: staying out past curfew, binge drinking, having "spontaneous" sex, certain that even if they are discovered that "I'll be able to talk my way out of it." This is a Pyrrhic victory for the adolescent, as over time he realizes that, "My parents really don't care what I do." Parents let kids' transgressions slide for a variety of reasons: because "she's such a good kid," or "she's so depressed already, I can't make things tougher," or simply because they are too exhausted or too unhappy themselves to enter into battle with their teen. Regardless, kids come to experience their parents' lack of limit setting and lack of follow-through as lack of concern.

Every psychiatrist and psychologist I spoke with over the course of writing this book mentioned a lack of firm limit-setting as one of the major contributors to adolescent dysfunction. "Kids want and need limits" is a common refrain among professionals who deal with troubled and not-so-troubled kids. Interestingly, many parents are skeptical of this conclusion. "Are you kidding? She goes crazy when we try to set a curfew!" is a typical response to the suggestion that even sixteen-year-olds need a curfew. But what all psychotherapists know is that, within the confines of their office, kids see a lack of limits as an open invitation to act out. There are many reasons for parents to set limits on their children—to promote safety, responsibility, thoughtfulness—but perhaps the most compelling one is that adolescents simply don't have the tools, the pre-frontal cortex development, the *judgment* to consistently and appropriately regulate themselves. Kids know this, and know that if their parents don't, they simply aren't paying attention.

MONITORING: "DO YOU KNOW WHERE YOUR CHILDREN ARE?"

Parents who monitor their children pay attention to, and keep track of, where their children are and what they are doing. The late-night public-service announcement "Do you know where your children are?" captures the essence of monitoring, and is a question parents should be able to answer nightly. Monitoring has been shown to have a protective effect on kids from childhood through adolescence. Parents may have to contend with all kinds of annoyed posturing the hundredth time they ask any of the following: "Where are you going?" "Who will be there?" "Will the parents be home?" "When will you be back?" But the payoff in terms of maintaining a healthy connection with our children, as well as helping to insure their safety, not only seems self-evident but is also well-documented.

Children who are actively monitored by their parents have evidence of less early drug use, less risky sexual behavior, better academic achievement, and higher self-esteem.[3] Clearly, optimal levels of monitoring vary, depending on the potential danger of a situation and your child's capacity to show good judgment. Not surprisingly, researchers have found that higher levels of monitoring are more salutary for kids who are at risk, while somewhat lower levels are adequate for low-risk kids. But this is a matter of degree, not a question of whether or not you should still be monitoring your sixteen-year-old. The answer is an unequivocal yes. Balancing your child's need for autonomy with the well-documented need to monitor can result in a considerable difference of opinion between you and your child about what constitutes appropriate parental oversight. At the very least, as long as your child lives in your house, you should know where they are and what they are doing.

Without adequate monitoring, children are vulnerable to bad decisions, but they are also vulnerable to being preyed on. Firm control always involves a parent who is monitoring, who is paying attention to their child's behavior, and who is ready to step in when their child is being threatened. Too often, affluent kids, particularly as they move into adolescence, are prematurely left to their own devices. Many adolescents are left home alone after school, some on weekends and even on school breaks. While some parents believe that they are fostering independence by leaving their child alone, others are too preoccupied to be available to their children, particularly since they are "almost grown-up."

One of my patients tells the story of an unfortunate Christmas vacation spent in Mexico with her parents and her sister. Her parents had booked the two girls in a separate room at the other end of the resort and left them, sometimes for days on end, while the parents were off exploring the sights. My patient was fourteen at the time and had her first sexual experience on this trip when she got drunk and was seduced by one of the older guests. Soon thereafter she began cutting and was brought in for treatment. While I see very few instances of abuse in my community, this kind of neglect is not uncommon. Kids who feel abandoned by their parents typically feel angry and depressed. These kids tend to act out in ways that force parental involvement: school failure, delinquency, substance abuse, promiscuity, and self-mutilation.

CONTAINMENT:
LETTING YOUR KIDS KNOW
WHEN YOU MEAN BUSINESS

In one family, an eleven-year-old child runs out of the house to meet a friend and is reminded by Mom that she forgot to make her bed. She turns around cheerfully, makes her bed, and then goes out. In another household the child meets this same request with an icy stare and with much sighing returns to her room to haphazardly throw the covers on the bed. In yet a third household an indignant child stops long enough for a "You've gotta be kidding" before she strides out the door. We would say that the first child has a good sense of containment, the second child has an adequate sense, and the third child lacks a sense of containment. Containment is not simply whether a child is well behaved or not. **Containment is the "child's belief that adults have the capacity to impose firm limits and to prevail if there is a conflict in goals."**[4]

There are families where bed making is an important part of daily routine, and there are other families where it's immaterial. Rules vary from family to family, with some households expecting adherence to a long list of responsibilities and chores while others consider a select few important. While developing a sense of responsibility and competence in our children is one of our most important jobs, there is considerable latitude in how this is accomplished. There are many things I consider more important than bed making, and over the years my kids' rooms could attest to this. On the other hand, there are things I consider mandatory: a firm handshake, "please" and "thank you," appreciation for help they have received. Day after day some mother in my office wonders whether she is being too "easy" because her child doesn't make the bed or clear the table or do the laundry. Basic self-management issues certainly matter, but the fact is that most kids eventually learn how to make a bed and wash dishes. The bigger issue is: When something is truly important to you, does your child believe that you have the power to enforce your position? So if you decide bed making can temporarily sit on the back burner, that's fine, as long as when, for one reason or another, it really matters to you—say, when company is coming—that your child complies with your request. Containment is another way of saying that when you "mean business," your kid gets it.

I like using the concept of containment because it has nothing to do with being told what your rules should be—the fact is, rules vary from household to household—and has a lot to do with helping parents understand that unless they have the power to enforce whatever their particular rules are, then their homes are likely to be chaotic and their children are likely to act out.[5] Not surprisingly, children and teenagers are more likely to show restraint and acknowledge parental supremacy when motivated by a loving relationship.[6] Restraint can be difficult to muster, especially when unrestrained behavior can be so appealing: stealing cookies (for a youngster), throwing back a dozen shooters (for an adolescent), cheating on a spouse (for an adult). In each of these situations, the *likelihood* of showing restraint is increased by our attachment to a loving parent or partner.

FLEXIBILITY: KNOWING WHEN TO SKIP THE SHOWDOWN

After writing so much about the need for firm, consistent monitoring, why a section on flexibility? After all, isn't flexibility one step away from lax parenting? Don't kids see this as an opportunity to manipulate their parents?

Flexibility has been shown to be a very important component of healthy parent-child relationships, which is why occasional lapses on the part of your child can and should be tolerated. But flexibility does not mean relinquishing responsibility altogether. In a good parent-child relationship, flexibility is a form of communication. The house rule may be that studying for exams should begin several days in advance. So what do you do when your son says, "I know I messed up that test. I felt lousy the last couple of nights and couldn't concentrate. Can we just let it go?" The mom who lets the incident slide, knowing that her son "bent" the rule because he wasn't feeling well, is showing flexibility. Mom's flexibility communicates to her child that she is more concerned with issues of health and honesty than test scores. In this instance Mom's "sticking to her guns" about studying in advance is unnecessary, counterproductive, and likely to impair feelings of warmth between her and her son.

Of course the child who regularly makes excuses, and doesn't hold up his end of the bargain, whether it's about school, chores, or other responsibilities, needs firmness. But even when we are being firm, we can still communicate warmth and concern by listening to our kids, by offering to help them find more effective ways of controlling their behavior, and by rooting for them to do better next time.

When we find ourselves "bending" the rules on a regular basis, we should reconsider the wisdom of the particular rule. "All homework has to be completed before television, talking to your friends, or getting on the computer" may work fine in some households, but in others a child may be much more capable of settling down to homework after a half-hour or even an hour of television, talking to a friend, or noodling around on the computer. Some kids really need and benefit from a period of decompression after school. Being more flexible about homework may take some initial monitoring on your part, but rather than constantly making exceptions to the homework rule, it makes sense to find a rule that suits you and your child's style better. We usually know when we are bending rules out of exhaustion or frustration ("Enough. You can watch television all night long for all I care"), out of manipulation ("A 2 A.M. curfew seems awfully late, but if that's what all your friends have I guess it's okay."), or out of sensitivity, flexibility, and common sense.

For a household to run effectively, and for a child to grow optimally, parents need to impose enough discipline to keep their children safe, to foster self-control, and to underscore good values. They also have to show enough flexibility to encourage independence and maintain warmth and connection. **The combination of containment** and flexibility has been shown to increase adjustment in children on almost all measures of personal and academic success.[7]

IT'S EASIER WHEN WE START EARLY (BUT IT'S NEVER TOO LATE!)

It is particularly difficult to begin to enforce discipline when your relationship with your child is poor or after he or she has been repeatedly let off the hook. Some parents I see complain that my suggestions regarding clearer and firmer discipline "don't work." There is some justification to this complaint. Relationships first and foremost are built on acceptance and trust. Without that, attempts to impose firm discipline on kids who have had the run of the house often lead to rebellion and acting out. At its extreme, parents who are unable to set limits and follow through on consequences often find themselves in the position of having kids whose acting out has become dangerous to their own health and safety. At that point, children may need to be sent to structured, therapeutic programs that can insure their safety as they begin to build both trust and the kinds of self-management skills that were never developed at home.

Imposing structure is hard for many of us who came of age during a time of "do your own thing" and quick gratification. But kids falter without structure. Anyone who has ever seen a young child having a temper tantrum knows how frightening and unmanageable overwhelming feelings can be to a young child. Parents' prohibitions function as a kind of holding tank that allows children to learn how to manage feelings and experiences that are beyond their reach. Within the safety of the holding tank, the young girl can say no to drugs because "my parents would kill me." This gives her an out, allows her to save face, keeps communication open with her parents, and buys her the time to more fully develop her own boundaries and judgment.

There is a substantial body of research that suggests that even when children have had poor early parenting, their deficits can be at least partly remediated by changes in parenting style.[8] In other words, it's never too late to start. Not all discipline is created equal, however. As we've seen, discipline runs along a continuum, from abuse through appropriate discipline to indifference. It also runs along another continuum one that has to do with whether we discipline by controlling our child's behavior or by psychological manipulation.

THE DIFFERENCE BETWEEN BEING "IN CONTROL" AND BEING "CONTROLLING"

Almost all conflicts that I see between my patients and their parents are embedded in the issue of control. From the mundane "My mother is so controlling, she won't let me wear low jeans," to the deadly "I won't eat because that's the only control I have in my family," control is a crucial issue for both parents and teenagers. Being willing and able to exert control is a critical part of parenting; it is how we socialize our children and keep them safe. How we exercise control; whether we are "controlling" or "in control," is central both to how our children develop and to the quality of the relationship we have with them. Control, its uses and misuses, has been the subject of extensive investigation. Researchers have distinguished between two types of parental control, **behavioral control** and **psychological control,** and find that a child's adjustment is closely related to which style of control prevails in the household.

- Behavioral control includes being an authority, making age-appropriate demands, setting limits, and monitoring children's behavior.

- Psychological control is characterized by two elements: it intrudes into the psychological world of the child and it attempts to manipulate the child's thoughts and feelings by invoking guilt, shame, and anxiety.

Not surprisingly, behavioral control has positive effects on child and adolescent development while psychological control has consistently been shown to have negative effects.[9] Parents who use behavioral control are "in control." Psychological control is experienced by children and teens as "controlling" and intrusive. The hallmark of psychological control is that it is nonresponsive to the *child's* emotional and psychological needs.

There is a world of difference between behavioral controls ("Sorry you did so poorly on your math test. TV is off-limits until you pull that grade up. Do you need some help?") and psychological control ("You're going to be flipping burgers for the rest of your life if you continue to be such a goof-off.") Every parent is well aware of the power of psychological control. It is often our strategy of last resort, used when we are so overwhelmed by our own anxieties that we cannot separate our child's needs from our own. When we hear our own needs being overemphasized, it's a good bet that we are sliding into the damaging territory of psychological control. "How could you do this to *me*?" "After all *I've* done for you."

As I write this section, I think about my three sons. Haven't there been times when I was so distressed by their choices that I would use any and every weapon in my arsenal—guilt, shame, whatever it took—to control them? I'm lucky to have great kids, but this doesn't mean they haven't made a few notable mistakes in their lives. But even when they messed up, even when my tolerance was pushed, I knew that the job I had to do would only be hindered by psychological control. We are way late in laying the groundwork for moral development in our children if we find that psychological control is all that is left to us when our kids are adolescents. Our children's conscience as well as their ability to control their behavior is born out of our willingness to discipline, and our love. When the bond between parent and child is strong and warm, our kids naturally don't want to let us down.

All parents struggle with issues of control, "experts" included, and so it is with the blessing of my tolerant oldest son, Loren, that I tell this story.

When Loren turned eighteen, he and his best friend threw a big party together at my house. They were careful about invitations, hired a bouncer to keep out unwanted guests, and locked any wine and liquor in the house upstairs in my husband's study as per my condition that there be no drinking.

The night of the party I spent some time downstairs with his friends, kids I had known for most of their lives, and went upstairs to watch TV at about eleven. My husband and two younger boys were out of town. I fell asleep watching TV and was awakened hours later by screaming sirens and the sound of general chaos. After I retired, several of the kids had brought out the alcohol they had smuggled into the house in backpacks and coat pockets. Some of them began drinking heavily, and one of the young men developed a full-blown panic attack. He was certain he was dying and my son's best friend was so frightened that he called 911. Well, the police, the fire department, the sheriff's department, and an ambulance arrived on the scene. I was dressed down by the police for allowing minors to drink and was cited. My son and his best buddy were sobbing, the police were chastising, kids were crawling out windows, and I had my first introduction to adolescent suburban parties gone bad.

The issue of behavioral versus psychological control is played out in scenes like this for almost every parent with adolescents. While my son had done his best, he still allowed drinking to go on when I had expressly forbidden it. He jeopardized his friends by allowing them to drink, knowing that they would be driving home, and he jeopardized my professional standing as well.

However, I knew there was nothing to be gained by humiliating my son. He already felt guilty, a much more effective punishment than any guilt trip I could lay on him. The lesson to be learned had to do with appreciating the consequences of his actions. A starter on the high school varsity basketball team, he had to miss many practices and games as he accompanied me to every meeting I had with my lawyer on how to handle my citation (which was thrown out). He had to enlist his friends in cleaning the house and writing letters to the DA, explaining what had happened and why the citation I was given was unwarranted. He had to pay for my legal fees by performing chores. And he was grounded for a month—all appropriate behavioral controls.

Psychological control, so tempting to use in this highly emotional situation, would have been counterproductive. The very skills my son still needed to develop would have been undermined by my manipulating him to feel guilty or ashamed. This is not to say that our children should never feel guilty or ashamed. On the contrary, if we do our job well, our children will have these feelings when they behave poorly. A child's conscience is built on years of clear expectations and loving connection with a parent, not on manipulation, criticism, and rejection.

If anything, we talked about the party at length. Whose responsibility was it? What went wrong? How could it have been handled differently? These are the kinds of questions that are essential for adolescents, who are confronted with new, often exciting, often dangerous, experiences on a regular basis. To drink? How much? To do drugs? What kind? To have sex? How often? With how many different partners? It is out of asking and considering questions like these that teens clarify their own sense of right and wrong, and develop confidence in their ability to handle different and sometimes difficult situations. Avoiding psychological control helps a kid turn inward—secure in the knowledge that a loving and respectful parent is available if necessary—and consider and take seriously his own point of view. Did I ever say, "How could you?" Probably once or twice that first night, but I knew that the real question was "Why did you?" My son needed to understand the pressures on him that kept him from sticking with his good intentions that particular night. He needed to think about why the party spun out of control and what skills were missing from his repertoire so that in the future he would be better equipped to handle the pressure of his peers. Discussions like these, even when we are angry or disappointed in our children, are mandatory if we value their safety and development over our own need to blow off steam.

Good judgment takes years to develop. Our kids are bound to run into situations where their lack of experience and underdeveloped judgment leads them to poor, sometimes regrettable, choices.

But understanding the tenets of the authoritative parenting style, with its twin emphasis on warmth and control, helps us navigate through difficult times with our children. Facing the twin tasks of socializing our children and supporting the development of their autonomy means we have to be clear about our own expectations at the same time that we respect the child before us. Sometimes there is not much difference between these two realities, and sometimes there is a yawning chasm.

We can become angry, disappointed, or withdrawn when we feel our child is letting us down. At those times it is tempting to exploit the power difference between parent and child, smacking the younger child who uses bad language, or shaming the older child who has forgotten our birthday. But before exerting control over your child, regardless of age, ask if what you are doing furthers your child's ability to make good choices or simply defends your own superiority. We are bigger, older, and more experienced. Most of us have little trouble making the better decision. The job is to make sure that our own children grow up with the skills that they will need to choose the wiser course themselves.

Ultimately, our ability to parent effectively depends on many things: how well we were parented ourselves, our interest and understanding of effective parenting styles, and the type of child we have been given to raise. Certainly some children are easier to raise than others; some of us were fortunate enough to have terrific parents, while others came from troubled families. But the most critical factor in how well we are able to parent has to do with our own feeling that we have enough inside of us, enough love, enough support, enough reserves, to go about the challenging task of raising our unique and singular child.

Part Four

WHY YOU HAVE TO STAND
ON YOUR OWN TWO FEET
BEFORE YOUR CHILDREN
CAN STAND ON THEIRS

CHAPTER 8

Challenges to Effective Parenting in the Culture of Affluence

Books that offer advice on parent-child relationships tend to focus on one side of this equation: the needs of the child. But what about the needs of the parent? What helps parents to do their job effectively and with zest? It's one thing to say that a parent with a slow-to-warm-up five-year-old should be patient, or that a fifteen-year-old needs to be respected when she withdraws; it's something else to have the resources to tolerate the dawdling of the child or the disconnection of the teenager. We may understand the importance of warmth, and still feel anything *but*, when our frustrated thirteen-year-old slams a door in our face. As for firm discipline, how easy is it to set limits on your teenage son's alcohol use when his friends' parents provide alcohol, claiming, "Since they're going to drink, I want it to be in my house." Materialism is found to be a destructive value to cultivate in our children, but how do we "deprive" them when our entire community appears to endorse the notion that a driver's license entitles a teenager to a car of his own.

Warmth, discipline, materialism—dealing with all these issues effectively demands that we address not only the *challenges* that parents face, but also the *needs* that they have as they try to be the best parent they can. Every parent I see in my office desperately wants to understand what has gone wrong, not only with their child, but with themselves as well. We all start out hoping to be terrific parents, and then any one of a number of things get in our way: a temperamental child, a difficult spouse, our own history, a demanding job, the community we live in. The culture of affluence that surrounds us, the values it promotes and prizes—poses particular challenges for the reflective parent. Just as our children are having difficulty getting their most pressing needs met in this culture, so are their parents.

While there are tremendous and obvious advantages to being affluent, there are also some real risks that go with the territory. The American Dream is pervasive and media messages insistently tell us that material wealth paves the route to happiness; the corollary, of course, is that among the affluent, unhappiness is rare.[1] This is clearly false, as is evident from the research that has been presented. And for those of us whose families are vulnerable to the unhappiness born of affluence, the first step to prevention is to clearly recognize the particular problems it can create.

Here are some of the common costs found in the culture of affluence. Not all of them will apply to you, but most of us confront at least some of these issues. Take a few moments to sit down and look at this list thoughtfully. Think about the direction your family is headed in and then decide whether or not you like the way your boat is being steered. Take a pencil and check off the items that seem pertinent to you; then consider your options. Not everything demands a major intervention; sometimes talking to a friend, joining a group, writing in a journal, or considering options and implementing change will do the trick. However, if it is apparent that your choices are truly unsatisfying and you and your family are suffering, then it's a wise idea to find a good therapist or counselor.

— When a family is affluent someone is usually working overtime. Often this means long hours and excessive time away from the family. Mothers (mostly) can feel like single parents raising their children.

— In families that are financially successful, there is often a power imbalance, with the parent who is making more of the money calling more of the shots.

— Parents from affluent families don't like to "rock the boat." Developing wealth takes tremendous effort and energy. An unhappy status quo may continue indefinitely out of fear of threatening the financial security of both parents and children.

— Busy schedules and/or preoccupation with material things interfere with those factors that are known to increase quality of life: friendships, spirituality, and community involvement.

— Loneliness can become a prominent part of an affluent lifestyle because perfection is highly valued and showing vulnerability is frowned upon. These values inhibit the development of truly close and nurturing relationships.

— Mothers become overly dependent on their children for emotional support and comfort. High-powered husbands are often physically and/or emotionally unavailable. While women (mostly) may be compliant toward their husbands, they know that in the long run their best emotional bet is on their children, increasing the risk of overinvolvement and intrusion.

— Highly capable people are accustomed to managing things on their own. While they may ask for help "fixing" their child, they may be reluctant to face their own weaknesses, neediness, and vulnerabilities.

— As a result of this reluctance to seek out help, problems may escalate from the easily treated to more difficult issues.

— Expecting excessively high levels of achievement, both from themselves and from their children, cultivates perfectionism, a well-documented precursor of depression.

— Affluent communities emphasize competition and extrinsic markers of success such as high grades, trophies, and admission to prestigious schools. This cultivates external, as opposed to internal, motivation, putting children at risk for a host of psychological difficulties.

— Substance use/abuse rates are high in affluent families. Whether acknowledged or not, someone may have an illicit drug, prescription-drug, or alcohol problem, often as a result of untreated depression.

The above items refer to a number of different factors known to cause problems in affluent families; some of them are primarily issues of the culture of affluence, while others are more directly tied to common personal problems found among the affluent. Being aware that there is a constant interaction between our own psychology and the pressures of the communities we live in, it's useful to try to distinguish whether our difficulties are primarily a result of the culture or a result of unresolved personal issues. Like most complex issues, it's usually some combination of factors.

BUCKING THE TIDE: IF EVERYONE IS DOING IT, THAT DOESN'T MAKE IT RIGHT

A major challenge to effective parenting is the feeling that we are out of step with our own communities. There are many parents who have an uneasy sense that something is wrong with the value system in their affluent community, with the enormous emphasis on "more." But all too often they stay silent, feeling like the odd person out. People all around us seem to be completely wedded to the cultural norms of achievement and status, so we are afraid to protest. As a result, nobody says that the emperor has no clothes!

Chris Mullin, one of the most well-known and best-loved former NBA players, relates the following story. His ten-year-old son, not surprisingly athletic, was chosen to be on the "select" soccer team in their suburban community outside of San Francisco. He enjoyed the competition and worked hard at being an outstanding player. The Mullins, who have four children, spend every summer in the East visiting family and old friends. When the family announced their summer plans to return east, their son's coach gave them an ultimatum: if he missed summer practice he would be cut from the select team. The parents of almost every other child on the team changed their summer plans to accommodate the coach's demand. It took Chris and his wife, Liz, a "nanosecond" to make their decision. They went back East; his son was cut, but continues to play on the local soccer team, and the world goes on.

Sometimes we lose sight of the fact that we have choices. While certainly kids try to manipulate their parents by saying that "everyone" is allowed to have unsupervised parties, or no curfew, or their own car, the fact is that sometimes we simply find ourselves with a different point of view. This can be lonely and very disappointing. However, it is imperative that when we have strong feelings about a subject related to our children, that we feel free to choose what we believe is the right path. Most parents have good instincts; trust them especially when you are being pressured.

Just as it is crucial for children to feel that they are making their own choices, we also need to feel that our parenting choices come from authentic places deep within us. Communities and schools can make decisions that are not in the best interests of children in general, or of your child in particular. If you disagree with a school policy, let your voice be heard. Some of the most important changes in a community come about when thoughtful people get involved. In my own community, many parents were fed up with the aggressive involvement of parents and the outlandish behavior of coaches at "select" soccer games. We rejected the idea that youth sports had to include excessive doses of competition, year-round commitment, and outrageous amounts of criticism directed at our children. A lacrosse league was developed with reasonable time commitments and clear sanctions against bad behavior. These games are a pleasure for both parents and kids alike and have become a much-needed opportunity for like-minded parents to socialize, free from the distraction of overzealous parents and coaches.

The problems outlined in this book—excessive pressure, isolation from adults, inappropriate intrusion, controlling behavior, lax discipline—have all found a home in affluent communities. Parents drink or get high with their teenagers. Kids use foul language in public and no one bats an eye, let alone confronts the child. Kids are pitted against each other for coveted positions on the playing field or in the classroom. While most of us are desperate to enhance our sense of community, we also need to work at creating the kind of community we want to be part of. When you find yourself swimming against the tide, you can retreat into disappointment or you can seek out people with similar concerns. Everyone needs to feel that they are part of a group; it is unlikely that you are the only person with a dissenting point of view.

The explosion of gear and products sporting college and university logos is emblematic of our need to identify with a group. While some people see this phenomenon as one more indication of competitiveness among parents, I think it has more to do with our hunger and our children's hunger to be clearly seen as part of a recognizable community. My undergraduate university didn't even have clothing in the bookstore. Now the clothing sections of campus bookstores are as large as the book sections, devoting enormous amounts of space to sweatshirts, T-shirts, hats, bathing suits, jackets, blankets, and more—all featuring the school's name in lettering that ranges from the unpretentious to the immodest.

Identifying with our kid's school is fun, but we need to find ways to feel that we are part of the communities we live in. We do this not by complaining, not by disconnection, but by becoming involved in issues that are important to us. Go to PTA meetings, parent education nights, school board meetings; join a local professional organization or volunteer at a political, religious, or social organization. Affluent kids are less altruistic than kids with fewer financial resources, and they become even less so as they get older. Model involvement for your kids. It teaches them to be aware of and value the needs of others, and it helps you to feel connected and involved in your own community.

HOLDING OURSELVES ACCOUNTABLE

For a year and a half I treated fifteen-year-old Andrew who came to therapy with a great deal of insight and a very big cocaine habit. A sweet and sensitive teenager, he attended an expensive private school where his quiet nature and artistic interests set him apart from most of the outgoing, often self-aggrandizing, popular boys. He found little solace at home, as his two charming, highly successful parents were preoccupied with their careers and their troubled marriage. His parents dutifully attended monthly sessions aimed at clarifying family dynamics and reporting on the results of their son's drug testing, but their engagement seemed superficial and distracted. As with many affluent boys, the combination of money and easy access to drugs made it easier for Andrew to self-medicate than to confront his feelings of anger and abandonment.

Cocaine is a powerfully seductive drug, and it is no small task to convince an angry and unhappy adolescent that a year or two of twice-a-week talk therapy is a better alternative than the quick relief of a couple of lines of coke. But Andrew's gentle nature and commitment to his art became powerful therapeutic allies as he felt increasingly "heard" in our sessions, and found that the crash that inevitably follows cocaine use interfered with his ability to concentrate on his painting. Little by little he learned how to express and then manage his anger, confronting his parents when necessary, and finding support among those who readily saw his admirable qualities. He quit chasing the "popular" crowd so valued by his parents and instead found a couple of boys and girls who shared his interest in the arts, and became part of a small but close group of friends. His cocaine use stopped altogether after about seven months, and he learned to avoid situations where the profoundly reinforcing effect of cocaine might tempt him back into using it again.

Toward the end of my work with Andrew, I received a frantic midnight call from him. He had been looking around the kitchen for a late-night snack and came upon a small plastic container filled with cocaine. He was terrified that he might use the drug, but, more important, he was beside himself that someone else in the house was using cocaine knowing the struggle he had just gone through. Together we decided that he would flush the cocaine down the toilet and that I would meet with him, and then separately with his parents, the next day.

To my amazement, both of Andrew's parents admitted to having secret cocaine habits themselves. Many of the same pressures that encouraged Andrew to turn to cocaine were present in his parents: pressure to conform, a distant relationship with their own parents, the easy availability of cocaine in their affluent community, and feelings of isolation and disconnection. After working diligently for close to a year to free their son from a habit that carries the risk of dependence, hallucinations, psychosis, stroke, cardiac arrhythmia, and death, Andrew's parents were unmoved by the warnings that they had so frequently presented to him. While they did not want their son to have a substance-abuse problem, they felt that they "could handle" cocaine; they were, after all, "adults, not kids." Somehow, the impact of their drug abuse on their child's resolve and sense of safety in the house escaped them.

If we hope to have children who are capable of being accountable for their behavior, then we must model accountability. Parents who bring to therapy their kids who drink too much while not addressing their own drinking problems—or kids with drug problems while parents maintain their own hidden stash—are short-changing their children and themselves. Andrew predictably backslid, albeit briefly. He quickly regained his equilibrium and faced the reality that in many ways he had passed his parents on the road to adulthood. This is a difficult and sobering lesson for an adolescent. Andrew's mom ultimately came to see the damage her cocaine use was causing her son and herself, joined a support group, and stopped her substance use. Dad, however, still maintains that his use is purely recreational and has no desire to change his behavior. Andrew's relationship with his father remains distant; an unfortunate but appropriate response to Dad's lack of responsibility. A parent who is "high" is an unavailable parent. We simply cannot expect our children to face the hard tasks of growing up with integrity if we are unwilling to pay attention to where we buy into bad behavior or poor values and face up to our own errors in judgment.

I tell the following story with more than a little self-consciousness, because it illustrates how vulnerable we all are to the pressures of the culture of affluence. In my worst parenting moment ever, I berated my youngest son when his A- in language arts slipped to a B+ the last week of school. Reduced to tears, he lay in miserable solitude in his bed with the covers over his head. I knew that I was way out of line, that my disappointment had nothing to do with him and everything to do with my own competitiveness and the unremitting emphasis on grades in my community. I waited long enough to be certain I understood what had been provoked in me, then went to tell him I was sorry and to talk about what had happened between us. The next week when he brought home his report card, next to his B+ his English teacher had written: "Hard worker. Kind and good-hearted person: considerate and thoughtful." I have never felt more properly chastised in my twenty-five years of parenting. I include this embarrassing story because as I ask parents to honestly inventory themselves, I want it to be clear that while this is a doable and extraordinarily valuable process, it can also be quite painful. We are constantly reminding our children to "think about what you're doing"; we need to make sure that we hold ourselves just as accountable.

We are all human, we all make mistakes, capitulate to peer pressure, and project our disappointments onto our children. When we make these kinds of mistakes, it is *imperative* that we apologize to our kids, explain ourselves, and model that while no one is perfect, we can strive for emotional honesty and integrity. While lapses are inevitable, making amends and taking responsibility is essential. Unfortunate as our mistakes can be, they also help us to learn where we need to watch our step, to be vigilant about our own issues, and to model the values of introspection and emotional honesty. Talking with our children about how community values can impact us for better or for worse helps them to begin thinking about these same issues.

THE POISON OF PERFECTIONISM

Affluent communities excessively emphasize individualism, perfection, accomplishment, competition, and materialism, while giving short shrift to more prosocial values such as cooperation, altruism, and philanthropy.[2] Many of us have become vigilant about our vulnerability to incorporating these unhealthy norms into our homes and are trying our hardest to set a different tone. This is not the whole story however. Even as we are watchful of what is around us in our communities, it is critical that we look inward as well. Affluent communities are full of people who are very talented, determined, skilled, competitive, self-centered, and successful—and we, not just our communities, may be prone to some unhealthy values and behaviors. Nowhere is this more true than in our tendency to be perfectionistic.

The term "effortless perfection" was coined at Duke University to describe the intense pressures on women to excel according to both traditional "male" standards (achievement, accomplishment, good grades, and high-powered careers) as well as traditional "female" standards (being thin, pretty, and wearing nice clothes). Not incidentally, young women who worked overtime to be outstanding in both these arenas found themselves troubled and with increased rates of alcohol and drug abuse as well as eating disorders.[3] "Effortless perfection" is an oxymoron, and the idea that we can be good at all things (or anything, for that matter) without effort is a disingenuous and dangerous notion. The effort it takes to *always* be at the "top of our game" is exhausting and can deprive us of those nurturing things that are likely to fuel our ability to be outstanding: relationships, downtime, freedom to think creatively, and a lack of self-consciousness.

The other night my husband dragged me away from the computer screen, insisting that I go out and see a movie with him. My passion for this particular section of this book had kept me secluded in my office for several weeks, emerging only to graze the kitchen and check homework. I was definitely missing in action, a temporary but nonetheless disconcerting state of affairs for my normally nondemanding husband. So that Saturday evening, I shut off the computer and went out—dressed in my frayed "writing" sweats, hair limp and badly in need of a touch-up, and without even the minimal slash of lipstick that would suggest I had cared enough to glance at a mirror before leaving the house. I prayed that we wouldn't run into anyone I knew.

We did, of course—several sets of friends, a few colleagues, and even a patient of mine. I found myself repeatedly apologizing for my appearance. By the time we left the movie theater I had pulled my sweatshirt hood halfway over my face and skulked back to the car. I had given up the opportunity to connect with colleagues and to spend some spontaneous time with good friends after the movie simply because I felt uncomfortable in my own skin that evening. How trivial and absurd to feel *"not good enough,"* and in typical upper-middle-class fashion I chastised myself for my superficiality instead of sympathizing with myself for being overworked and frazzled.

"Not good enough" is a phrase that rings in my office day after day. It bounces off the walls, spoken by teary, athletic twelve-year-olds who don't make the "A" team, by discouraged high school students with admirable but not outstanding grades, and by exhausted mothers engaged in the useless exercise of trying to make their homes and their children perfect. I was distressed to find myself victim to the very insecurity I work so hard to lessen in my patients. Certainly I looked "good enough" for someone who was under a deadline and working around the clock. But "good enough" simply isn't enough in communities where mothers toil to create perfect homes, working parents toil to reach the pinnacle of professional success, and kids toil to be the best and the brightest. I understand the contempt of my teenage patients who roll their eyes in session when a parent says, "Your grades aren't good enough, we know you can do better," or the ubiquitous "Just do your best." Too often these duplicitous statements are used to mask a disturbing truth, that what is expected by many parents in affluent communities is not a personal best but the absolute best.

"The enemy of the good is the best," said Voltaire, and, as most of us know, that enemy has set up shop in our homes.

One of my patients, a charming and bright mother of three, a lawyer turned full-time homemaker, spends her days "making sure everything is just perfect." She polishes her house, her children, and herself. On the surface everything shines, but underneath, Mom is depressed, drinks too much, and abuses painkillers. Why are so many otherwise bright, thoughtful women obsessed with their appearance, their kids' performance, and whether or not White Linen is a better paint color choice than Navajo White? Do perfectionists naturally find themselves part of the upper middle class or is there something about belonging to the upper middle class that cultivates perfectionism? Are perfectionism and affluence bound together for other, less obvious, reasons?

Bright, hardworking people are more likely than others to find themselves working their way into the upper middle class. Aside from inherited wealth, most people who make money do so because they have put their heart and soul into a profession or career that values achievement and advancement. Perfectionism is likely to stand you in good stead when you're poring over medical or law or business texts. So when does perfectionism that is useful slide into the kind of maladaptive perfectionism that is strongly linked not only to depression but to a host of serious emotional problems—eating disorders, obsessive-compulsive disorders, psychosomatic disorders, and, most disturbingly, suicide?

Maladaptive perfectionism is driven by an intense need to avoid failure and to appear flawless. It has its roots in a demanding, critical, and conditional relationship with one's parents. When approval is conditional on performance, then closeness and affection are bound to suffer. Maladaptive perfectionism hides deep-seated feelings of insecurity and vulnerability.[4] In particular, the feeling that excessively high standards are expected and necessary to win approval and acceptance can lead to intense feelings of hopelessness.

The tendency of affluent communities to focus on and overly value external measures of accomplishment is directly related to high rates of depression and substance abuse, but it is also related to a general sense that living can be unbearably difficult. One of my patients describes her exhausting attempts to create a "perfect" Christmas for her family. She worked for months redecorating her house and importing gifts, ornaments, and foodstuffs from around the world so that her friends and family would have a "Christmas they would never forget." As trivial mistakes mounted—a cracked ornament from Thailand, napkin rings that were the wrong shade of red, toffee bars instead of pecan rolls from Neiman Marcus—she became increasingly irritable and finally depressed. On Christmas morning her husband presented her with a Porsche 911, but she was too exhausted and depressed to get out of bed and look at it, let alone drive it. Far from being a perfect Christmas, she had succeeded in turning a generally festive, and often trying, family holiday into a nightmare. There is no perfect Christmas, child, outfit, family, vacation, home, marriage, or friendship. This is real life, and we would do well to cast the notion of perfection out of our lives and get on with the real business of living with strengths and weaknesses, abilities and deficits, accomplishments and failures. This is how we help our children learn the art of living: by encouraging them, to take pleasure from their efforts and successes and to tolerate their limitations.

Certainly there are times when people need to perform as well as they can: we'd like our surgeon and airline pilot and the person driving the car next to us to be interested in optimal performance. But this is different from chasing perfection. Chasing perfection is a good way to have your life pass you by. It keeps you focused on the future, and out of the moment. It means you miss small pleasures as you chase larger ones. It means you can't see the child in front of you because you're looking for a child that doesn't exist. And it means that your own life is stripped of real feeling, love, and connection as you pound yourself and those around you with fantasies instead of welcoming realities. The pursuit of perfection is a diversion from the messiness of real life. If your real life isn't working, don't push your children, push yourself to make a change. One cannot be perfect and vulnerable at the same time. To truly love, to truly nurture and protect both ourselves and our children, we need our eyes open to the people in front of us, real people with varying degrees of talent and ambition and capacity and desire. We need to understand that often, close is good enough, and perfect is far too costly.

While parents often find themselves making bad deals with their children to maintain the appearance of perfection—a car for high grades, a later curfew for making the more competitive team—this is not simply about shallow parents who are happy only when their children "shine." The reasons why we push our children to look good, or to excel, are complicated. Sometimes it's about our depression or unmet needs, other times about our own excessive perfectionist strivings, but often it's a desire to ensure that our children will lead lives that are financially equal to, or easier than, our own. For many of us who came out of difficult economic circumstances—my family was on state assistance for a while after my father died—this is not an insignificant concern.

OVERCOMING MYOPIA ABOUT THE "GOOD LIFE"

We want opportunities for our kids because we know that life can be easier and perhaps more satisfying when money is not a worry. Every generation of parents hopes for an easier and more rewarding life for their children. When we push for excellence and achievement, it is because we believe that in the long run our kids will be happier. For many of us who are passionate about our professional lives, it is hard to imagine that our children will be happy without experiencing the kind of gratification that our own work brings us. We can be myopic when we insist that high grades, well-known schools, or particular professions are the royal road to happiness. A life well lived takes many forms. Carlos Castaneda cautioned: "All roads are the same. . . . Choose the one with heart."[5] "Heart" differs for each of us, and when we insist that our children be gratified by the same things that have gratified us, then we limit the roads they can travel on, roads that may be closer to *their* own hearts. In addition, we miss out on the opportunity to see the world differently, to see it through the singular and vivid eyes of our child.

My husband and I often kidded that our middle son, Michael, was "a creative kid in a house full of obsessive-compulsives." It was always said with pride and a bit of apprehension. The hours he spent watching the light shift across the grass in our backyard or transforming our living room into a tropical island with colored sheets and crepe paper, and the endless games he created out of household kitchen items, while interesting, were somewhat foreign to his parents, who rarely dallied, preferring to put one foot in front of the other. When Michael was quite young he would creep into our room in the early morning hours, trying to rouse his late-to-bed mother to watch the sun come up with him. The mother of three young boys, I'd wave him off with an exhausted hand, desperate for the extra sleep. As he grew older, his persistence also grew, and finally I started watching the sunrise with him, something I had never done in my life. I was so startled by the beauty of not just the spectacle, but the awe in my young son's face, that I became increasingly interested in the world through his eyes—in the tiny colored pebbles that he would craft together into trivets, in the collages made of pictures and magazines and found objects that adorned his room, in the parts of life I had neglected as I focused mightily on "getting things done" and "staying on track."

Michael has gone on to be a theater and film major. He has taught me that creativity is like a river, something that flows so strongly that you can either go with the flow or it will flow around you, leaving you in its wake. My choosing to go with the flow has probably made things easier for my son, but it has also enriched my life in ways I would have been helpless to imagine had I not gotten up on those early lavender mornings. I've stopped worrying about whether he'll find work or how he'll make a living. These will be his challenges to face, not mine. But I know for sure that the "good life" has less to do with money and more to do with the good fortune of finding one's particular "path with heart."

Affluent communities overvalue a very narrow range of academic and extra-curricular accomplishments. While my children were in junior high school, I sat through scores of ball games for my two sons who were interested in athletics and a single evening of poetry for my son who was interested in the arts. Schools hold far more assemblies for academic excellence than for other kinds of personal achievement or community involvement in spite of the fact that personal achievement and community involvement are equally valuable parts of becoming a successful, well-educated person and a good citizen. Parents swarm to highly publicized "education nights" featuring admissions directors from prestigious colleges and universities, hoping to glean some little-known fact that will give their child an advantage, no matter how small, in the admissions process. We are a huge market for businesses that profit from our anxiety—from toy manufacturers that push absurd "educational toys" for infants, to scholastic services that promise to increase our children's AP, SAT, LSAT, MCAT, and GRE scores. We are made to feel guilty by books and magazines that label us as vain, indulgent, and childish parents, as if we couldn't possibly raise a child without a map and a guidebook. To counter all these pressures, to prove our own worth, to keep our own worries and anxieties at bay, we focus on our children, hauling them from activity to activity, tutor to tutor, camp to camp, to bolster their performance, and to help us feel that we are doing, if not a perfect job, then one that's damn near close.

There are thousands of schools in this country, hundreds if not thousands of jobs, careers, and professions, and an endless number of artistic, intellectual, mechanical, physical, and recreational hobbies and learning opportunities. Having three children with very different areas of strength has made me acutely aware of how myopic a view of education I have shared with my community. My oldest son is persistent, verbal, and linear in his thinking. A "perfect suburban kid," as one of his teachers once remarked (something I now hear as a questionable compliment). Schools are made for kids like him, and he barreled through school easily, happily, and successfully. My middle, creative, son found less support for his interests. He was regularly reminded to "stay on task," even when the roads he wandered down were rich and far more intellectually challenging than the deadening "teaching to the test" of his classroom. Supplementing his education, however was not that difficult, as our community vigorously supports the arts, and so finding theater, dance, and voice classes for him outside of school was relatively easy. As for my youngest, nonverbal, visual-spatial child, school has not been rewarding in the same way that it was for his verbal brothers. In spite of a terrific ability to see things in space and work with his hands, the only relevant course his junior high offered was a six-week woodworking shop. Finally in high school he has found an engineering and architecture track filled with kids just like him, and with a set of courses that interest and excite him. But first he has to undo the damage of an educational system that until ninth grade had no interest in the children who will one day build our bridges, buildings, and transportation systems.

Parents need to pay attention to the particular strengths of their children. Sometimes this is obvious, but often it takes a bit of digging. Exposing kids to a wide array of work opportunities and fulfilling leisure activities helps them to imagine a larger world than their neighborhood, which is often filled with investment bankers, businessmen, entrepreneurs, and assorted professionals. My office has seen an endless stream of bright, talented children who are disinterested in school because "My parents think there are only two things to be in the world: a doctor or a lawyer." In the same way that we encourage our children to make friends with a wide group of people so that they don't shut off their social opportunities too early, so should we encourage them to keep their options open when it comes to potential careers, interests, and colleges. Some of the most interesting people I have known are those who have had more than one career, people who have had the curiosity and the courage to try their hand at different things in life.

If we can expand our horizons, quiet our perfectionist strivings, and recover the spunk most of us had in our youth, we can rediscover the thrill and the adventure of new learning. While writing this book, I decided to take a course in American Sign Language with my youngest son. I can honestly say that I am absolutely the worst student in a class where the subject requires a good deal of visual-spatial not verbal ability. But I'm having a ball—sharing time with my son, seeing the pride he has in excelling at something that challenges me, and choosing to do something well beyond my comfort zone of the spoken word. There are schools besides the Ivies, fulfilling work besides the professions, and worthwhile activities that are never practiced at private clubs. While there is nothing wrong with being a tennis-playing Harvard cardiologist (and many things satisfying about it), there is also a world of options that we need to let our children know are just as interesting, just as valid, and just as valuable.

HANDLING THE ISOLATION THAT MAKES US VULNERABLE TO BEING BULLIED

Several years ago, outside my local grocery store, I witnessed the following scene. A middle-age mother, arms full of groceries, is imploring her teenage son, probably thirteen or so, to help her with the groceries and put his bike in the back of their SUV. He looks at his mother with what can only be described as contempt and tells her to "Fuck off." Mom continues to struggle with her bundles, alternately begging and cajoling her son. She reminds him that she is making his favorite dinner, that they have to get home and feed the dog, and besides she still has the laundry to do so that his gym uniform will be clean for the next day. He is unmoved by her entreaties and refuses either to help or to put his bike in the back of the van. Mom's shoulders slump and she starts to cry. At least two dozen adults walk quickly past this defeated mother and her bullying son without saying a word. Accustomed to dealing with kids and parents in conflict, I walk over to the mother and ask if I can help. "Could you please get him to come home with me?" she asks. In my very best professional voice, I turn to the boy, put a hand on his bike (big mistake), and say quietly, "Son, you need to go home with your mother now. Put your bike in the car and help load up the groceries." Without a hint of the wariness that children typically show when they are addressed by strangers, this young man looks me right in the eye and says, "If you don't take your fucking hand off my bike, I'm going to break it." With that he turns his bike around and pedals furiously off.

I turned to Mom, feeling I'd somehow blown the interaction, but also knowing that I just happened to walk into a drama of great and probably long-standing pain. "Why don't you just go home and talk it over with your husband. Your son will show up, I'm sure." "There is no one at home," she says plaintively. "Call a friend then, someone who knows you two, maybe that will help." Mom looks at me with desperation and spits out, "There *is* no one." "I'm sorry," I mutter as I back off toward my own car, overwhelmed by this woman's hopelessness and my own sense of helplessness.

I have no way of knowing what happened to this woman and her son. I don't know if she was divorced or her husband was out of town. I don't know if her relationship with her son was always so troubled or if they were in the middle of a temporary rupture. But her anguished "There *is* no one" has stayed with me for the years since this incident happened. It has become for me an iconic example of the feelings of isolation that so many affluent parents experience and their resultant vulnerability to being manipulated, bullied, and even abused.

I have a file in my office with examples of parents being bullied by their kids, parents bullying each other, and parents bullying teachers and other service providers sent to me from professionals around the country who were interested in the subject of this book. After reading dozens of anecdotes, the pattern of escalating bullying and manipulation in the absence of the protective factor of a strong, involved community becomes evident.

- In Fairfield County, Connecticut, a twelve-year-old boy and six of his friends get into his parent's liquor cabinet after school. They drink to the point of intoxication and two of them have to be taken to the local hospital to be treated for alcohol poisoning. When the boy whose home this took place in is questioned by the police, he is belligerent and not remorseful. When the police suggest to his parents that counseling might be in order, the youngster says, "We don't have to listen to them, they're just cops." His parents decline treatment.

- In Morris County, New Jersey, a seventh-grade boy is caught red-handed stealing a wallet out of a classmate's backpack. Called into the principal's office, where he is joined by his parents, he puts his feet up on the principal's desk, takes a pen from her desk, and begins doodling on her stationery. Neither of his parents tell him to behave respectfully. When the principal suggests that the boy may be suspended for his theft, the father reminds her that he is a lawyer.

- In Fairfax County, Virginia, a well-liked and successful physician shows up in the emergency room with multiple facial fractures. This is her fourth visit in as many years. A dogged social-service worker finally gets her to admit that she has been in an abusive marriage for over a decade, and that her husband, a pillar of the community, has shifted from verbal abuse to increasingly life-threatening physical abuse. Living on a large estate, he would taunt her by telling her she could scream as loud as she wanted since no one would hear her.

- In North Dallas, Texas, three high school boys lure a retarded girl to the home of one of the boys after school. They promise to "like her" if she will perform sexual acts on them. When she becomes frightened and tries to run away, they hold her down and force her to perform fellatio on them. The parents of all three of these boys show up at the police station with lawyers in tow and post bail for their sons. On leaving the police station, one of the fathers remarks, "Boys will be boys."

These examples, chosen because they bring into high relief a serious problem among the affluent, are far more common than we would like to believe. While they may represent manipulation, bullying, and abuse in the extreme, *every* parent is familiar with the more ordinary manifestations of these problems. The child who refuses to make her bed because "the cleaning ladies are coming." The preadolescent who challenges his parents' ban against homophobic and misogynistic music by saying, "You can't tell me what to do. I've got my own money." The husband who demands quiet when he comes home from work, because "Someone around here has to support this lifestyle." The misuse of power in affluent families is pervasive and troubling. Since we are raising the children who are most likely to be our next generation of power brokers and policy makers we need to be particularly sensitive to cultivating fairness and justice, not arrogance and a willingness to exploit.

Sociologists have long recognized the important function of a strong, involved, and cohesive community. These types of communities socialize children to value the needs of the group as well as individual needs. Alternatively, when community cohesion is low and values are highly competitive and individualistic, its members feel unsupported and wary of each other. Affluent communities suffer from both a lack of cohesion and a lack of values that stress the needs of the community. In this environment, individuals come to feel that it's "every man for himself." Kids don't return phone calls to classmates asking for help with a math assignment because one child's disadvantage becomes another child's advantage. Here is an issue that warrants the zeal typical of affluent parents. Make it clear that you value good citizenship just as much as academic excellence. Make certain that your children see you treat others respectfully. Bring them along to events that include the community, whether it's a Fourth of July parade or a day of doing good deeds sponsored by your church or synagogue. Watch your children for signs of arrogance or bullying or lack of cooperation. This is the place to show disappointment.

In the type of blue-collar community that many of us grew up in, community support and involvement was essential to the successful management of its children. With dozens of eyes watching the comings and goings of neighborhood kids, a cigarette smoked in the garage quickly became public knowledge. While it would be naïve to suggest that bullying did not exist, the neighborhood bully was easily identified and, far from being popular, was often shunned. Adults acted as a group in not tolerating kids who were "fresh," and if your parent was not clear on this point, then your neighbor or teacher usually was. Children were expected to be respectful toward adults, and the grocery-store scene that opened this section was inconceivable on two counts. First, kids simply did not curse at their parents, and, second, other parents quickly came to the aid of a parent in distress. I can remember many a time when one neighbor or another asked my policeman father to have "a word or two" with a misbehaving child. Bullying and manipulation feed off the indifference of the community.

These same kinds of cohesive communities banded together in times of trouble, sharing resources and providing support. People tend to remember the kindnesses that are shown to them during difficult times. One of the reasons that life in an affluent community can feel so lonely is because affluent people have the resources to buy their way out of many types of trouble and are reluctant to turn to neighbors for fear of being rejected or humiliated. This is not idle worry. In many affluent communities, the tremendous emphasis on individual accomplishment can make attempts at community unsuccessful. But parents who are committed to changing the pervasive sense of isolation that exists in their communities can begin to change the tide. When each of my sons in turn hit early adolescence, I'd call the mothers of all of their friends to see if we were all "on the same page" in terms of acceptable behavior. While there were always some minor differences about the acceptability of R-rated movies, or whether or not it was okay for them to hang out at the gas station in the evening, in general we all shared the same concerns that our sons be responsible, respectful, and safe. I asked to be informed if my son was rude, inconsiderate, or stayed out past whatever curfew had been set when he was staying at a friend's house. These informal arrangements helped our sons know what would be tolerated, regardless of whose home they were at, and, equally important, helped me to feel that I wasn't going it alone. **The antidote for isolation is involvement.** We make our job easier and fortify ourselves against abuse and manipulation when we reach out and develop relationships with like-minded people.

THE THREAT OF DIVORCE AND THE POTENTIAL LOSS OF "WIFESTYLE"

Apart from the extremely rich, who tend to have high rates of divorce, the divorce rate among upper-middle-class parents is lower than for other socioeconomic groups. This may reflect the fact that more educated people are more likely to marry later—marrying at a young age is the single greatest predictor of divorce—or the reality that leaving a financially comfortable marriage can be particularly difficult. While more women than men initiate divorce proceedings, it is not clear that this is the case among the well-to-do. Affluent women are often hesitant to entertain the possibility of divorce even when they are extremely unhappy or even abused in their marriages. Divorce is shown, *in general,* to increase the risk that children will run into emotional problems. In particular, the children of divorce are significantly more likely to have difficulty entering into committed loving relationships in young adulthood than children from intact marriages. This does not speak to any particular child, but it does mean that women are right to carefully consider the alternatives when thinking about divorce.

While many of the concerns of affluent women focus on the effects of divorce on their children, they also focus on their own potential loss of lifestyle, or "wifestyle." These two concerns are often hard to separate: women rightfully fear a significant decline in their socioeconomic status and worry that they will be unable to provide their children with the educational and extracurricular activities they so highly value. A not uncommon exit plan among women is to wait until their children have entered or graduated from college before leaving a bad marriage. But they also worry about their own ability to tolerate the loss of a lifestyle that has provided them with many "perks." The extent to which a woman is dependent on her husband, not just financially, but for an identity as well, affects her ability not only to consider divorce but even to ask for change in a dysfunctional marriage. Similarly, men are concerned that the demands of their work schedule minus the support of someone handling the details of home life will leave them with insufficient time and contact with their children. The fear of a greatly attenuated relationship with their children often keeps men from confronting the difficulties in their marriages.

A colleague tells me of a middle-age, well-to-do woman whose wealthy husband tells her when to go to sleep, when to wake up, and how long she is allowed to be on the phone when he is home. When questioned about why this otherwise bright and capable woman tolerates such unconscionable levels of control, her answer is simple, "Besides him, I love my life." In fact, there are aspects of her life that certainly can be seen as enviable: outstanding private schools for her children, exciting travel, several beautiful homes, and the opportunity to engage in extensive and meaningful philanthropic work. She does not see divorce as an option, but what is more intriguing is that she cannot conceive of altering the relationship she does have with her husband. "We've worked so hard to get to this place, I'm afraid to rock the boat" is her response to suggestions about how she might begin to talk to her husband about their inequitable relationship. Instead of turning to her husband, she consistently turns to her children for emotional support. Her sixteen-year-old son has already begun plotting his escape from his bullying father and his passive mother. Under his bed are a stack of college view-books, all from the other side of the country.

When there is a large power imbalance in a marriage, the financially dependent spouse can feel helpless about effecting change, or even exploited by their monied partner. An heiress decides to end her twenty-year marriage to her marginally employed husband. They have two sons. Because of her extremely comfortable financial situation, the court rules that she must pay her husband a not insignificant lump sum. She does this easily and then proceeds to hire the most expensive lawyers in town, who spend two years filing motions and generally harassing the father until his resources are exhausted. In the end he is given the choice of severely limiting his relationship with his sons or being forced into bankruptcy by continued legal actions. Tolerating emotional and financial manipulation by a controlling spouse who holds the pursestrings is striking a bargain with the devil. In this case, as in many others I see, the real victims are the children, who become pawns in the battle between their parents. Money is a seductive ally, and children are often drawn to the parent who offers more "goodies," better vacations, a swimming pool perhaps, and certainly a bedroom of their own. It is important that parents understand how destructive it is to use the attraction of material goods to win affection from their children following a divorce. It sets the stage for materialism at a time when research tells us that children are vulnerable, and most in need of emotional security, not material goods.

Why would any parent allow himself or herself to be manipulated, even abused, on the basis of money? One reason is that revealing a damaged marriage is anathema to people who have difficulty tolerating minor failures, let alone the "failure" of a bad marriage. The façade of a good life afforded by affluence helps to mask problems that might otherwise be transparent and inescapable. Materialistic pursuits provide temporary respite from unhappiness at home; sadness is drowned in vintage wines and expensive vodkas; affairs are carried on in distant cities and high-end hotels. While these "solutions" can offer temporary relief, they often exacerbate both marital and personal problems in the long run.

Certainly some marriages are unbearable and abusive and need to end for the good and sanity of all concerned. Being a single parent is difficult, trying to manage a blended family is difficult, and, yes, marriage is also difficult. Hallmark sentimentality has knocked many of us senseless when it comes to the realities of relationships. But whatever our difficulties may be, we need to make the compromises that we can live with and address the issues we can't live with. This book has stressed the value of authenticity in leading an independent, productive, loving life. We cannot ask our children to dig down and find their own authentic voices when they observe our lives to be inauthentic. If you are having trouble, it is important that you explain to your child, in a way that is understandable and not overly anxiety-provoking, that you are having some problems but that you are doing your best to work them out. In the case of divorce, older adolescents benefit from understanding the mistakes made by both parents, thereby increasing the odds that they will be able to go on and succeed in creating more lasting and successful relationships for themselves.

While the topics in this chapter address some of the more common problems associated with parenting in a culture of affluence, it is by no means exhaustive. There are communities that are completely caught up in the values of individualism, competition, and materialism, while other, equally affluent communities, are doing their best to establish a healthier environment for their children. Affluent people and affluent communities are not all the same and what one individual or one community experiences as valuable another may consider problematic. In general, it is clear to me that parents are fed up with and disillusioned by the culture of affluence and are looking to provide healthier alternatives for their children. Unfortunately, how to make this shift is often less clear.

Possibly because I see more adolescents than adults, or possibly because teenagers are more pliant and less wedded to their choices, it is often my adolescent patient who takes the lead and forces her family to confront the unhealthy compromises they have been making in order to keep the status quo humming (or, more accurately, stumbling) along. While it is unlikely that your family is a showcase for the personal problems and the ills of affluence to the same extent as Samantha's family, it's important to bear in mind that most of us have made some regrettable choices, and that few of them are irreversible.

SAMANTHA'S STORY: DANCING IN THE DARK

Samantha is one of those beautiful, golden California girls that songs are written about. Long blond hair, clear blue eyes, tall and athletic, she exudes a kind of robust confidence that rarely makes its way into my consulting room. However, Samantha, not her parents, had requested therapy, and that fact alone alerted me to the seriousness of her problems. Kids do not ask for therapy lightly. Both of Samantha's parents agreed that she had been an "easy" child, showing no indication of emotional problems. They were baffled by her insistence that she be allowed to see a psychologist, although they had two older sons who had both done stints in rehab.

The daughter of a wealthy CEO and his eager-to-please wife, Samantha understood the position of privilege she occupied. She lacked for nothing and, like many of the adolescents I see, was grateful for, if somewhat uncomfortable with, her parents' largesse. She was embarrassed by the new black convertible Saab that had been her sixteenth-birthday present, but she enjoyed her many travel opportunities and her trendy clothes. Samantha knew that she was smart, appealing, and popular. It didn't take her long, however, to reveal how sad, alone, and misunderstood she felt. Samantha spent much of her free time sleeping, was frequently teary, and felt hopeless about both her future and the possibility of ever being truly happy. She had a frighteningly well-thought-out suicide plan. She was clearly depressed.

Samantha was terrified of being evaluated, certain that she would be judged a failure. She was a talented dancer and cheerleader who could only practice her routines in the dark, fearful that if she caught a glimpse of herself in the mirror, she would be disappointed with what she saw. She was desperate enough to avoid most cheerleading tryouts by faking bouts of migraines or intestinal problems, once even walking into tryouts with a sling she had purchased at the local drugstore simply to make her appear to be incapacitated. Her talents were well known, however, and she was invariably offered a spot on the team. Samantha did not behave this way because she was untruthful; rather, she was driven to extreme behavior by her distorted view of how harshly she would be treated if she did not perform perfectly. Samantha had adopted her father's rigid code, which insisted that anything less than excellence was failure.

Samantha's father ran his family the same way he ran his corporation. Standards were high and inflexible. Samantha was ridiculed for her preoccupation with dancing, an activity "you can't make a living at." After two sessions, Dad refused to attend ongoing sessions (I usually have a session with the parents of the kids in my practice at least once every couple of months), saying that such "bullshit" was better left to his "neurotic" wife and daughter.

Away from home a great deal of the time, he expected his wife to raise the children and to present the kind of home he envisioned for his family—perfect, polished, and achievement-focused (a world light years away from his original disheveled, chaotic, alcoholic household). He was abusively controlling at home and had little interest in examining how his behavior contributed to the unhappiness felt by all members of his family.

Mom, compliant and fearful, allowed her husband to bully the family. While Dad was distant and aggressive, Mom was overinvolved and anxious. When her three children were younger, Mom was "delighted" with being a mother. She enjoyed her babies and toddlers as they offered physical and emotional comfort as well as relief from her husband's unrelenting criticism and harshness. Mom's depression and drinking began in earnest when her older sons hit puberty and became preoccupied with their own early-adolescent issues. Unfortunately, Mom experienced their individuation as rejection and became increasingly withdrawn from them. She spent weekends and sometimes weeks away from the family, leaving her kids to manage on their own, which they did—poorly. She was, however, able to maintain her connection to Samantha, at least partly because she could identify with her daughter's depression, as opposed to her sons' acting-out behavior.

Samantha's mom was terribly isolated. Living in a huge house behind electronic gates, she spent a great deal of her time renovating her already lovely home. She drank excessively and was well aware of the extent of her depression. However, she felt unable to change her situation because "I have everything." In fact, she had very little: an emotionally abusive relationship with her husband, a strained relationship with her children, a lack of community involvement or support, and virtually no sense of self-efficacy or control over her own life. Eager to protect her daughter from her own humiliating fate, she made sure that Samantha's slightest efforts at autonomy were kept well hidden from Dad. Samantha's acceptance at a prestigious summer program for the arts was labeled "camp" so that Dad would not challenge Samantha's desire to further her dance skills. Mom often colluded with Samantha, helping her daughter to pursue her interests without interference from Dad. She considered the deception necessary, lest she run the risk of "rocking the boat and finding myself and Sam alone and poor."

Whenever possible, Samantha tried to present her best self, scoffing at her problems as "trivial" and denigrating her astute psychological observations about her troubled family. Over time, however, Samantha revealed the many ways in which she felt deprived rather than indulged. She was left alone frequently with only an overwhelmed housekeeper for company or support. She experienced her parents' absences, particularly her mother's, as a lack of concern. "I could be screwing the football team and they wouldn't know the difference." While her brothers had responded to the lack of parental monitoring by acting out and getting in trouble with the law, Samantha retreated to her room and her depression. Without parents around to keep an eye on their activities, all three siblings felt prematurely ejected from the family.

When her parents were home, Samantha worked overtime to avoid conflict with her controlling father and to nurture her depressed mother. Samantha often said, "I lack substance," and her assessment was accurate. Samantha knew what was expected of her but had little sense of what she wanted to do with her life or expected to accomplish in the future. Dad's control and Mom's depression robbed Samantha of the opportunity to develop the building blocks of a strong sense of self: the ability to self-soothe, to tolerate adversity, to think creatively and flexibly, and to feel safe and loved for one's unique self. Samantha felt a special kinship with the blond, freckled, athletic-looking girls in Ralph Lauren ads, noting that "They look so open, you think you know something about them, but it's just an image."

Samantha had a good outcome after three years of therapy. Medication alleviated the worst of her depression. She became increasingly capable of fending for herself and was a willing student in my office: eager to learn to navigate life in spite of her feelings of anxiety and helplessness. Her autonomy was encouraged by my support and ability to tolerate, and even encourage, her risk taking. I was unimpressed by Samantha's façade but intrigued by her sparks of authenticity. When Samantha worked up the nerve to tell her parents that she was performing in a dance recital, I went to watch her, applauding wildly, not just for her talent but also for her emerging courage and independence.

While Samantha's parents were never fully on board in the sense of being willing to examine their own histories, they became more cooperative as they saw Samantha's depression lift. Like almost all parents, in spite of their particular strengths and weaknesses, Samantha's parents wanted "the best" for their daughter and were pleased as she regained some of her zest. In the process, they also gained some appreciation for their own deprived childhoods.

Samantha is currently in college and is doing well. We still have regular telephone contact. Her ability to separate from her parents and attach to me—a predictable and encouraging adult—helped this case have a good outcome. However, had Samantha's parents been more willing to engage in the psychotherapeutic process, I think we would have had an excellent outcome, not only for Samantha, but for her parents as well. Children cannot be dropped off at psychotherapy the way they are dropped off at ballet or soccer. Parents need to commit to doing the hard work of confronting their own "ghosts in the nursery," a particularly lyrical phrase coined by child analyst Selma Fraiberg to describe the leftover, unresolved parts of our own past that still influence how we parent in the present. I'm regularly amazed at the capacity of the teens I treat to step up to the plate and take a hard look at themselves and the choices they are making. Parents need to show the same courage.

Samantha's story carries all the hallmarks of many of the unhappy affluent families I see. The polished façade that hides a raft of emotional problems and personal pain. The unequal power relationship between parents, the loneliness, perfectionism, substance abuse, reliance on material goods, and fear that seeking change will result in ruptures and divorce. Am I satisfied with the outcome of this case, a not unusual outcome in my practice? Yes and no. I'm delighted that Samantha was able to get back on track and I'm optimistic that she will be able to lead a happy life. I believe that Samantha will be capable of being a good mother, should she choose to have children, ending the unhappy cycle of her own family. However, I'm also aware of how much suffering could have been avoided in this family had Mom and Dad been able to explore their own troubled past instead of turning to the culture of affluence to ease their pain.

From time to time I run into Samantha's mom. She carries a beautiful leather-bound photo album in her purse and shows me pictures of Samantha at various dance recitals at her small liberal-arts college. She is incredibly proud of her daughter, and in her eyes I often think I catch a glimpse of wistfulness about whether she, too, might have found a way to free herself, either literally or emotionally, from her unhappy situation. Mom was too scared to fight on her own behalf; fortunately, she could fight on Samantha's.

The competing pressures on mothers frequently feel unmanageable. Affluent mothers often say they feel that they have run out of alternatives, that their dilemmas will either be trivialized or they will be called on to change in radical ways that are beyond their capabilities. Most mothers, in most homes, are the emotional heart of the family. We busily tend to the needs of others—our children, our partners, our homes, and our jobs. In the process, we neglect one of the most basic principles of psychology: that a happy child always begins with a mother who has had her own needs reasonably met. To fully appreciate the importance of this tenet, the next, and final, chapter focuses on the necessity of mothers acknowledging and attending to their own needs.

CHAPTER 9

Having Everything Except What We Need Most: The Isolation of Affluent Moms

Having waded through the culture of affluence, child development, parenting styles, and the mistakes we've all made, we now come to the difficult part of this book: being kind and gentle with ourselves in spite of everything. A critical factor in a child's well-being is the serenity of his mother. We need to be compassionate toward ourselves both for the good of our children and for our own good as well.

There are many ways to frame the issues surrounding the disproportionately high rates of emotional problems experienced by children of privilege. We've examined the contributions of pressure, disconnection, and the culture of affluence. We can point to the deadening role of the media, or irrational educational trends that focus on performance instead of learning. Additionally, we can blame drugs, materialism, overwork, or a lack of government support for social programs that prioritize the needs of children and parents. All these factors certainly contribute to why children from affluent homes are troubled. But most of us will find it difficult, in the immediate future, to bring about any major changes in media emphases or social policies. Considering what we *can* affect most immediately, I believe that the critical question to address is: "How do we help affluent mothers to be happier and less troubled themselves?" While I primarily treat teenagers, I know that my constant background question is: "How can I maximize good parenting for this child?" And I know that—not always, but most of the time—I am relying on Mom to effect this change.

Certainly good parenting takes all the resources that both mothers and fathers can muster. But we ignore both our instincts and scientific evidence when we fail to acknowledge the distinctions between mothering and fathering. While children get 50 percent of their genes from their mothers and 50 percent from their fathers, they get their entire prenatal experience in their mothers' bodies. We know that there are positive consequences for the developing child when Mom is in good health and obtains consistent prenatal care, just as there are negative consequences when Mom is depressed, drinks too much, or receives inconsistent prenatal care.

Mothers and fathers do not participate equally in bringing up children. There are many critical areas in child development where a father's impact is great, perhaps none more so than his ability to nurture his wife. And as we've seen, adolescence is a time when fathers can have a particularly great impact on their children's lives, as well as a time when teens often feel more at ease with their fathers than their mothers. But because the responsibility for child rearing falls overwhelmingly on mothers in most homes, it is both our strengths and our weaknesses that are more likely to influence our children's development.[1] *Most* children, at *most* times in their lives, feel closer to their mothers than to their fathers.[2] So it should come as no surprise that research confirms that a child's *best shot* at healthy emotional development depends on his own mother's emotional health.[3] For this reason this chapter is written for mothers and recognizes their unique and critical contribution to raising children.

I know that emphasizing the role of mothers carries with it the risk of being seen as blaming mothers or further burdening them. On the contrary, my hope is that every mother who reads this chapter feels the sense of relief that comes when what we intuitively know to be true is recognized and validated. You are not imagining it when it feels like "It's all up to me." Moms do the lion's share of child rearing, and it's a much tougher job when we're unhappy. Experienced clinicians find an unexpectedly high amount of depression, anxiety, substance abuse, loneliness, and plain old unhappiness among well-to-do mothers. It is critical that we also understand the political, economic, and cultural pressures that have combined to strip American mothers of the infrastructure support common in most of the industrialized world. For a thorough analysis of these larger social issues look at *The Mommy Myth* by Susan Douglas and Meredith Michaels, a well-researched, insightful book that through some alchemy on the part of the authors is at once illuminating, profoundly depressing, and riotously funny.

ACKNOWLEDGING HOW VERY HARD OUR JOB IS

In a maddening paradox, the media, often aided by "experts," idealizes motherhood while it devalues actual mothers. We are regularly scolded and chastised and warned that our smallest mistakes can have negative lifetime consequences for our children. We are put on notice to "get it right"—how to toilet train, how to deal with sibling rivalry, how to make certain our youngsters aren't traumatized by separation—or risk turning out permanently damaged kids. Leafing through parenting magazines one gets the impression that while motherhood is beautiful, mothers themselves are boneheads in need of constant instruction and reassurance.

While parenting magazines may have sporadic vignettes of mothers truly distressed by turbulence at home, they are far more likely to feature various versions of domestic bliss—happy, smiling babies with their beaming mothers. If that's not you at 2:00 in the morning with your impossibly colicky baby, you just haven't mastered mothering yet. Article after article breezily presents the major tasks of parenting: first, the need to learn about developmental milestones, and second, how to be an authoritative parent, warm and loving but with consistent and firm limits. What we rarely hear or read about is how very hard it is to accomplish these tasks and how none of us can (or should) get it all right.

When the popular media portray problems between mothers and children—as in Eminem's *Eight Mile,* for example—the mothers are typically shown as quite disturbed, so that it seems no wonder that the child is troubled—"He's only reacting to his crazy mom." What we see far less often is how parenting adolescents can be an extremely daunting, challenging task even for the relatively "sane" parent. So when we find ourselves struggling with our own adolescents, we end up feeling inadequate.

In reality, the task of parenting presents unexpected challenges on an ongoing, often daily, basis. Each one of us has had moments when every bit of parenting advice we've ever heard has flown out the window in the face of a stubborn two-year-old or a defiant teenager. We've all had lapses in judgment when our children, who typically are bright enough and intuitive enough, attack us in our very weakest spots. Mothers and fathers are not saints; we all come to this job of parenting only partially prepared. Understanding the cross-currents of joy, connection, pride, pain, rejection, loss, and disappointment that parenting inevitably entails should make us more charitable toward ourselves, which in turn will make us more capable of being loving, effective parents.

Parenting adolescents can hit us particularly hard, psychologically. Larry Steinberg, an expert on family-adolescent relationships, has written extensively on this topic.[4] Among various other challenges to parents, he has described the hurt we can suffer at our adolescents' hands. When we have a fight at home with our teenage children, they go to school, get busy with their friends and schoolwork, and don't give it another thought (at least not until they come home). We, on the other hand, obsess throughout the day, chastise and second-guess ourselves about either having been too strict or too lenient.

Among the hardest things about parenting a teenager is the inevitable emotional and physical separation. A colleague tells of the struggles she went through. Her firstborn son and she were simpatico right from the start. She described him as having the soul of a poet, and the mind of a philosopher. As he grew, they took great and obvious pleasure in each other's company. But as he approached the teen years, he became increasing distant and belligerent. Mom, being a psychologist, knew intellectually that he was doing what he was supposed to do: he was trying to separate. She knew too that the need might have been particularly keen for him, because of his strong attachment to his mother. Intellectually, she recognized all this. Emotionally, however, she felt bereft—it was a huge loss. The pain of our children separating from us, after we have been so deeply immersed in their development for years, can be searing.

The various challenges of being a mother are greatly aggravated when we ourselves feel fragile. This can be the result of many things. Being a single parent, or just feeling like one. Not having really close friends to help assure us that we are loved even if our kids are not being particularly loving. Our own neediness, vulnerability, and sense of neglect are all activated when we find ourselves at home alone with an angry child who is hell-bent on punishing and disconnecting from us. There is no quick fix for scenarios like this; either you are willing and capable of enduring your child's anger or you are too depleted to do so. If you find yourself *regularly* too depleted to parent effectively, then you must first turn your attention to yourself before you can begin making better parenting decisions. Our best shot at good parenting comes when we have enough internal resources of our own to make it through tough patches—this means friends, interests, sources of support, clear priorities, and clarity about our own life story.

So how do we get to a point where we can both bask in the gratification *and* tolerate the disconnection that comes with the territory of parenting? First and foremost, we need to identify and attend to our own emotional needs. This is not a selfish preoccupation. It is a realistic acknowledgment that Mom's "self" is critical to the healthy development of her child's "self." A mother's needs must be reasonably met so that she has the capacity to lay aside her own needs, when necessary, for the benefit of her children.

Anyone who is overworked, empty, lonely, or depressed has a harder time functioning than someone who is happy or content. If you've been dying of thirst, you can't share your first glass of water. But if you've had plenty to drink, not only can you share, you can even go without for a bit. Mothers are often called on to "go without for a bit." To the extent that we have been given to, by ourselves and those around us, we are more capable of giving to our children. This has nothing to do with whether we work or not, whether we are married or divorced, whether we have one child or six. The issue here is whether or not we can muster enough love, support, and encouragement inside ourselves to carry on, to maintain perspective, to feel that there is purpose and meaning in our lives. You can't fake happiness. **As we are able to feel generally loved, valued, and connected, so will our children.**

While what I have stressed so far is the fact that happier women make happier mothers, this is not the only reason for women to tend to their own needs. We do ourselves a great disservice when the only reason to feel better is so that we can become better mothers, or wives, or workers. Affluent women are the least likely of any socioeconomic group of unhappy women to seek help for their problems.[5] This is a result of our impossibly high standards, our commitment to never appear either self-absorbed or vulnerable, and our fervent guarding of our privacy, lest the façade of perfection be torn away. Like the Wizard, when Dorothy finally pulls back the curtain, we fear being exposed as imposters. Worries like this engender profound feelings of isolation, feelings that often result in our drinking too much, abusing drugs, and depression. It is time that affluent women consider their own needs as reason enough to get help or fight on their own behalf.

TAKING OUR PROBLEMS SERIOUSLY

Researchers and clinicians have looked at and tried to understand the lives of mothers living in poverty, of single mothers, of adoptive mothers, of lesbian mothers, of working-class and middle-class mothers. Such undertakings have never been considered trivial, as their goal is to alleviate suffering and shed light on how to help the family, the basic unit of society, function more effectively.

We need to cast the same inquiring and empathic eye on the issues faced by financially comfortable mothers. It is both inaccurate and misleading to characterize these mothers' unhappiness as unfounded, neurotic, or selfish. Most of us are loving and generous. We do our best, in spite of intense personal and cultural pressure, to "count our blessings," to show the world how perfect and capable we are, and to hide our vulnerabilities. The particular obstacles and challenges faced by affluent women are real; and no amount of "boo-hoo" trivialization by the media or negative self-talk that scolds "You have nothing to complain about," can change the fact that the personal and social demands made on many affluent mothers are considerable and sometimes overwhelming.

In psychology, there is the concept of the IP, or "identified patient." Often, when one member of a family is brought into therapy, they carry with them the problems of the whole family. A depressed or eating-disordered daughter, or a substance-abusing or rule-breaking son draws attention away from a family system that has gone awry. An alcoholic mother, a bullying father, a bad marriage—these give way to the immediacy of treating a self-destructive kid. While the outcome for the child who is receiving treatment may be good, as we saw in Samantha's case, it is less than optimal if the parents cannot obtain some relief as well. In at least half of my cases, what begins as a therapy for a depressed or acting-out child eventually comes to include a mother who, often encouraged by her child's success, decides that she might also benefit from therapeutic help and support. In many ways, affluent kids have become the IP of their struggling families, their unhappy mothers, and the larger damaged culture. Most of the time it is Mom who calls to make the first appointment for an unhappy child. Why is it so difficult for us to call and make that same appointment for ourselves? Why is help for our children reflexive and natural, while help for our own problems smolders on the back burner for years, if not decades?

THE FEAR OF VULNERABILITY

Affluent moms can be many things: bright, competitive, persistent, protective, interesting, and funny. They are not vulnerable—at least not publicly. Vulnerability is a kind of admission: an admission of hurt feelings, of neediness, of things not going well. This is not the territory affluent moms are comfortable in. We like the high ground, the places that feel secure and capable and accomplished. At PTA meetings, at the gas station, at the florist or the nail salon, even at our social events, our conversations tend to center on our children's accomplishments. There might be some passing comment, in hushed tones, about another mother's kid who was packed off to rehab or picked up for a DUI, but it's never our own kid. In public we shine, and so do our children.

Certainly the fear of appearing vulnerable is not limited to affluent moms. Many people choose not to expose their emotionally tender spots. For many of us, being wary comes from repeated experiences of not having our needs met when we were vulnerable, either as children or as adults. It makes sense to keep our guard up. It helps protect us from disappointment, anger, and sadness.

Somewhere back in our ancestral history it made perfect sense to hide our wounds from our enemies so we wouldn't be clubbed over the head and dragged off to a cave. For women who continue to fear that those around them will exhibit aggression rather than compassion, presenting a "perfect" and formidable front is the best insurance against being exploited and misunderstood. It is also an exhausting and ultimately empty performance. We are human exactly *because* we love and hate, *because* we excel and fail, *because* we are independent and needy. We cannot embrace only our strengths and disregard our weaknesses. Children need to see their mothers being competent, but they also need to see them struggling with challenges. How else does a child come to see that challenges, even failures, are a part of life? Moms who appropriately share some of their difficulties can help model resilience, active approaches to problem solving, and compassion for oneself.

Try to remember a time in your own childhood when you felt afraid and unprotected. Perhaps it was the first time you were left alone in your house and every noise and creak made you jump. Remember the sound of your parents' key in the door and the relief that flooded you when you knew you were safe. Or perhaps you remember your first broken heart when you were young, and how everyone made light of it, except for one dear person who took your grief and your heartache seriously and quietly stroked your hair while you sobbed into your pillow. We were all once very vulnerable, just as our children are now. Mothers who reflexively put up a "good front," who deny the hurt or sadness or depression that is so clearly seen by their children miss the opportunity to teach that while life isn't always fair, pain is always eased by love and connection.

Children are exquisitely tuned to their mother's state of mind. We never fool our children, regardless of how convinced we are that "the children don't know a thing." A mother's mental state is a child's lifeline, and to the extent that a mother works overtime to hide her unhappy feelings, her child has to work that much harder at making sure that Mom is okay. Kids do this in seemingly adaptive ways: they study and become good students, hoping to see Mom brighten because of their accomplishments; and in maladaptive ways: they act out and try to divert Mom from her unhappiness. Either way, they expend too much energy trying to further their mother's cause and too little energy furthering their own. The work of childhood and adolescence is growing yourself, not your parent.

A mother sits in my office. She is a pillar of the community, articulate and personable, well-coiffed and well-dressed. She has a good marriage and two sweet, if quiet and tentative, young children. She comes to see me week after week, sitting forward on the couch, her back ramrod straight, filling me in on the incidental details of her life. She constantly reminds us both how "blessed" she is. I have no idea why she is coming to see me, but have grown accustomed to feeling that way in the early stages of treatment with some of the affluent women I treat. I know I have a long wait. I tell myself I should be thankful for this "easy" hour in my difficult day, but instead find myself feeling restless and disconnected. I wonder what it's like to be one of her children. In spite of her well-honed social skills, my office feels sad and lifeless as soon as she walks into it.

One day, out of desperation, I move out of my chair and sit next to her on the couch. I take a chance, look directly into her eyes, and tell her I feel she has come to see me for reasons that are terribly hard to talk about. I feel sad when I'm with her and I think it's because she is very sad. She is absolutely startled and I wonder if I've said too much. I stop talking, but stay next to her on the couch. At first she doesn't move, but slowly her hands begin to shake and her eyes dart back and forth between the floor and mine. In a low, almost mechanical voice, she begins to tell me her story. How at twelve her older brother sexually abused her, and how her own mother refused to believe her, calling her a whore and a slut. A good student, she buried herself in schoolwork, becoming an outstanding student, even as the abuse continued over three years, until her brother finally left for college. She doesn't cry. I can feel tears sting my eyes.

For the next four months this woman lies on my couch, wrapped in the blanket I keep there, sharing the secrets she has kept from everyone, including her husband, and allowing me to bring her tea and take care of her. She can't believe that she will ever feel better; she worries that her husband will leave or her children will act out. Interestingly, aside from the first week or two after what she calls her "nervous breakdown," she continues to go about her business, running the school board and showing up for her multiple volunteer jobs. Little by little she reveals parts of her history to her husband and parts of herself to her children. Hell doesn't freeze, her husband doesn't leave, and her children start sharing bits and pieces of their own lives.

This mother, like many of the women I see, had decided that the cost of vulnerability was too great. Not having a mother she could rely on, she came to the logical but unfortunate conclusion that she was better off not relying on anyone. Bright and capable, she developed the hardworking, organized parts of herself that allowed her to stay busy in the world, while shutting down her emotional life. Little by little, she came to see that while she did not have control over her early traumas, she did have choices as an adult, and that by choosing to be "strong" over vulnerable she had simply papered over the fragile walls of her childhood.

In the process of shutting herself down, she could see the beginning of the same pattern in her cautious and quiet children. Like most mothers, when push comes to shove about our children's emotional health, we will do whatever it takes to ensure that our children suffer less hurt and abandonment than we did. I learned something very important from this woman. Sometimes we have to get out of our chair, look a patient (or a spouse, or a friend, or a child) in the eye, and say out loud that something is wrong and we want to help. Alternatively, sometimes we have to say out loud that we need help. Extending a hand or asking for help can make us feel vulnerable. The friend may be puzzled, the husband dismissive, the child defiant, the patient angry. But go back to your own life, remember the times when you couldn't accept a helping hand, and then remember the times when one saved you.

THE RISKS OF STAYING UNHAPPY

For those of us struggling with unhappiness over extended periods of time, it is critical to get help—for our own sake as well as our children's. One of the most well-researched aspects of parent-child relationships is the effect of depression on child development. The impact of parental depression on children is particularly strong when the depressed parent is Mom. In a review of ten years of studies on the effects of parental depression on child development, researchers have come up with the following conclusions:[6]

1. Depressed mothers are less able to be sensitive and responsive to their children, resulting in less secure attachments. This is particularly damaging for infants and young children.

2. When a parent suffers from depression, his or her child has a 61 percent chance of developing a psychiatric disorder during childhood or adolescence. This is four times the rate of kids who do not have a depressed parent.

3. When a child or adolescent has a depressed mother, that child has a 45 percent chance of developing depression, as compared to 11 percent for children who do not have a depressed mother.

4. Maternal depression poses a substantially higher risk for adolescent depression in girls than in boys.[7]

5. Marital conflict is a major contributor to depression, particularly in mothers.

6. Depressed mothers tend to be irritable and negative with their children. They are often critical. Persistent maternal criticism leads to a host of problems in their children, including substance abuse and conduct disorders.

While these statistics are bound to be disturbing, particularly if you are a parent who suffers from depression, it is important to put them in context and understand how you can lessen the impact of your depression on your child. **First and foremost, a parent who currently suffers from untreated depression needs help.** Unfortunately, the reluctance to expose vulnerabilities can extend even to the confidentiality of the therapist's office. Depression is tough to hide though, and most of the teens I see are excellent diagnosticians when it comes to identifying their parents' depression. Like the children of alcoholic parents, who, as they approach their house after school, become adept at anticipating what they will find there, simply by noticing if the curtains are open or drawn, the children of depressed parents quickly learn how much "grayness" is in the house in the first moment or two of interaction. "Gray" is a term used by several of my astute adolescent patients to capture the lack of energy and interest of a depressed parent. When the house feels very "gray," these kids make a quick exit, either out the door or into their rooms, which helps protect them emotionally but leaves their parent feeling even more miserable and abandoned.

Depression has a genetic component, which makes it all the more critical for parents who are suffering from depression to do what they can to ensure that their children are at the least risk possible. Remember that the healthy sense of self that we want so desperately for our children must first exist in ourselves. Importantly, it is only current depression in parents that seems to have such a negative impact on children. If you were depressed earlier in life and received appropriate treatment, your past depression is unlikely to impact your child. It is your current, day-to-day behavior with your child that is critical.[8] We cannot parent effectively when we are depressed, and *equally important,* we cannot live our own lives with enthusiasm and purpose. With the advances in treatment of depression, medication, psychotherapy, and cognitive-behavioral therapy, the chances of a good treatment outcome for depression are high.

TEND AND BEFRIEND:
THE CRITICAL IMPORTANCE
OF FRIENDSHIPS

Do you remember the last time someone asked, "Do you want to be friends?" It was probably in grade school and you probably felt pretty good about the question. Now that we've grown into independent, highly capable, and privileged adults, it's a question we don't hear much anymore, nor are we likely to pose it. As a result, many of us feel isolated, in spite of our busy lives.

Psychologists have long written about the importance of strong, intimate relationships for women and the benefits of connectedness when dealing with problems.[9] Recently, there has been evidence that in response to threats or stress, women cope by gravitating toward others. The pattern they show is called "tend and befriend"—as opposed to "fight or flight," which is more characteristic of men. Tending involves nurturing activities designed to protect children and reduce their distress; befriending is the creation and maintenance of friendships. Both animal and human studies have shown the protective effects, for females experiencing stress, of affiliation with groups of other females.[10]

In *Crash*, a 2005 movie that deals with stereotypes and prejudice, a wealthy, self-centered woman finds that while expensive material things surround her, she has absolutely no friends she can depend on in a pinch. At the end of the movie, she sobs in the arms of her Hispanic housekeeper, "You're the only real friend I have." Painful as this moment is in the movie, it is far more painful in real life. There are few things less tolerable than isolation—and this is especially true for women. All cultures have rituals that include the community for major life events—births, deaths, marriages, coming of age—because life without connection and support is unthinkable. Yet many affluent women soldier on alone, desperate for connection and terribly tentative about "making the first move" toward connection, friendship, and, ultimately, intimacy. Many of us, caught in the press of child rearing, marriage, and work, have forgotten how to make friends. While we may give the appearance of having many friends—being busy, working on committees, or having coffee with coworkers and acquaintances—this is not the same as having a good friend, as having a best friend.

The importance of connection and social support for ourselves cannot be stressed enough. But how exactly does one create a community, or even close friendships when it's all we can do to keep up with the demands that are already on us? There is, of course, a question of priorities that needs to be acknowledged. If we are lonely enough, disconnected enough, isolated enough, and really believe the premise that we wither without strong connections, then we will find the time. The bigger issue is how difficult it can be to put ourselves out there, to risk rejection, to appear needy, but nevertheless to ask: "Do you want to be my friend?" If we want to be seen, then we have to show ourselves.

The women who have undertaken this task have made it clear to me that it is best accomplished by taking "baby steps." One does not go out and ask anyone and everyone to "be friends."

Rather, it makes sense to think about one or two women who might be a good match for you and then to have lunch or dinner or coffee or a walk. What is critical is that we feel we can open our hearts enough to take some risks in these contacts. This means that the entire walk is not spent talking about what a great athlete your youngest is, or how many AP classes your oldest is taking. It means, at a pace that feels reasonable to you, opening up about *your* internal life. Most people appreciate, even feel flattered, when someone reaches out to them.

There are no guarantees of course, and you may also bump into rejection as you pursue more emotionally open relationships. You will win some and lose others. But if you don't try, you can't win any. It helps if you feel good enough about yourself that an unreturned phone call or an unresponsive lunch date doesn't throw you into a tizzy. Like any skill, the more you practice approaching people openly and honestly, the more you cultivate deep and meaningful friendships, the easier it gets.

Having strong friendships has been found to be predictive of everything from general well-being to increased longevity. These friendships are mandatory for us as we struggle with the isolation that often comes as part of the territory of affluence and the multiple demands that are placed on us during the child-rearing years. Reaching out means we give, but it also means we get. Competent people like goals: try to connect with someone you like every day. *Guard against being too easily disappointed, it's a way of maintaining distance.* Every time you reach out and give a little or get a little you are fortifying yourself, which in turn helps to fortify your children. Remember that warmth protects child development; but it protects our own development as well.

If this prescription for reaching out to others seems overwhelming or too threatening, then think about therapy. It's very important to find a therapist who makes you feel comfortable and accepted, not judged. Don't worry about "hurting the therapist's feelings," if he or she is not the right one for you. Believe me, we are just as anxious to have a good match as you are. Shop around until you find a therapist who feels right to you. In the meantime, continue taking little steps, no matter how small, to connect with others.

THE DISTRACTION OF THE WORK DEBATE

The debate about whether or not a mother's work status affects her child's emotional development has been around for decades. Certainly the popular press seems to feature a never-ending stream of stories about the pros and cons of being a working mother and its impact on child development. It had been a long time since I'd looked at the research on mother's work, childcare, and child development. I knew that the quality of childcare was extremely important, but for the most part, affluent women can afford the type of daycare/childcare that ensures consistency, affection, and attention. I had only dim memories of research on how children were affected by having a working mother; the one finding I remembered clearly was the quirky fact that children with working mothers were more likely to be ambidextrous! I looked forward to what I assumed would be a lively debate about how children are affected by their mother's choice to work outside the home. I was surprised (and, as a working mother, frankly relieved) to find that research has consistently found that a mother's work status has no impact on her child's adjustment. Of course this doesn't speak for any particular mother or family. Still, it was reassuring to find that social science research spoke with one voice in debunking the myth that a mother's work status is an important variable in her child's emotional development.[11]

There is something counterintuitive about this finding. After all, aren't stay-at-home moms more available to their children? And isn't availability a positive factor in parent-child relationships? Why would there be no impact on child development if Mom were home 100 percent of the time, versus 50 percent or 25 percent?

There probably would be a difference if time alone were the variable that predicted healthy child development. But there is nothing to suggest that time in and of itself is what is beneficial to children.

What is beneficial is time that is spent in healthy and satisfying inter-action. Children's needs shift as they grow, but what remains constant is the benefit of having a mother who is free enough from distress herself to be able to "tune in" to her child's needs. An unhappy stay-at-home mom is far less likely to nurture healthy child development than a happy mom who works full-time.

When talking about working moms versus stay-at-home moms, there is often less, rather than more, that meets the eye. It is very difficult to define either the "typical" stay-at-home mom or the "typical" working mom. Working moms encompass everything from the mother who is a teacher's aide two days a week to the career mom who puts in a seventy-hour plus workweek. Stay-at-home moms can spend a lot of time playing tennis and lunching, or they can run the PTA the local arts council, and be a volunteer at one of dozens of community agencies. Children's complaints rarely match up with their mother's work status. "I wish my mom would get a hobby besides me," comes from a teenager whose mother works a full-time-job. "My mother always seems to disappear when I need her," comes from a preteen whose mother prides herself on being a stay-at-home mom. Mother's have enough to worry about without fretting about whether or not working outside the home is damaging to their child's emotional development. It isn't, as long as we are able to maintain a satisfying balance in our own lives.

Regardless of work status, most moms worry about pretty much the same things. They also feel guilty about pretty much the same things. They worry about their children's safety. They worry about access to pornography on the Internet, sexual activity, drugs and alcohol, and the "wrong" peer group. They feel guilty about not doing enough. They feel guilty when they have interests and passions other than their children. They worry *and* feel guilty about whether they are giving their children too much freedom, involvement, money and material goods, or, alternately, not enough of these things. Whether a mother works or not, worry and guilt appear to be equal-opportunity employers.

While there are many similarities in the worries and challenges faced by mothers whether they work outside the home or not, it would be naïve not to acknowledge the differences as well. Mothers who choose to work outside the home, particularly mothers with careers, are constantly juggling the competing demands of family and work. Skip the report that's due the next day in order to make it to the soccer finals or skip the game? As most career moms know, the solution is usually to go to the game and then stay up half the night writing the report. Exhaustion becomes our constant companion. While many of us love our work, there is a nagging suspicion that we're not doing a very good job of balancing career, family, and personal needs. When something has to give, it's usually our own needs, heightening our feelings of isolation, resentment, and guilt. The popular fantasy that women can "have it all"—family, career, money, and opportunity—takes on a disturbing, rather than a rewarding, cast, as ambitious women with high expectations of themselves and others find themselves not happy, but overwhelmed. Retreating further into work accelerates family problems, while backing off from work limits opportunities for advancement. Most of the women I know—whether within my practice or among my friends and colleagues—are at "loose ends" as to how to make the various parts of their lives, which are individually rewarding, into a rewarding whole.

Mothers who choose to stay home and raise their families face a different set of challenges. These are the neighborhood "go-to" moms. At the beginning of every year, faced with a packet of papers from my children's school, I would have to list a "contact person" in case I could not be reached in an emergency. I would choose one of the stay-at-home moms in the neighborhood. So did every other working mother. Stay-at-home moms end up picking up the sick children of working moms from school, shuttling them to after-school activities, and fielding a host of weekly questions about when soccer tryouts are being held, and what time is back-to-school night for those of us unable to effectively coordinate the school calendar and our Palm Pilot. Volunteerism is high among homemakers, and many of these women work as many hours driving on field trips, working on school committees, or involved with philanthropic endeavors as those mothers who work outside the home.

Many women who gave up careers of their own find that they miss the camaraderie, stimulation, and appreciation they once felt at work. Many plan on returning to work when their children are older. But most of the women I've spoken with who have made the decision to stay home and be "full-time" moms are happy with their decision, particularly when their children are young. They occasionally feel derided by working moms, or ignored by the media, which tend to focus on the problems of working mothers. A fast click on Amazon.com shows that there are exactly twice as many books under "working mothers" as there are under "stay-at-home mothers." This may be because working mothers are more conflicted and guilty about their dual roles and so buy more books, or it may simply reflect the fact that even in well-to-do communities the majority of women work outside the home.

We are focused on the wrong question when we ask, "Should mothers work outside the home?" The right question is: "How do we find the balance between our children's needs and our own needs so that we can be both effective mothers and fulfilled, happy women?" Clearly, these two sets of needs are not mutually exclusive; they can be tightly bound to each other. The first question is easily answered. Yes, mothers should work if they want to, if their work is fulfilling and nourishes their sense of self. They should work if the extra income they provide allows for enriching educational and life experiences that they consider important for themselves and their children. The second question, however, is far more complex.

CHOOSING WHAT WE CAN LIVE WITH

One of the women I see in my practice is the CFO of a large well-known corporation. Marilyn is capable, in high demand, and overworked to the gills. She travels an average of two days a week, often jetting to London or Hong Kong for a single meeting. In the meantime, her household is in shambles. Her adolescent son is starting to abuse drugs, and her preteen daughter goes to school looking like a hooker. A succession of housekeepers has not been able to stem the tide of difficulties in this family. Dad also works a high-pressure job. Both parents are overly permissive, feeling that the children "get so little attention" that whatever opportunities or gifts they can provide are warranted. Marilyn and her husband spend little time together, reserving whatever bit of energy is left at the end of the day for a few minutes with the children. The kids, for their part, are demanding and self-centered. This case, distinguished only by the intensity of mom's work schedule, hit close to home, reminding me of a time when I was not yet able to find a balance in my own life.

Soon after my third son was born, when my practice was full and my books on kids and the media kept me busy with a steady stream of speaking engagements, I noticed that instead of being pleased with my success, I was becoming edgy and unhappy. My two older boys, typically quite easy, were becoming increasingly demanding, and I seemed to be giving in to an assortment of unreasonable requests. With no extended family to rely on, married to a busy surgeon, trying to juggle the demands of being a psychologist, a writer, and raising three children, too busy to cultivate friendships and too exhausted to participate in either civic or religious activities, I knew that I would be unable to sustain myself or my family without some major realignment.

I moved my office to my home and cut my practice in half. I don't mean to make this sound like an easy decision. It wasn't, and it involved plenty of strife between my husband and myself about the uneven distribution of parenting responsibilities in our house. In the end I decided that whatever my "position" might be, my kids mattered more. I chose an intact marriage and being a more relaxed mother over professional advancement. I believe I made the right choice, both for my children and for myself *at that time*. Was it a perfect solution? Not at all. But it solved more problems than it created; and it allowed me to feel I was doing a pretty good job at most things, as opposed to a pretty lousy job of everything. It was *work-*

able for me. Not ideal, not what I had imagined, but workable nonetheless. Instead of feeling constantly fragmented, I felt reasonably intact. The reason our own "intactness" is so crucial is exactly because we are called on to forgo parts of our own lives for the benefit of our children. This self-sacrifice began the moment we looked down at our newborn and knew that we would lay down our lives for theirs in a heartbeat. While the form and intensity of this self-sacrifice lessens as our children grow, we have, in one form or another, gone to Disneyland instead of Paris, bought a minivan instead of a sports car, and given up good movies and better novels for back-to-school nights and basketball games.

I learned from that experience that part of being a mother and part of being a grown-up has to do with being clear about priorities and understanding that all decisions involve taking one road and forgoing another. Fortunately, I happen to be passionate about a field in which working part-time is rather easy to do. Now, since two of my three children have grown and left home, I find that I can return to the intellectual pursuits I treasure without anxiety or guilt, or exhaustion for that matter. Do I feel I lost some time professionally? Maybe a little, but not much. If anything, now that my children are almost grown, I mostly regret the time I wasn't around. I also need to remind myself that it's easy to romanticize the past, to forget about periods of boredom and frustration that nearly drove me out of my mind. But I understand that there are no perfect solutions, that we have to learn what causes us the *most* pain, and the *most* gratification, and make our decisions accordingly. What worked best for me might not work at all for some women, or might not be possible for others. The decisions that we have to make about work and children are among the toughest decisions we will ever face.

Marilyn's work did not allow her the luxury of working part-time. For many professional women, taking themselves out of their careers, even temporarily, results in an inability, perceived or real, to reestablish themselves. For these women, the most productive and ambitious years of their career come at the same time as they are raising children. Addressing the inadequacies of a society that refuses to put resources into building institutional structures that would enable women to more effectively combine work and motherhood is the subject of another book. In the meantime, women are forced on a day-to-day basis to make choices that have taken many of us by surprise.

Growing up along with the feminist movement, all doors seemed open, and we are shocked that our husbands aren't full participants, that society has not prioritized childcare, and that the glass ceiling is real, despite all our sacrifices. Certainly women's choices are greater than they once were, but choice also creates conflict about competing roles. And the unfortunate ascendancy of the super-mom myth suggests that now we should excel at two jobs, not just one.

In the end, Marilyn decided to reevaluate her work schedule. She knew that it was her demanding travel schedule that was taking the greatest toll on her family, and so she took an interesting if slightly less prestigious job that entailed far less travel. Unlike my part-time schedule, Marilyn continued to work full-time, but she eliminated the greatest stressor in her family—her frequent absences. Dad was brought into the picture, limits and consequences were set for their acting-out teenagers; Mom and Dad were encouraged to rediscover their own relationship; and over time, quite a bit of time actually, their household settled down. Children who have never been expected to wash dishes, make beds, or rake leaves do not take to such new requirements gracefully. Mothers who have been staggering from day to day take a while to slow down and return to the job of cultivating their own equilibrium while helping their children learn self-control and responsibility. Withered marriages need tending before they can sprout again.

Marilyn and I still have sessions here and there. We mostly talk about the kinds of inevitable problems that come up for ambitious mothers who are still raising children. D.W. Winnicott coined the term the "good enough mother." It's an important tonic for women who tend not only to be perfectionists but who expect everything to fall into place with the appearance of minimal effort. Life simply isn't like that. The old saying "Never let 'em see you sweat" needs to be exposed as inauthentic and unreasonable. We do sweat, and too often we sweat alone. While financially comfortable women can afford nannies to help with the kids and housekeepers to help with the house, we cannot buy the kind of camaraderie and friendship that is necessary to sustain us through the many years of being tugged in so many different directions.

Motherhood as we know it today is a unique invention of an affluent society. Few women in the world are so isolated, so cut off from the easy back-and-forth of communal relations, as financially comfortable American mothers. While we love our children madly, truth be told, many of us have problems with parts of motherhood, with the distance from our own families, with the preponderance of responsibility for child rearing, and with the lack of connection to others who share our joys, our problems, and our values. There was a time in this country, a time that still exists in much of the world, where an extended family and a community shared the responsibilities of child rearing. Children did not always demand the full time and attention of their mothers. Mothers were able to go about a variety of tasks—cooking, cleaning, sewing, gardening, laundering, and socializing, to name a few—without the gnawing worry that somehow the needs of their children were not being adequately met.

Children thrive best when their mothers take care of themselves as well as their children. Keep in mind that when the flight attendant goes over emergency procedures, she instructs you to "Put your own mask on first." If *you* can't breathe you can't effectively help anyone else. **Be absolutely certain that you value your own growth and development.** Make sure that there is room in your life for the things that give you pleasure outside of the family. That could be your work or your friends, a creative pursuit or connection with nature. Interests and passions help fill you up, allowing you to bring a revitalized, giving, and satisfied mother back into the family. Over and over in my office, teenage girls beg me to help their mothers "get a life."

It astounds me that we can find time weekend after weekend to travel to some distant site, spend the entire time watching our child play in one more soccer, baseball, or basketball tournament, and yet can never find the time to spend a weekend away with girlfriends, free to kick back, brainstorm and bask in the congeniality that women have historically enjoyed with each other. Marriages flounder as parents divvy up the job of being at one child's soccer game and another's piano recital, forgetting the fact that the best gift you can give your children is a good marriage.

This is what I have learned from over fifty years of life—twenty-five years of mothering and twenty-four years of being a psychologist: that life can be difficult, that we all have been injured, neglected, "unseen," or missed in some ways. These experiences are simply part of living, part of the fact that the group, or the tribe, or the family has many things to take care of, and the needs of children are just one of these things. As a result, parents cannot be perfectly tuned to the needs of their children. The notion of a perfect mother is a childhood fantasy—one we would all do well to give up. None of us had perfect mothers, just as we cannot be perfect mothers. In spite of this, generations move forward and children manage to grow up and have children of their own. There is no point in being angry or bitter about what you didn't get. We cannot change our past. We will always carry around the disappointments from our own childhood. While the world, our children, our husbands, our friends cannot heal all our wounds, we can be compassionate toward ourselves.

Our privileged children, the ones we adore and work overtime for, are experiencing levels of emotional distress never before documented by researchers in child development. These problems are not likely to "work themselves out"; depression in adolescence predicts depression in adulthood, substance abuse predicts a dark and uncertain future, anxiety disorders severely compromise the quality of life. While the causes of any epidemic are complex and often hard to disentangle, our love, our unflinching honesty about our own strengths and weaknesses, and our willingness to consider the value of parenting from warmth and acceptance instead of pressure and criticism can help our children return to a healthier childhood and adolescence. When we protect our children from excessive control, outsized competition, and persistent academic pressure, and choose instead to commit to nurturing them with warmth, clear limits, firm consequences, and a delight in their potential and uniqueness, then our children are free to return to their essential task—the development of a sense of self, sufficiently robust to weather the inevitable ups and downs of a lifetime. We must love and protect our own development with the same zeal and seriousness of purpose that we bring to the protection of our children.

All of us—mothers, fathers, children, adolescents, and young adults—yearn to be loved for who we are, not just for what we do. Make certain that your children know every day how much they are loved, not for their grades, honors, or awards but for their striving to be independent, capable, good, and loving people. We need to be certain that our emphasis is on those things that have been shown to contribute to healthy self-development: encouraging autonomy and self-management skills, valuing relationships and reciprocity, allowing space for the development of self-efficacy, and being able to truly see, truly appreciate, and truly love the child who stands in front of us. If we can keep our sights properly focused on what really matters, and not buy into the destructive values of the "culture of affluence," we can begin to bring down the shocking and unacceptable levels of emotional suffering documented in our privileged children.

ACKNOWLEDGMENTS

No one writes a book alone. Through the swirl of patients, family, friends, colleagues, and researchers a book begins to take shape. This is not false modesty, but rather the reality of what happens when one is alone night after night at a computer, with the tearful admission of a patient or the insightful comment of a colleague as companions in the writing process. So my first acknowledgment is to all of the above who have shared their thoughts, concerns, ideas, and insights with me. Thank you.

In particular, the shape and substance of much of this book grew in the crucible of my relationship with Suniya Luthar, Chair of the Department of Clinical and Developmental Psychology at Columbia University's Teachers College. In addition to being one of the most highly regarded researchers in the fields of childhood resilience, Dr. Luthar is also at the vanguard of exploring the relationship between economic status and emotional development. An extraordinary scientist, she is at heart an indefatigable teacher. Her willingness to share with me her thoughts and insights as well as her research gave both life and gravitas to this book. Her empathy and thoughtfulness about the dilemmas faced by affluent moms profoundly informed the final chapter of this book.

Other researchers who were generous in sharing their thoughts and their work include Diana Baumrind, Mary Main, Edward Deci, Richard Ryan, Brian Barber, Joseph Allen, James Youniss, Clyde Hertzman, and Roy Baumeister. Special thanks to Tim Kasser for his availability and generosity. I'm also grateful to Elliott Stein and David Goldman, M.D., neuroscientists from the National Institutes of Health, for keeping me humble and helping me understand the wonder and complexity of the human brain.

To Richard A. Lannon, who has helped me navigate through the complexities of the self, thank you for your consistent generosity and unwavering and ultimately contagious conviction, that it is love and connection that have the power to heal and give meaning to our lives.

To my agent, Eric Simonoff, thank you for your unflagging faith in my abilities, your wit, and your willing and spirited sharing of ideas. It is a privilege to work with you. And to his ever kind and patient assistant, Eadie Klemm, thanks once again for the sympathetic ear.

To Gail Winston, my smart, wise, and patient editor at HarperCollins. Thank you for your faith in this project. And thank you for your unflappable patience in helping a global-thinking clinician learn that while global may be the way to think, linear is the way to write. To her assistants, Katherine Hill and Annie Weissman, and my publicist, Erin Cox, thank you for your enthusiasm, attention to detail, and creativity. To Ed Cohen, thank you for your meticulous copy-editing and your gentle reminders that periods, commas, and semi-colons are not, in fact, interchangeable. To Jeanette Sawyer, who somehow managed to clean up the scrawled citations I was too carried away to note properly, thank you for your hard work. And to Scott Wood, who rescued me over and over from a temperamental computer at all hours of the night, thank you for your being a skilled and patient night owl.

Special thanks to the ever gracious Merla Zellerbach, who reminded me that I was loved, and that my friends would actually be there at the end of this long and time-consuming process. And they were—thank you, Sharon, Judy, Lori, Bonnie, Maggie, Susan, Phyllis, and David. Special love and thanks to Ann Buscho, who, in addition to being a best buddy is also an insightful and available collaborator. To my dear friend DeeDee Epp, who fought a good fight and lost during the time I was writing—I miss you every day.

Thank you, Margarita, for the endless supply of coffee, for feeding me at whim, for taking care of the kids, and for tolerating the sound of my keyboard night after night until three or four in the morning. And to my mother, Edith Levine, who shared this project with me from the moment of acceptance to the exhale of completion, thank you for your unflagging love, support, and good cheer. To my dad, Louis Levine, who has never left me in spirit and who still guides my heart and my hand, I hope I've done you proud.

No psychologist can ever thank their patients enough for the privilege of being allowed access to their hearts and minds. With my office cluttered with drafts and my enthusiasm for this project spilling over, each and every one of them provided insights, examples, and encouragement. While their identities have been obscured, their contributions have not.

As this book grew from an interest to a preoccupation to an obsession, it was my family—my husband, Lee Schwartz, and our three children, Loren, Michael, and Jeremy—who bore the brunt of a wife and mother who could talk of nothing but this project. I owe you guys big time. Loren, Michael, and Jeremy, who keep me laughing and delighted, and Lee, my biggest booster and a terrific editor to boot—your love, support, and tolerance for this project is a big part of its realization. I can't imagine my life without the richness and joy that you have all brought me.

NOTES

CHAPTER 1 · The Paradox of Privilege

1. Maguire, K., & A.L. Pastore, eds. (1996), *Sourcebook of Criminal Justice Statistics 1995* (Washington, D.C.: U.S. Government Printing Office). See also U.S. Public Health Service (1999), *The Surgeon General's Call to Action to Prevent Suicide.* (Washington, D.C.: Department of Health and Human Services).
2. Grolnick, W.S. (2003), *The Psychology of Parental Control: How Well-Meant Parenting Backfires* (Mahwah, NJ: Lawrence Erlbaum Associates), p. 12.
3. Harter, S., et al. (1996), "A model of the effects of perceived parent and peer support on adolescent false self behavior," *Child Development, 67* (2), 360–74.
4. Arora, R., & L. Saad, (March 10, 2005), "Marketing to mass affluent women—They're smart, educated, and have considerable discretionary income. How should you target this powerful group?" *Gallup Management Journal,* available at: http://gmj.gallup.com/content/Default.asp?ci=15196&pg=2

CHAPTER 2 · The Not-So-Hidden Mental Health Epidemic Among Privileged Youth

1. Luthar, S. S. (1999), *Poverty and Children's Adjustment* (Newbury Park, CA: Sage). See also McLoyd, V.C. (1998), "Socioeconomic disadvantage and child development," *American Psychologist 53,* 185–204.
2. Luthar, S.S., & C. Sexton, (2005), "The high price of affluence," in R. Kail, ed., *Advances in Child Development* (San Diego, CA: Academic Press).
3. Csikszentmihalyi, M., & B. Schneider (2000), *Becoming Adult: How Teenagers Prepare for the World of Work* (New York: Basic Books).
4. Luthar, S.S., & S.J. Latendresse, (2005), "Comparable 'risks' at the SES extremes: Pre-adolescents' perceptions of parenting," *Development and Psychopathology 17,* 207–30.

5. Luthar & Sexton, (2005).

6. Luthar, S.S., & K. D'Avanzo, (1999), "Contextual factors in substance use: A study of suburban and inner-city adolescents," *Development and Psychopathology 11*, 845–67.

7. Becker, B.E., & S.S. Luthar, (in press), "Peer-perceived admiration and social preference: Contextual correlates of positive peer regard among suburban and urban adolescents," *Journal of Research on Adolescence*.

8. Luthar & Sexton (2005); see also Walters, E., & K. Kendler, (1995), "Anorexia nervosa and anorexic-like syndromes in a population based female twin sample," *American Journal of Psychiatry 152*, 64–75.

9. Price, D. (2004), *Feast or Famine: The Etiology and Treatment of Eating Disorders*, Continuing EdCourses.Net.

10. Luthar, S.S., & B. Becker, (2002), "Privileged but pressured? A study of affluent youth," *Child Development 73*, 1593–1610.

11. Ibid.

12. Luthar, & D'Avanzo, (1999).

13. Gilligan, C. (1982), *In a Different Voice: Psychological Theory and Women's Development* (Cambridge: Harvard University Press). See also Pipher, M. (1995), *Reviving Ophelia* (New York: Ballantine Books).

14. S.S. Luthar and L. W. Tell (2005), "Exploring the relationships between achievement pressures, family dynamics, and psychopathology in a private urban high school," (poster submitted for 2006 meetings of the Society for Research on Adolescence).

15. Last, J. (2001), *A Dictionary of Epidemiology*, 4th ed. (New York: Oxford University Press).

16. Luthar & Sexton, (2005).

17. Clark, C., & H. Mokros, (1993), "Depression and suicidal behavior," in Tolan, P. & B. Cohler, eds., *Handbook of Clinical Research and Practice with Adolescents* (New York: John Wiley and Sons), p. 342.

18. Price, (2004).

19. Fitzgerald, J. (Nov. 13, 2002), "Study links teen drinking pressure," *Associated Press Online*.

20. Prisching, J., (May 7, 2003), "Powder puff hazing turns ugly," *USA Today Online*.

21. www.pbs.org/wgbh/pages/frontline/shows/georgia/outbreak

22. Galen, B.R., & S.S. Luthar, (2005), "Negative behaviors linked with middle schoolers' popularity: A three-year longitudinal study," manuscript submitted for publication.

23. Dishion, T. J., J. McCord, & F. Poulin, (1999), "When interventions harm: Peer groups and problem behavior," *American Psychologist 54*, 755–64.

24. Scaramella, L.V., et al. (2002), "Evaluation of a social contextual model

of delinquency: A cross-study replication," *Child Development* 73, 175–95.

25. Evans, D.L., et al. (2005), *Treating and Preventing Adolescent Mental Health Disorders* (New York: Oxford University Press).

26. Ibid.

27. Montoya, A.G., et al. (2002), "Long-term neuropsychiatric consequences of 'ecstasy' (MDMA): A review," *Harvard Review of Psychiatry* 10, 212–20.

28. Evans, et al. (2005)

29. Puura, K., et al. (1998), "Children with symptoms of depression—What do adults see?" *Journal of Child Psychology & Psychiatry & Allied Disciplines* 39, 577–85.

30. Luthar, S.S. (2003), "The culture of affluence: Psychological costs of material wealth." *Child Development*, 74, 1581–93.

31. Luthar, S.S., & S.J. Latendresse (2005), "Children of the affluent: Challenges to well-being," *Current Directions in Psychological Science* 14, 49–53.

32. Ablard, L.E., & W.D. Parker (1997), "Parents' achievement goals and perfectionism in their academically talented children." *Journal of Youth & Adolescence* 26, 651–67; see also Mukhopadhyay, P., & J. Kumar (1999), "Academic pressure: Its impact on the mental health of children," *Social Science International* 15, 39–45.

33. Weisse, D.E. (1990), "Gifted adolescents and suicide," *School Counselor* 37, 351–58; see also Farrell, D.M. (1989), "Suicide among gifted students," *Roeper Review* 11, 134–39.

34. Blatt, S.J. (1995), "The destructiveness of perfectionism," *American Psychologist* 50 (12), 1003–20.

35. Luthar, & Latendresse (2005).

36. Hochschild, A.R., & A. Machung (2003), *The Second Shift* (New York: Penguin Books).

37. "White House Conference on Teenagers: Raising Responsible and Resourceful Youth," available at: http://www.whitehouse.gov/WH/EOP/ First_Lady/html/teens/transcript.html. See also Kohn, A. (1999), *Punished by Rewards* (Boston: Houghton Mifflin).

38. LeBeau, J. (1998), "The 'silver spoon' syndrome in the super rich: The pathologic link of affluence and narcissism in family systems," *American Journal of Psychotherapy* 21, 425–36.

39. Csikszentmihalyi, M., & B. Schneider (2000), *Becoming Adult: How Teenagers Prepare for the World of Work* (New York: Basic Books).

40. Latendresse, S.J., & S.S. Luthar, "Perceptions of parenting among affluent youth: Antecedents of middle school adjustment trajectories." (manuscript submitted for publication).

41. Ibid.

42. Eisenberg, M., et al. (2004), "Correlations between family meals and psychosocial well-being among adolescents," *Archives of Pediatrics and Adolescent Medicine 158*, 792–96.

CHAPTER 3 • Why Money Doesn't Buy Mental Health

1. Ryan, R.M., & E.L. Deci (2001), "On happiness and human potentials: A review of research on hedonic and eudaimonic well-being," *Annual Review of Psychology 52*, 141–66.

2. Myers, D., & E. Diener (1996), "The pursuit of happiness," *Scientific American 274* (5), 70–72.

3. Lykken, D. (1999), *Happiness* (New York: St. Martins Press), p. 17.

4. Myers, D.G. (1993), *The Pursuit of Happiness* (New York: Avon), p. 53.

5. Diener, E., J. Horwitz, & R.A. Emmons (1985), "Happiness of the very wealthy," *Social Indicators Research 16*, 263–74.

6. Inglehart, R. (1990), *Culture Shift in Advanced Industrial Society* (Princeton: Princeton University Press).

7. Brickman, P., D. Coates, & R.J. Janoff-Bulamn (1978), "Lottery winners and accident victims: Is happiness relative?" *Journal of Personality and Social Psychology 36*, 917–27.

8. Myers, D. (2000), "The funds, friends, and faith of happy people," *American Psychologist 55* (1), 60.

9. Tellegen, A., et al. (1988), "Personality similarity in twins reared apart and together," *Journal of Personality and Social Psychology 59*, 291–97.

10. Seligman, M., et al. (1995), *The Optimistic Child* (New York: Houghton Mifflin).

11. Campbell, A. (1981), *The Sense of Well-Being in America* (New York: McGraw-Hill).

12. Myers, (2000), 61.

13. Kasser, T. (2002), *The High Price of Materialism* (Cambridge: MIT Press).

14. Garchik, L. (Aug. 31, 2005), "Public Eavesdropping," *San Francisco Chronicle Online*.

15. Sax, L., et al. (1998), *The American Freshman: National Norms for Fall 1998* (Annual: Higher Education Research Institute; Los Angeles: University of California).

16. Winokur, J. (1996), *The Rich Are Different* (New York: Pantheon Books).

17. Maslow, A.H. (1970), *Motivation and Personality*, 2nd ed. (New York: Harper and Row).

18. Kasser, T., R.M. Ryan, & M. Zax (1995), "The relations of maternal and social environments to late adolescents' materialistic and prosocial values," *Developmental Psychology 31* (6), 907–14.

19. Kasser, T., & R.M. Ryan (1993), "A dark side of the American dream: Correlates of financial success as a central life aspiration," *Journal of Personality and Social Psychology 65*, 410–22.

20. Sheldon, K.M., M.S. Sheldon, & R. Osbaldiston (2000), "Prosocial values and group assortation in an N-person prisoner's dilemma," *Human Nature 11*, 387–404.

21. Csikszentmihalyi, M. (1997), *Finding Flow: The Psychology of Engagement with Everyday Life* (New York: Basic Books).

22. Grolnick, W.S. (2003), *The Psychology of Parental, Control: How Well-Meant Parenting Backfires* (Mahwah, NJ: Lawrence Erlbaum Associates). See also Kohn, A. (1999), *Punished by Rewards* (Boston: Houghton Mifflin).

23. Caskey, W.H. (Nov. 25, 2004), *Providence Journal Online.* "Perilous Privileges for Teens of Means"

24. Grolnick, (2003).

CHAPTER 4 · What Is a Healthy "Self"?

1. Baumeister, R. (1997), "Esteem threat, self-regulatory breakdown, and emotional distress as factors in self-defeating behavior," *Review of General Psychology 1* (2), 145–74.

2. Ramey, C.T., et al. (1982), "The Abecedarian approach to social competence: Cognitive and linguistic intervention for disadvantaged preschoolers," in Borman, K., ed. *The Social Life of Children in a Changing Society*. (Hillsdale, NJ: Erlbaum), pp. 145–74.

3. Bandura, A. (1997), *Self-efficacy: The Exercise of Control* (New York: W. H. Freeman and Company) p. 169.

4. Ibid.

5. Shoda, Y., W. Mischel, & P.K. Peake (1990), "Predicting adolescent cognitive and self-regulatory competencies from preschool delay of gratification: Identifying diagnostic conditions," *Developmental Psychology 26* (6), 978–86.

6. Goldberg, S., R. Muir, & J. Kerr, eds. (1995), *Attachment Theory: Social, Developmental, and Clinical Perspectives* (Hillsdale, NJ: Analytic Press).

7. Lewis, T., F. Amini, & R. Lannon (2001), *A General Theory of Love* (New York: Vintage).

8. Main, M. (2000), "The Adult Attachment Interview: Fear, Attention, Safety, and Discourse Processes." *Journal of American Psychoanalytic Association 48* (4), 1055–1096.

9. Rutter, M. (1987), "Psychosocial resilience and protective mechanisms," *American Journal of Orthopsychiatry 57,* 316–31.

10. Roisman, G.I. et al. (2002), "Earned-Secure Attachment States in Retrospect and Prospect," *Child Development,* 73(4), 1204–1219.

11. Hesse, E. (1999), "The Adult Attachment Interview: Historical and Current Perspectives," *Handbook of Attachment,* Guilford Press (New York).

CHAPTER 5 · Different Ages, Different Parenting Strategies

1. McGhee, P.E. (1976), "Children's appreciation of humor: A test of the cognitive congruency principle," *Child Development 47* (2), 420–26.

2. Ames, L.B., F.L. Ilg,. & S.M. Baker (1989), *Your Ten-to-Fourteen-Year-Old* (New York: Dell).

3. Grolnick, W.S. (2003), *The Psychology of Parental Control: How Well-Meant Parenting Backfires* (Mahwah, NJ: Lawrence Erlbaum Associates).

4. Lewis, M., S.M. Allesandri, & M.W. Sullivan (1992), "Differences in shame and pride as a function of children's gender and task difficulty," *Child Development 63*(3), 630–38. See also Eccles, J.S. & P. Blumenfeld (1985), "Classroom experiences and student gender: Are there differences and do they matter?" in Wilkinson & Marrett, eds., *Gender Influences in Classroom Interaction* (Orlando, FL: Academic Press).

5. Dweck, C.S., Davidson, W., Nelson, S., & Erra, B. (1978), "Sex differences in learned helplessness." *Developmental Psychology, 14,* 268–276.

6. DeBellis, M.D., et al. (2001), "A pilot longitudinal study of hippocampal volumes in pediatric maltreatment-related posttraumatic stress disorder." *Biological Psychiatry, 50,* 305–309.

7. Curtis, J.W. & D. Cicchetti (2003), "Moving resilience into the 21st century: Theoretical and methodological considerations in examining the biological contributors to resilience." *Development and Psychopathology, 15,* 773–810.

8. Buckner J.C. (2003), "Characteristics of resilient youths living in poverty: The role of self-regulatory processes." *Development and Psychopathology, 15,* 139–162.

CHAPTER 6 · How We Connect Makes All the Difference

1. Baumrind, D. (1966), "Effects of authoritative parental control on child behavior," *Child Development 37,* 887–907; Baumrind, D. (1967), "Child care practices anteceding three patterns of preschool behavior," *Genetic Psychology Monographs 75* (91), 43–88; and Baumrind, D. (1971), "Current Patterns of Parental Authority," *Developmental Psychology Monographs, 4.*

2. Lamborn, S.D., et al. (1991), "Patterns of competence and adjustment among adolescents from authoritative, authoritarian, indulgent and neglectful families," *Child Development* 62 (5), 1049–65; see also Baumrind, D. (1991), "The influence of parenting style on adolescent competence and substance use," *Journal of Early Adolescence* 11 (1), 56–95; see also Cohen, D.A. & J. Rice (1997), "Parenting styles, adolescent substance use, and academic achievement," *Journal of Drug Education* 27 (2), 199–211.

3. Baker, B.L. & T.L. Heller (1996), "Preschool children with externalizing behaviors: Experience of fathers and mothers," *Journal of Abnormal Child Psychology* 24 (4), 513–32.

4. Lamborn, S.D., et al. (1991).

5. Ibid. See also Steinberg, L., et al. (1994), "Over-time changes in adjustment and competence among adolescents from authoritative, authoritarian, indulgent and neglectful families," *Child Development,* 65 (3), 754–70.

6. Luthar, S.S. & A.S. Goldstein, "Substance use and related behavior among suburban late adolescents: The importance of perceived parent containment." (manuscript submitted for publication).

7. Forehand, R. & S. Nousiainen (1993), "Maternal and paternal parenting: Critical dimensions in adolescent functioning," *Journal of Family Psychology* 7 (2), 213–21.

8. Ibid, pp.218–19.

9. Maguire, K. & A.L. Pastore, eds. (1996), *Sourcebook of Criminal Justice Statistics 1995* (Washington, D.C.: U.S. Government Printing Office). See also U.S. Public Health Service (1999), *The Surgeon General's Call to Action to Prevent Suicide* (Washington, D.C.: Department of Health and Human Services).

10. Baumeister, R.F., et al. (2003), "Does high self-esteem cause better performance, interpersonal success, happiness, or healthier lifestyles?" *Psychological Science in the Public Interest* 4(1), 109.

11. Ibid.

12. Luthar, S.S., K. Shoum, & P.J. Brown, *Developmental Psychology,* "Extracurricular involvement among affluent youth: A scapegoat for 'ubiquitous achievement pressures'?"

**CHAPTER 7 · Discipline and Control:
The Tough Job of Being the "Bad Cop"**

1. Forehand, R. & S. Nousianinen (1993), "Maternal and paternal parenting: Critical dimensions in adolescent functioning," *Journal of Family Psychology* 7(2), 213–21.

2. 2003 *National Survey of Drug Use and Health: National Finding* (2004), available at: https://nsduhweb.rti.org/.

3. Dishion, T.J. & K. Kavanagh (2003), *Intervening in Adolescent Problem Behavior: A Family-Centered Approach* (New York: Guilford Press).

4. Schneider, W., T. Cavell, & J. Hughes (2003), "A sense of containment: Potential moderator of the relation between parenting practices and children's externalizing behavior," *Development and Psychopathology 15*, 94–117.

5. Ibid.

6. Cavell, T. (2000), *Working with Parents of Aggressive Children: A Practitioner's Guide* (Washington, D.C.: American Psychological Association), 27–47.

7. Luthar, S.S. (2006), "Resilience in development: A synthesis of research across five decades," in Cicchetti & Cohen, eds., *Developmental Psychology: Risk, Disorder, and Adaptation*, 2nd ed. (New York: Wiley).

8. Belsky, J., et al. (2001), "Childrearing antecedents of intergenerational relations in young adulthood: A prospective study," *Developmental Psychology 37*, 801–14.

9. Barber, B., ed. (2002), *Intrusive Parenting: How Psychological Control Affects Children and Adolescents* (Washington, D.C.: American Psychological Association).

CHAPTER 8 • Challenges to Effective Parenting in the Culture of Affluence

1. Luthar, S.S. (2003), "The culture of affluence: Psychological costs of material wealth," *Child Development 74*, 1581–93.

2. Luthar, S.S. & C. Sexton (2004), "The high price of affluence," in Kail, ed., *Advances in Child Development, 32* (San Diego, CA: Academic Press).

3. Farrelly. M.J. (March, 28, 2005), "Freshman women at Duke University battle 'effortless perfection,'" (available at: www.imdiversity.com/villages/woman/education_academia_study/voa_duke_freshmen_0405.asp)

4. Blatt, S.J. (1995), "The destructiveness of perfectionism," *American Psychologist 50*, (12) 1011

5. Castaneda, C. (1969), *The Teachings of Don Juan: A Yaqui Way of Knowledge* (Los Angeles: University of California Press).

CHAPTER 9 • Having Everything Except What We Need Most: The Isolation of Affluent Moms

1. Connell, A.M. & S.H. Goodman (2002), "The association between psychopathology in fathers versus mothers and children's internalizing and externalizing behavior problems: A meta-analysis," *Psychological Bulletin 128*, 746–73.

2. Ibid.

3. Durbin, E.E., et al. (2005), "Temperamental emotionality in preschoolers and parental mood disorders," *Journal of Abnormal Psychology* (*114*)1, 28–37. See also Luthar, S.S. (2006), "Resilience in development: A synthesis of research across five decades," in Cicchetti & Cohen, eds., *Developmental Psychopathology: Risk, Disorder, and Adaptation*, 2nd ed. (New York: Wiley).

4. Steinberg, L., & W. Steinberg, (1994), *Crossing Paths* (New York: Simon & Schuster).

5. Wolfe, J.L., & I.G. Foder, (1996), "The poverty of privilege: Therapy with women of the 'upper' classes," *Women & Therapy 18*, 73–89.

6. Beardslee, W.R., E.M. Versage, & T.R.G. Gladstone (1998), "Children of affectively ill parents: A review of the past ten years," *Journal of the American Academy of Child and Adolescent Psychiatry* (*37*)11, 1134–41. See also Luthar, S.S. & N.E. Suchman (2000), "Relational psychotherapy mothers' group: A developmentally informed intervention for at-risk mothers," *Development and Psychopathology 12*, 235–53.

7. Sroufe, L.A., et al. (2005), *The Development of the Person* (New York: Guilford Press), p. 260.

8. Luthar, S.S. & C.C. Sexton, "Maternal drug abuse versus maternal depression: Vulnerability and resilience among school-age and adolescent offspring" (manuscript submitted for publication).

9. Gilligan, C. (1982), *In a Different Voice: Psychological Theory and Women's Development*. (Cambridge: Harvard University Press). See also Luthar, S.S. & N.E. Suchman (1999), "Developmentally informed parenting interventions: The relational psychotherapy mothers' group," in Cicchetti & Toth, eds., *Rochester Symposium on Developmental Psychopathology, Volume 9: Developmental approaches to Prevention and Intervention*. (Rochester, NY: University of Rochester Press), pp. 271–309.

10. Taylor, S.E., et al. (2000), "Biobehavioral responses to stress in females: Tend-and-befriend, not fight-or-flight," *Psychological Review 107*(3), 411–29.

11. Harvey, E. (1999), "Short-term and long-term effects of early parental employment on children of the National Longitudinal Survey of Youth," *Developmental Psychology, 35*(2), 445–59.

INDEX

abuse, physical or psychological, 153, 186–90, 209

acceptance, 133–34
  perfectionism and lack of, 180, 181

accountability (taking responsibility), 122–23, 128, 130, 153
  affluence and lack of, 187–88

achievement pressure, 28–30, 33, 53, 68, 89–90, 173, 177

acting out, 6, 20, 135, 148–51, 156, 159, 197, 218–19, 221

adolescence
  affluence and, 10, 12–15, 16–24, 26–28, 30–35, 41–45, 47–59, 66–70, 75–79, 84–85, 88–94, 124, 122–23, 124, 128, 151, 153, 169–99, 183–90, 194–99, 223–24
  brain development in, 114–15, 156
  causes of emotional problems, 28–33
  cognitive development, 113–15, 120
  "internal home," creation of, 85–88
  overstimulation and, 87
  parenting challenges, 12, 30–33, 116–20, 122–23
  premature mortality, 21
  professional help for, 26–28
  self, development of, 12, 63–94
  social development, 115–16, 121–22
  symptoms and warning signs of serious problems, 34, 68, 88–92, 145
  traditional trajectory and conflicts, 10, 19, 43–44
  truncated development, 41–44, 63

  See also boys; girls; self (identity); *specific areas of concern*

advertising, 50–51
  consumerism and, 38, 128

affluence and privilege, 13, 169–99
  accountability of child and, 122–23, 128, 130, 153, 187–88
  behaviors and psychological problems associated with, 17, 18–24
  case history, "Allison," 41–45
  case history, "Andrew," 174–77
  case history, "Samantha," 194–99, 206
  case history, "Tyler," 88–92
  causes of teen problems and, 28–33
  common "costs" to families of, 170–72, 198–99
  competition and, 52–53, 171, 172, 174, 177, 178, 189, 194
  dependency issues and, 140–41, 171, 192
  development of self, 66–70, 75, 78–79, 85, 88–92
  development of self, "Kate vs. Marissa," 66–70
  discipline of children and, 130, 153, 155–56, 159, 173, 187–88 (*see also* discipline)
  divorce and marriage, 191–94, 223
  entitlement and inflated sense of self, 142, 187–88
  epidemic of teen problems and, 12–15, 16, 40–41, 223–24
  fathers, emotional or physical unavailability, 171, 176